Stories from Palestine

STORIES FROM PALESTINE
Narratives of Resilience

MARDA DUNSKY

University of Notre Dame Press

Notre Dame, Indiana

University of Notre Dame Press
Notre Dame, Indiana 46556
undpress.nd.edu

Paperback edition published in 2023

Library of Congress Control Number: 2020950373

ISBN: 978-0-268-20033-6 (Hardback)
ISBN: 978-0-268-20034-3 (Paperback)
ISBN: 978-0-268-20032-9 (WebPDF)
ISBN: 978-0-268-20035-0 (Epub)

for

MUFID

CONTENTS

ACKNOWLEDGMENTS

The greatest opportunity I have received in writing *Stories from Palestine: Narratives of Resilience* is that of *access*.

I have chosen narrative storytelling as the means to support a framework of inquiry asserting that there is more to consider about Palestinians and their society—in this context, within the geographical parameters of the West Bank, east Jerusalem, and Gaza Strip—than the information and characterizations that reach the general public through the news media and a significantly smaller audience through scholarly studies.

In order to tell stories of Palestinians as creators and producers in their daily lives—their endeavors impacted by the various circumstances of living under occupation but not overcome by them—I needed access. I needed access to sources who were willing to make time in their busy schedules for me—a stranger identifying herself as a scholar-journalist—and who were willing to answer my questions and share their perspectives about living life in this conflict zone.

After having done so, these sources were also willing to grant me a second round of access when I contacted them after writing narratives based on our interviews. Once again, they indulged me, patiently confirming and/or correcting certain details about which I asked them a second time in order to try to attain the greatest possible degree of accuracy.

And so the first debt of gratitude that I wish to express is to each and every one of the thirty people whom I quote by name in the pages of *Stories from Palestine*. They have let me into their lives and believed in my objective. They have trusted me to convey the details of their personal and professional lives, experiences, and worldviews.

Twenty-seven of these thirty sources are Palestinians who were working, when I interviewed them, as creators and producers in agriculture, education, science and medicine, media, business, and culture and the arts. One source is Italian, representing a United Nations agency, and one is Japanese, representing a Japanese government agency; one source is an American who established a website for young Palestinian writers. Approximately three-quarters of these sources met with me face-to-face in their homes, offices, and places of business in Jerusalem and the West Bank. All but one of the remaining sources gave me their time through internet-based, real-time voice interviews—several of them in multiple sessions—and one provided me with written answers to my questions via email.

To each and every one of these thirty sources named and quoted herein, I express my heartfelt and humble thanks—for without them, the creation of *Stories from Palestine* in its present form would not have been possible.

The genesis of this work began in late 2015, when I began reporting what eventually became the basis of chapter 1, "Made in Palestine." This narrative of agricultural producers in the northern West Bank is based on a piece of reportage published under the same title in 2017 by *The Cairo Review of Global Affairs*, an English-language quarterly journal based in Egypt at the American University in Cairo. I wish to thank Scott MacLeod, founding and former managing editor of the *Review*, for originally commissioning the piece, and to thank the management and editors of the journal, among them Sean David Hobbs, for granting me permission to publish a revised version of "Made in Palestine" in *Stories from Palestine*.

My access to many of the sources I have quoted herein was direct, the result of my own initiative. However, I also depended to a significant degree on guidance and assistance from many others in locating and/or reaching out to sources whom I wished to interview. Their efforts on my behalf contributed richness and texture to the mix of sources.

Chris Gunness, the formidable and fearless former chief spokesperson for UNRWA, the United Nations Relief and Works Agency for Palestine Refugees in the Near East, provided me with multiple leads and connections to sources in the Gaza Strip and within the humanitarian community in Jerusalem.

The fulcrum of assistance for my reporting on Palestinian agricultural producers in the northern West Bank has been, since 2015, Ahmed Abufarha, administrative manager of the Burqin-based Canaan Palestine, which processes and markets Palestinian olive oil, grains, and other agricultural products.

Bill van Esveld and Sari Bashi of Human Rights Watch; Catherine Cook of OCHA, the United Nations Office for the Coordination of Humanitarian Affairs, Occupied Palestinian Territory; and Michelle Gyeney of the Food and Agriculture Organization of the United Nations also provided valuable assistance to me in accessing sources and information for chapter 1.

Areej Shalbak of the Arab American University in Jenin provided me with invaluable assistance in sourcing chapter 1 and chapter 2, "Lessons in Liberation," which focuses on education in the West Bank. I also wish to thank Jihan Samoudi for helping me access sources for this latter chapter.

From the outset, I believed that including a chapter about Palestinian life in the Gaza Strip was essential, and my original intention was to travel there to interview sources and observe the current landscape. I had visited the Gaza Strip on an informal research tour in 1987 and as a journalist in 1989 and 2000, but conditions there have changed radically since Israel unilaterally withdrew its soldiers and settlers in 2005 and Hamas, the Islamic Resistance Movement, came to power in Gaza in 2007.

My first step was to contact Israel's Government Press Office—for which I received guidance from my friend and former *Chicago Tribune* colleague Judy Peres and from Isabel Kershner of the *New York Times*—to inquire about permission to enter Gaza through the northern Erez crossing, which is controlled by Israel. After being notified that I was not eligible to obtain a permit, and considering the potential complications and risks of entering the Strip through Rafah, the southern crossing, which is controlled by Egypt, I decided to try to find credible sources and interview them remotely. It was an option less desirable than face-to-face contact, but it seemed the most pragmatic course. Nevertheless, I was able to produce chapter 5, "In Gaza, They Are Not Numbers."

In this effort I was assisted to a great extent by Najwa Sheikh-Ahmad. Within the framework of the extremely challenging conditions of her work as acting public information officer for the UNRWA field office in the Gaza Strip, she expended considerable effort on my behalf to connect me with a particular refugee source I was seeking to interview for one of the chapter's two main narratives. In addition, I also interviewed Najwa as an official source for the chapter. I also wish to acknowledge Matthias Schmale, director of UNRWA operations in Gaza, for granting permission for me to interview her.

For assistance in sourcing the second narrative for the Gaza chapter, I wish to thank Pam Bailey, the journalist who created the We Are Not Numbers website for young Palestinian writers, and my friend Sabah Fakhoury, who directed my attention to WANN in the first place.

I cite the Birzeit-based Palestinian Circus School as an example of a glittering narrative via an interview with one of its performers in the concluding chapter 6, "Imperatives of Narrative." For facilitating my access and visit to PCS, I wish to thank Shadi Zmorrod, cofounder; Mohammad Rabah, executive director; and Rana Nasser, coordinator.

I wish also to thank professors Rashid Khalidi of Columbia University, Craig Duff of Northwestern University, Ebrahim Moosa of the University of Notre Dame, and Marwan Darweish of Coventry University for their support.

Academic publishing requires peer review by experts in the field who read and critique the project proposal and manuscript. In this process, the reviewers' identities are not known to the author. However, I wish to thank the reviewers of *Stories from Palestine* just the same for their insightful and otherwise valuable input. My former *Tribune* colleague Charles Madigan also made helpful suggestions based on his reading of early chapter drafts.

Eli Bortz, editor in chief of the University of Notre Dame Press, was quick to appreciate the potential of this project when I pitched it to him in late 2017. His enthusiasm and support for seeing it through have been invaluable. I am grateful to manuscript editor Bob Banning, who added precision and clarity to my prose, but I am solely responsible for its content.

Ultimately and essentially, I wish to thank my husband, Mufid Qassoum. He has been my singular source of support, understanding, and inspiration for this undertaking and for much, much beyond.

Marda Dunsky
October 2020

Introduction

The Story behind the Stories

Madees Khoury is holding court, regaling thirty or so members of an Episcopal church from Cambridge, Massachusetts, who have ridden a big white tour bus to the Taybeh Brewing Company, owned and run by Khoury's family.

Translated from Arabic, *taybeh* means good or delicious, and it is the name of Khoury's village, situated about ten miles northeast of Jerusalem, three thousand feet above sea level. Khoury is dressed in a short-sleeved T-shirt and jeans, her long brown hair pulled back in a ponytail. A soft zephyr is blowing as she describes the shipping woes she recently faced sending her company's beer to a festival in Copenhagen. The bottom line behind the snafu, which involved security inspections further north in the West Bank and delays at the Israeli ports of Ashdod and Haifa, was, she says, "because we are Palestinian."[1]

But Khoury, at age thirty-two the brewery's operations manager, is in her element. Undaunted, she speaks without a trace of complaint or bitterness as she lays out details of the story: She finally shipped a smaller quantity of the beer by air, and it arrived on time, but her profits got zeroed out. No matter. Her family business is thriving, the thrum of the brewery vibrating in the background. In the center of the village, the Khourys operate the Golden Hotel, where they also sell a line of wines.

Khoury speaks to her American guests in their language, English—which is one of her own languages.[2] Born in Boston and a graduate of Hellenic College in nearby Brookline, where she earned a bachelor's degree in business, she makes her life in Taybeh, the village of her ancestors in Palestine for countless generations.

"I hate the snow in Boston," she tells the tour group, laughing. "My cousins are still there. They're stuck—they come here to visit but get only two weeks." But she speaks of her American background with pride. "How well do you know Brookline?" she asks the Bay Staters, describing the whereabouts of Foley's Liquor, about which she beams: "That's my family's."

The group moves inside the brewery, where they watch bottles of Taybeh beer clink along on the assembly line. Visitors sample the wares and buy Palestinian beer and wine to take back home. Khoury is at the cash register with a ready smile for her customers. Her uncle David Khoury is on hand to observe the day's production and mingle. He and Madees's father, Nadim, founded Taybeh Brewing Company in 1994 when they returned from eighteen years in the U.S. "We come from a family of priests," David says; Khoury means "priest" in Arabic.

Their Greek Orthodox community in Taybeh lives alongside Melkites and Roman Catholics in this village of about eighteen hundred. Silhouettes of churches dot the panorama of the sloping landscape filled with boxy white houses built among olive trees. Jesus is said to have retired to a nearby hilltop with his disciples after the resurrection of Lazarus. The original Greek Orthodox St. George church was built here in the fourth century; in the twelfth century, Crusaders built a castle.

On this day, the brewery is treating visitors to samples of white beer, one of its six varieties. The lager is crisp, smooth, and delicious, made from Palestinian wheat, coriander, and orange peel. And, of course, Palestinian spring water—which is key but difficult to access "because," Madees Khoury says, "we are Palestinian."

From Taybeh to Jenin in the West Bank, from the Old City of Jerusalem to the Jabalia refugee camp in the Gaza Strip, *Stories from Palestine: Narratives of Resilience* is a journey. It is a pathway meant to create a new space in the literature on contemporary Palestine by profiling Palestinians engaged in everyday pursuits in the West Bank, east Jerusalem, and Gaza. The Palestinian people also encompasses the Palestinian minority living as citizens in Israel and Palestinians living in the diaspora in refugee camps, towns, and cities in Jordan, Lebanon, and Syria and in Palestinian communities elsewhere in the region as well as in Europe, North America, and beyond.[3] However, *Stories from Palestine* focuses on the five million Palestinians who live in the West Bank, Jerusalem, and Gaza Strip—as these areas form the territorial basis envisioned for eventual Palestinian independence. Still, it has been observed, Palestinians who exist within this particular context "thrive on a continuum of Palestinian history, people, and geography and do not exist (though they sometimes function) as separate from the whole" of the Palestinian people.[4]

The narratives herein reflect the humanity of their protagonists, exploring dimensions and textures of contemporary Palestinian life in these locales not often represented in American mainstream media reports and scholarly studies. *Stories from Palestine* presents an alternative to prevalent framing of Palestinians as victims of injustice and/or perpetrators of violence while contextualizing their stories with relevant impacts that the conflict imposes on their lives. Their hardships are considered, but their perseverance and achievement are paramount.

Glimpses of Palestinians as producers, creators, and even champions don't often appear—and when they do, they are often either tightly framed by protest or fleeting in duration. Consider Abdelfattah Abusrour, founder of the Alrowwad children's theater program in the Aida refugee camp next to Bethlehem, who was interviewed by Anthony Bourdain for his "Parts Unknown" series on CNN in 2013.[5] Bourdain noted that at the camp "children play in the streets beneath walls covered in images of martyrs, plane hijackers, political prisoners" and that two-thirds of the camp's six thousand residents were under the age of eighteen—"pretty much a recipe for unruly behavior." Abusrour responded:

Well, yes. Especially when you don't have any possibilities to evacuate the anger and the stress in a creative way. So after I finished my studies, I came back here and I started using theatre as one of the most amazing, powerful, civilized and nonviolent means to express yourself. To tell your story. To be truthful.

And this is for me the remedy to build peace within. And hopefully help [children] to think that they can grow up and change the world and create miracles. Without the need to carry a gun and . . . explode themselves or burn themselves. But to stay alive.

Such a Palestinian perspective, which expresses constructive agency emerging from an environment with few apparent sources of hope, is not typically given voice in mainstream reporting of the conflict—yet it represents a crucial human dimension that deserves consideration. But the CNN snippet, though enlightening, literally appears one minute and is gone the next. *Stories from Palestine* spends time with Palestinians, including Abusrour, to go beyond the sound bite, rendering their humanity fuller and deeper.

Or consider Areej Al-Madhoun, who at age fourteen as a ninth grader in the Jabalia refugee camp in the Gaza Strip won first prize in the 2012 Intelligent Mental-Arithmetic Competition in Malaysia. Her achievement—coming less than a month after Israel and Hamas fought an eight-day war in Gaza—merited a write-up on the website of UNRWA,[6] the United Nations agency that serves Palestinian refugees, and on some social media sites, but did not attract international media coverage. *Stories* follows up on her story in depth.

The tremendous human potential that vibrates through Palestinian society is often overlooked in media reporting, which tends to represent Palestinians' humanity empirically and anecdotally, focusing instead on easily observable modalities of conflict. Scholarly studies across a range of social science disciplines provide valuable context about the Israel-Palestine conflict but do not often delve beyond surface details into the everyday human stories coexisting behind, inside, and sometimes even in front of it.

Stories from Palestine attempts to strike a balance, placing in the forefront narratives of Palestinians in the West Bank, east Jerusalem, and Gaza Strip who are engaged as producers and creators, illuminating their human resiliency and agency. The aim is to present a fresh, parallel way of seeing—in essence, to challenge prevalent, reductive representations of Palestinians as victims of oppression and/or perpetrators of violence and their society as mired in, if not stymied by, the Israel-Palestine conflict. The protagonists' narratives of achievement and perseverance are based on personal interviews, the majority of which were conducted in person, in the field. The contextualizing subtext of their stories—the difficult conditions of life under occupation—is quantified and otherwise characterized based on data drawn from a range of nongovernmental, governmental, scholarly, and media secondary sources.

Stories from Palestine takes up Palestinian productive and creative capacity across a broad spectrum: women and men, Muslims and Christians, professionals and entrepreneurs, students and teachers, family farmers, cultural curators, and refugees. They are engaged in agriculture, education, and culture in the West Bank; persist in east Jerusalem as a sizable minority within the city; and confront the harsh circumstances and uncertainties of life in Gaza. *Stories* is informed by an analytical framework that focuses on Palestinians' everyday lived experience—their many quotidian ways of pushing forward under occupation. Characterized variously as perseverance, agency, and resilience, this framework is rooted in the examination of Palestinian lived lives that maintain their presence—past, present, and future— in the highly contested space of the Israel-Palestine conflict zone.

In Arabic, the term *sumūd* denotes steadfastness or perseverance, and *sāmid* the one who is steadfast or persevering.[7] In his *Samed: Journal of a West Bank Palestinian*, Raja Shehadeh explains that *sumūd* came to the fore of regional Arab discourse at the 1978 Baghdad Conference, the ninth summit of the Arab League.

> It was then that Arab politicians outside officially acknowledged the urgency of stemming the mass exile of Palestinians from the occupied territories and of trying to halt the Israeli government's expropriation of huge tracts of land on the West Bank. We, who had been living under occupation for ten years, were now called on to be *samidīn* and urged to adopt the stance of *sumūd*: to stay put, to cling to our homes and land by all means available.[8]

Three decades later, in a series of field interviews with Palestinians in the West Bank in 2009–10, scholars Alexandra Rijke and Toine van Teeffelen found that

> *sumūd* has developed from a nationalist symbol emphasizing the shared goals and values of Palestinians to a way of life lived by individuals and communities. *Sumūd* has come to represent the struggle to preserve a certain "Palestinian" way of life, with its own rhythms and customs, its discourses and lifestyles, and also its joys. The added dimension of daily life has democratized the concept of *sumūd*. The interviewees suggested that *sumūd* is relevant to the daily life of Palestinians who actively wish to maintain their identity and dignity through small acts of what is sometimes called "everyday heroism."[9]

In Bethlehem, the Sumud Story House collects stories of Palestinian daily life and posts them on the Wall Museum of art and graffiti covering the Israeli separation barrier that slices through the town, thereby "creating a narrative community based on solidarity and caring."[10] Abusrour of Alrowwad in the Aida refugee camp told the researchers: "*Sumūd* is continuing to live in Palestine, laughing, enjoying life, falling in love, getting married, having children. *Sumūd* is also continuing your studies outside, to get a diploma, to come back here. . . . That I am here is *sumūd*. To reclaim that you are a human being and defending your humanity is *sumūd*."[11] *Sumūd* has been interpreted by other academic observers as "an attitude, a cultural trait, or an 'inward-directed' life stance—a term that captures the underlying values of the Palestinian struggle or an art of living 'manifested in building living stones, building human beings, and building relationships between people.'"[12]

The scholar Lori Allen argues that with Palestinians living under conditions "where the routine and assumptions of daily life are physically disrupted," their ability to deflect through adaptation—pursuing everyday, nonviolent acts of *sumūd*—is crucial and "the result of concerted, collective production. There is something beyond political motives and awareness that inspire the incorporation of disorder into a quotidian order, however. The necessities of survival, and the physical and psychological capacities that people have to learn and adapt to sustain themselves in changing circumstances, also feed into a kind of agency that is no doubt quite prevalent in situations of ongoing violence."[13]

Acts of *sumūd* also fit the typology of "everyday resistance," a concept pioneered in the mid-1980s by political scientist James C. Scott. Distinct from political mobilization, protest demonstrations, and acts of violence, which often spur the powerful (and usually sovereign) agents being opposed to impose harsh countermeasures, "everyday acts of resistance make no headlines," Scott has written. While "less explicitly confrontational" than armed revolt, he argues, "these acts still qualify as resistance, to the extent that they 'deny or mitigate claims made by appropriating classes.'"[14] "Everyday resistance" is seen through a theoretical lens as informal and nonorganized; Scott has referred to it as "infra politics."[15] It is a practice (rather than an intent or outcome) that can take varying forms in different contexts and situations. Relationships between agents—actor/s, target/s, and observer/s—are fluid, and spatial (relating to space) and/or temporal (relating to time) characteristics of each individual act vary.[16]

Shehadeh's notion that "it is the day-to-day living that is the test of *sumūd*" has stood the test of time, from the early 1980s when he wrote his *Journal* to the present day. Advocating for Palestinians in their struggle against the Israeli occupation and chronicling the legal structures and stories behind his clients' cases became Shehadeh's "third way." In this, he wrote that he chose a state of mind and course of action that rejected alternate paths of submission/exile or vengeance/hatred: "This is where you are free, your own master—because your mind is the one thing that you can prevent your oppressor from having the power to touch, however strong and brutal he may be."[17]

In chronicling his life and work as a lawyer in Ramallah during 1980–82, Shehadeh emphasized the importance not only of *sumūd* but also of making it resonate.

> One of the greatest threats to our *sumūd* is the feeling of isolation. The Palestinians' political activities and demands are well known and reported. But we *samidīn* are silent about the actual day-to-day experience of living under occupation. It is not only

military orders and the threat of banishment that make us keep our thoughts and feelings to ourselves. Our struggle for survival is totally consuming. It was to break out of this silence that I began writing about my life and the lives of other *samidīn*.[18]

In 1979 Shehadeh became a founding member of Al-Haq: Law in the Service of Man, established in Ramallah by Palestinian lawyers. In 1980 the Geneva-based International Commission of Jurists published *The West Bank and the Rule of Law* in affiliation with the organization, coauthored by Shehadeh.[19]

In his *Journal*, Shehadeh recorded the story, among others, of Hani, a fifteen-year-old neighbor who was shot in his left leg on April 28, 1980, by an Israeli soldier while running away from the direction of a demonstration in Ramallah that day in which he did not participate. Demonstrators were protesting an appearance by the ultra-right-wing Israeli politician Meir Kahane, founder of the extremist Kach party, which advocated expulsion of Arabs living in Israel and the occupied territories.

Immediately after the shooting, Shehadeh reported, the soldier stood over Hani and falsely asserted that he had thrown stones and petrol bombs at soldiers from a moving car. Hani required a series of surgeries on his leg; Shehadeh wrote that he recorded the story to keep it alive, to assert the truth, to take the writing of a page in his people's history into his own hands. "If my sumūd as a lawyer is to mean anything, I must at least be able to tell my people's stories. . . . So I am writing Hani's story, for the record; and for Hani and his mother. It is one of many thousands of stories that should at least have been documented."[20]

In their day-to-day living and acts of creativity and production, those whose narratives illuminate *Stories from Palestine* continue along this path.

W hat, though, makes these narratives significant? Beyond its borders, is the Israel-Palestine conflict still relevant?

On January 28, 2020, the conflict made headlines around the world when the Trump administration unveiled *Peace to Prosperity: A Vision to Improve the Lives of the Palestinian and Israeli People* [*sic*].[21] President Donald Trump, facing impeachment proceedings in the U.S. Senate, announced the peace plan, his so-called "deal of the century," at the White House with Israeli prime minister Benjamin Netanyahu, facing multiple corruption charges in his own country, at his side. Palestinian president Mahmoud Abbas was absent.

Three years in the making, the plan followed the blueprint that Trump had already laid out during those years: recognition of Jerusalem as Israel's capital and relocation of the U.S. embassy there; cutting aid to the Palestinian Authority and UNRWA; and recognition of Israeli settlement in the West Bank and control over the Golan Heights. The Trump "deal" announced in early 2020 would cede the Jordan Valley to Israel and allow it to annex virtually all of its settlements in the West Bank and east Jerusalem, which "matched the Israeli leader's hard-line, nationalist views while falling far short of Palestinian ambitions,"[22] the Associated Press reported, noting that the plan "supports the Israeli position on nearly all of the most contentious issues in the decades-old conflict."[23] According to the International Crisis Group, the plan would result in "a discontiguous Palestinian archipelago state, surrounded by a sea of Israeli territory."[24]

The plan would also freeze Israeli settlement building in areas designated for the Palestinian state for four years, but Israel was already bypassing these areas for settlement activity. Under the plan most of occupied east Jerusalem would remain under Israeli control, including the Old City and holy sites; and Israel would maintain overall security oversight of the demilitarized Palestinian state, including control of its borders. The plan would significantly enlarge the land area currently under Palestinian control through land swaps, including territory currently within Israel proper inhabited by Arab citizens. The Palestinians would be allowed to establish their capital on the outskirts of Jerusalem in Abu Dis, outside the Israeli separation barrier. Palestinian refugees would not be granted the right of return to locales they had inhabited in Palestine prior to 1948 that subsequently became part of Israel—despite having that right under international law. Rather, they would be allowed to live in the Palestinian state or become absorbed by other countries and possibly receive some degree of compensation from the U.S.[25]

Announced five weeks before the third round of Israeli elections—with Netanyahu having been unable to form a government after two elections held in 2019—Trump's plan, in the estimation of the embattled Israeli leader, was a green light for immediate Israeli annexation of the Jordan Valley and West Bank settlements, which would boost support from his hard-right constituency in advance of the March 2020 vote. The Associated Press reported that following the announcement ceremony, Netanyahu told reporters: "This dictates once and for all the eastern border of Israel. Israel is getting an immediate American recognition of Israeli sovereignty on all the settlements, without exceptions."[26]

However, within days of Trump announcing the plan, Jared Kushner—one of its chief architects and the president's son-in-law-turned-Mideast-policy-adviser—put the brakes on annexation, telling Israeli officials that the matter should be decided only after their next government was in place; Netanyahu's planned cabinet meeting to approve annexation was canceled.[27] As the dust settled, the *Financial Times* reported that "the plan was far-fetched and with little chance of ever materialising but it was important as an official document rewarding long-held Israeli rightwing positions—from annexing settlements, holding on to East Jerusalem and stripping a third of the occupied West Bank from any future Palestinian state."[28] In the third round of Israeli elections within a year, held on March 2, 2020, Netanyahu once again failed to secure a parliamentary majority for the right-wing bloc with his Likud party at its center; defiant, he resisted calls to resign.[29]

Having opted out of attending the announcement of the plan at the White House, Abbas took the Palestinian case to the international community at the United Nations, appearing before the Security Council on February 11, 2020, to denounce the Trump "deal" as making "Swiss cheese" out of territory mapped out for a future Palestinian state, leaving it "without any control on our land, air, and sea. This plan will not bring peace or stability to the region," the Palestinian president said, "and therefore we will not accept this plan," *Foreign Affairs* reported. Abbas called for an international peace conference that would replace U.S. mediation of bilateral Israeli-Palestinian negotiations; having previously proposed such a conference, France indicated willingness to begin discussions.[30] At the Security Council session, pressure from the Trump administration forced withdrawal of a resolution drafted by Indonesia and Tunisia rejecting the Trump plan in favor of traditionally accepted parameters of a two-state solution as envisioned a generation ago in the Oslo Accords—for which all fourteen of the council members except the U.S. declared their support in a debate that the *Times of Israel* characterized as "rancorous."[31]

The approach in the Trump plan had been amply foreshadowed by measures serving to disrupt rather than bolster prospects for peace. Unilateral fiat, not negotiations, was the means by which Trump had declared in December 2017 that the U.S. recognized Jerusalem as Israel's capital and would relocate the U.S. embassy there from Tel Aviv—a move seen to have "shattered decades of unwavering U.S. neutrality" on the issue of the divided city.[32] Trump's action was widely condemned by European and Middle Eastern leaders and seen as an "alarming break" by American diplomats, who have considered U.S. neutrality on Jerusalem "a bedrock principle and essential for peace."[33]

Of the eighty-seven countries that have embassies in Israel, all prior to Trump's proclamation located them in Tel Aviv. Nevertheless, the U.S. president said he was merely acknowledging "the obvious" and called his act of fiat "a long overdue step to advance the peace process."[34] Trump did not take a position on the ultimate sovereignty of Jerusalem, and he did not endorse the 1980 Jerusalem Law proclaiming the "complete and united" city to be Israel's capital, widely seen as de facto annexation of east Jerusalem, captured by Israel in the Six-Day War of 1967. But Trump did not reject this notion, and he made no mention of the longtime aspiration of Palestinians that east Jerusalem become the capital of their future state.[35] Since 1967 Israel has confiscated thousands of acres of land in and around east Jerusalem, incorporating them into the city's municipal boundaries and establishing twelve settlements populated exclusively by Jewish Israelis.[36]

In 2018 Trump wielded the cudgel of foreign aid in order to compel the Palestinian Authority to negotiate with Israel under U.S. mediation.[37] When the PA refused to receive Vice President Mike Pence during his visit to the region in January 2018, a month after Trump made his Jerusalem embassy declaration, Trump said: "And when [the Palestinians] disrespected us . . . by not allowing our great vice president to see them, and we give them hundreds of millions of dollars in aid and support, tremendous numbers, numbers that nobody understands, that money is on the table and that money is not going to them unless they sit down and negotiate peace."[38]

The opening of the new U.S. embassy office in Jerusalem on May 14, 2018, observed at a ceremony marking the seventieth anniversary of Israel's independence, was reported to exacerbate ongoing protests by Palestinians in the Gaza Strip, with fifty-eight killed by Israeli forces that same day.[39] The following summer and early autumn, Trump's policies were to continue in a serial fashion noted to put maximum pressure on Palestinian leaders to accept forthcoming U.S.-dictated terms regarding territory, refugees, and sovereignty.[40]

From late August through mid-September, the Trump administration announced that it was cutting more than $200 million in bilateral aid to the Palestinian Authority for programs supporting good governance, health, education, and civil society in the West Bank and Gaza Strip (while days earlier having released $60 million for ongoing projects enhancing security cooperation between the PA and Israel);[41] cutting $60 million already allocated for UNRWA—which provides education, health, and other social-welfare support for 5.6 million Palestinian refugees in the West Bank, Gaza Strip, Lebanon, Jordan, and Syria—as well as discontinuing all future funding to the agency, accounting for a quarter of its budget;[42] and cutting $25 million in aid for the East Jerusalem Hospital Network.[43] Trump then closed the Palestine Liberation Organization office in Washington[44] and ordered the visas held by its ambassador and family members to be revoked.[45]

The series of punitive measures was seen by Aaron David Miller, former policy adviser on the conflict to six U.S. secretaries of state, as an "economic and political war" waged against the Palestinians. Miller told NBC News that in forty years, he had not witnessed an administration "simultaneously support Israel so uncritically and go after Palestinians so harshly both without logic, purpose or national security rationale."[46]

In 2019 the Trump administration continued to flout international consensus in favor of unilateral fiat. In March Trump signed a decree during a meeting with Netanyahu, two weeks before hotly contested Israeli elections, stating that the U.S. recognized Israeli control over the Golan Heights,[47] Syrian territory that Israel occupied following the Six-Day War and imposed its jurisdiction over in 1981, in contravention of international law. The European Union rejected Trump's move.[48]

In November 2019 Secretary of State Mike Pompeo announced that the U.S. did not consider Israeli settlements in the West Bank to be in violation of international law—despite four decades of American policy and numerous UN Security Council resolutions to the contrary, based primarily on the Fourth Geneva Convention prohibiting an occupying power from transferring its own civilian population to occupied territory.[49] Stating that the Trump administration had "recognized the reality on the ground," Pompeo's logic appeared counterintuitive if not contradictory in his assertion that the U.S. policy shift would enhance opportunities for Israel and the Palestinians to negotiate a peace deal and that the issue should be left for Israeli courts to decide. "There will never be a judicial resolution to the conflict, and arguments about who is right and wrong as a matter of international law will not bring peace," he said.[50]

The *New York Times* characterized the move as "the latest political gift from the Trump administration to Prime Minister Benjamin Netanyahu," who at the time of the announcement had been unable to form a government following a second inconclusive round of elections and had taken a hard-right stance signaling intent to annex much of the West Bank. The European Union opposed the U.S. policy shift, with EU foreign policy chief Federica Mogherini maintaining that the settlements are illegal and harm chances for peace.[51]

Although the grand sweep of Trump administration policy on the conflict militates against chances for restarting peace negotiations, for decades U.S. policy toward Israel (and, by extension, the Palestinians) already had been profoundly impacting the trajectory of the conflict—establishing the foundation, brick by metaphorical brick, for Trumpera policy. Crystallized by U.S. geostrategic interests shaped during the Cold War and spurred by domestic politics, the U.S.-Israel alliance has remained uncompromisingly strong and a lynchpin of American policy in the region. In the wake of the announcement of the Trump "deal," Nathan Thrall, director of the Arab-Israeli Project at the

International Crisis Group and a veteran observer of the conflict, asserted: "It prioritizes Jewish interests over Palestinian ones. It rewards and even incentivizes settlements and further dispossession of the Palestinians. But none of these qualities represent a fundamental break from the past. The Trump plan merely puts the finishing touches on a house that American lawmakers, Republican and Democrat alike, spent dozens of years helping to build."[52]

The United States for decades has supported Israel with billions of dollars of annual grants of military and economic aid. The U.S. has also actively defended Israel in a range of international fora, exerting political pressure on international courts and investigative bodies not to censure Israel for its settlement, land confiscation, and military policies toward the Palestinians.[53] In the UN Security Council, more than half of the total vetoes that the United States has cast from 1970 to 2019—forty-four of eighty-three, or 53 percent—have been to shield Israel from international censure regarding its settlement actions and other measures taken in occupied Palestinian territory, as well as regarding military and other actions taken toward Lebanon and Syria. These U.S. vetoes have been noted to be "far more than any other permanent member [of the council], most frequently to block decisions it regards as detrimental to the interests of Israel."[54]

The net effect of U.S. policy, Thrall maintained—noting that in addition, "the European Union and much of the rest of the world applaud and encourage this charade, solemnly expressing their commitment to the resumption of 'meaningful negotiations'"—has given Israel "cover to perpetuate what is known as the status quo: Israel as the sole sovereign controlling the territory between the Jordan River and the Mediterranean Sea, depriving millions of stateless people of basic civil rights, restricting their movement . . . and dispossessing them of their land."[55]

For lack of a more precise and concise term, the interaction between Israelis and Palestinians since 1948 until the present day is often characterized in shorthand, referred to in media, academic, and policy discourse—as well as within the pages of *Stories from Palestine*—as the "Israel-Palestine conflict." But the obvious should be clearly stated: There is no parity in this asymmetrical conflict; it is hardly a contest of equals, due significantly but not exclusively to the last half century of U.S. policy. Further, as many Palestinian and international observers have long noted, the current map of the West Bank—on the ground and in real time, dominated as it is by Israeli settlements and de facto control of the Jordan Valley as aggressively rendered by Israel with longtime tacit acceptance by the international community and more recently outright backing from the Trump administration—precludes the feasibility if not the possibility of the two-state solution envisioned in the Oslo Accords a generation ago that is still in vogue in much international discourse.

Israel is the largest cumulative recipient of U.S. foreign aid since World War II, receiving $142.3 billion (in noninflation-adjusted dollars) in bilateral assistance and missile-defense funding from 1949 to 2019,[56] with 99 percent granted since 1967.[57] Since 2008, when the majority of economic aid was discontinued,[58] U.S. bilateral aid to Israel has been almost exclusively in the form of military grants, officially designated as Foreign Military Financing or FMF. In the 2016 Memorandum of Understanding between the two countries, the United States pledged $38 billion in aid through fiscal years 2019–2028: $33 billion in annual military grants plus $5 billion in annual missile-defense appropriations.[59]

The U.S. commitment to Israel dates to its creation in 1948, with "robust" support for its security and shared strategic goals for the region.[60] To ensure Israel's strength, U.S. military aid for Israel has been designed to maintain its "qualitative military edge," or QME, over neighboring countries, the Congressional Research Service reports.[61] In 2012 Congress passed the United States–Israel Enhanced Security Cooperation Act, which stated that the policy of the United States is "to help the Government of Israel preserve its qualitative military edge amid rapid and uncertain regional political transformation."[62] Further legislation in 2014 changed mandatory reporting on Israel's QME from every four years to every two.[63]

FMF aid has also advanced Israel's own interests at home and abroad. U.S. military support has helped transform Israel's armed forces into one of the most technologically sophisticated militaries in the world[64] and its domestic arms industry into one of the world's top suppliers of arms, becoming the eighth-largest weapons exporter worldwide from 2012 to 2016.[65] Israel is the largest recipient of U.S.

foreign military financing, accounting for approximately 57 percent of total FMF funding requested by the Trump administration for fiscal 2020 worldwide. Annual FMF grants to Israel represent approximately 18 percent of its overall defense budget; its defense spending as a percentage of its GDP (4.3 percent in 2018) is one of the highest in the world.[66]

Israel was also the first foreign country to operate the U.S.-built F-35 joint-strike fighter jet, considered the most advanced of its kind. From its FMF allocations, by 2018 Israel had purchased fifty Lockheed Martin F-35s of the seventy-five it was allocated to buy by agreement with the U.S. in 2008. Israel also receives "offset" reciprocal purchases by the U.S. from Israeli defense companies, the value of which could reach $4 billion if Israel buys all seventy-five jets.[67]

Despite the fact of its consistent settlement building and settling of Jewish citizens in occupied territories in contravention of international law and consensus—settlement policies that successive U.S. administrations until Trump had criticized for hindering prospects for peace and which, in January 2020, the Associated Press reported had culminated in the number of Israeli settlers in the West Bank and east Jerusalem surpassing seven hundred thousand[68]—Israel has been virtually immune from U.S. sanctions. Penalties imposed for settlement activity have totaled approximately $1.1 billion, deducted from available loan-guarantee allocations in fiscal years 2003 and 2005.[69]

By contrast, U.S. aid to the Palestinians, while greatly expanded since the Oslo Accords of 1993, has been comparatively limited and significantly restricted by stringent congressional oversight. The United States has granted approximately $5 billion in bilateral assistance to the Palestinian Authority from 1994 to 2018.[70] From 1975 to 1993, prior to the establishment of the PA, U.S. development and humanitarian assistance for Palestinians in the West Bank and Gaza totaled approximately $170 million, channeled mainly through nongovernmental organizations.[71] Since 1950 additional, separate U.S. contributions to UNRWA in support of Palestinian refugees throughout the region have totaled more than $6 billion, the most from any country.[72]

From 2008 to 2012, annual U.S. humanitarian and development aid and budgetary support for the PA averaged $400 million, with an addition $100 million in nonlethal assistance for PA security forces and the criminal justice sector in the West Bank.[73] Created largely to stifle activity in the West Bank by supporters of the Gaza-based Hamas, Palestinian security forces were reported in 2016 to number twenty-five thousand to thirty thousand employed in at least eight branches and work in close cooperation with the Israeli military.[74] Hamas, whose name is an Arabic acronym for "Islamic Resistance Movement," has been designated as a foreign terrorist organization by the U.S. government since 1997[75]—a designation that continues to the present despite Hamas having been democratically elected in 2006 and controlling the Gaza Strip since 2007. Since then, parallel to its military activity, Hamas has continued to serve the population in social-service capacities; not affiliated itself with other armed Islamic groups in the region, including Al-Qaeda and ISIS; and through Arab states negotiates indirectly with Israel to reduce the occurrence of military clashes.[76]

U.S. aid to the PA declined from 2012 through fiscal 2017, averaging $310 million a year for humanitarian and budgetary assistance and $71.5 million for security-related support.[77] In addition to political tensions based on the Palestinian Authority's rejection of Trump administration policies and tactics, delays in and reductions to U.S. aid have also been linked to the Taylor Force Act. In March 2018 Congress passed the legislation, augmenting existing conditions to suspend aid to the Palestinian Authority due to payments it makes that are deemed under U.S. law to be "for acts of terrorism"—even though there is no standard definition for "terrorism" used by the U.S. government[78]—but are considered by Palestinians and others to be legitimate acts of resistance to the Israeli occupation.[79] The payments are made to Palestinians imprisoned for such actions as well as to families of such individuals killed by Israeli forces.

As these events and phenomena have continued to play out, the Israel-Palestine conflict has continued to fester while a steady population trend between the Mediterranean Sea and the River Jordan progresses. The imminent if not already virtual population parity between Jews and Arabs—the number of Israeli Jews compared with the number of Palestinian Arab citizens in Israel and Palestinians in the occupied territories—rarely makes headlines but is inching the conflict ever closer to a tilting point.

By September 2020 the population of Israel had reached 9.25 million, according to Israel's Central Bureau of Statistics: 6.841 million Jews, accounting for 74 percent (including settlers in the West Bank and east Jerusalem); and 1.946 million Arabs (including those residing in east Jerusalem), accounting for 21 percent; with the remaining 459,000 (5 percent) identified as members of other groups.[80]

Meanwhile, in March 2018 it was reported that the Palestinian population of the West Bank and Gaza Strip had reached 4.78 million by the end of 2017, according to a census taken by the Palestinian Central Bureau of Statistics and funded by the Palestinian Authority and a host of European governments and nongovernmental organizations (NGOs). The census reported 2.88 million Palestinians in the West Bank and 1.9 million in the Gaza Strip.[81]

In 2018 Israel's leading demographics expert, Sergio DellaPergola, reported that the numbers of Jews and Arabs are nearly equal when the latter includes the populations of the West Bank, Gaza Strip, east Jerusalem, and Israel—and the razor-thin gap is likely to disappear within the next fifteen to twenty years.[82] Population statistics for 2018 indicated an average of 3.11 births per woman in Israel (Jewish and Arab),[83] but nearly 5 births per Palestinian woman in the West Bank and Gaza Strip.[84]

The looming population parity scenario is echoed in Israel's policy and orientation toward its Arab citizens, who account for one-fifth of the country's population. In July 2018 the right-wing Netanyahu government effectively devalued their citizenship status to second-class, adopting a law that officially defines the country as the nation-state of the Jewish people—including Jews who live outside its borders—and downgrading Arabic from an official language to one with "special standing."[85] The Trump peace plan announced in early 2020 went beyond the politics of exclusion to that of removal, stating that it "contemplates the possibility, subject to the agreement of the parties, that the borders of Israel will be redrawn such that the Triangle Communities become part of the State of Palestine"—which would strip upward of two hundred fifty-seven thousand Arab citizens living in ten towns and villages in the "Triangle" region in the center of Israel of their citizenship and involuntarily deport them, in situ, to the Palestinian state.[86]

Against this backdrop, the Israel-Palestine conflict continues to be of essence not only for Israelis and Palestinians. It also holds continuing importance for Arabs and Muslims in the region and beyond, for whom Jerusalem is holy and the conflict represents Western domination if not an ongoing colonial struggle of sorts—despite normalization deals engineered by the Trump administration in 2020 between Israel and a few autocratic Arab states. As such, the conflict continues to affect, directly and indirectly, stability and American interests in the region. Thus, the flow and quality of information about the conflict are significant—even as other events and developments in the region and surrounding it, including the continuing U.S. military presence in Afghanistan and Iraq, civil wars in Yemen and Syria, ISIS, and the Iranian nuclear question, continue to demand attention.

Stories from Palestine is informed by the theory of action that broadening discourse can potentially impact public opinion, affect policy making, and perhaps in turn pave new paths toward peace.[87] *Stories* presents narratives of Palestinians as self-actualizing change agents whose constructive social engagement in the face of occupation is seldom explored in depth by the media and academy.

Geopolitics often flattens, if not obliterates, the humanity of those most directly affected by it. *Stories from Palestine* aims to magnify that humanity in the Palestinian context.

Much if not most information about the Israel-Palestine conflict reaches the public—including policy makers—through the media, in particular television news, and to a lesser extent through academic studies that sometimes filter into popular discourse but generally remain confined to narrower audiences with specific theoretical or otherwise esoteric interests. Western mainstream media coverage of Palestinians tends to represent them as victims of oppression and/or perpetrators of violence.

A leading exemplar, the *New York Times* arguably devotes more resources to producing original reporting and other coverage of the conflict than any other U.S. media outlet. On March 17, 2013, the *New*

York Times Magazine devoted its cover story to an eight-thousand-word freelance report headlined "The Resisters."[88] The piece was a masterful rendering of the landscape of Palestinian resistance to Israeli occupation in the West Bank through a finely drawn portrait of the person, family, and fellow villagers of Bassem Tamimi in Nabi Saleh, where reporter Ben Ehrenreich had spent three weeks. With conflict at the heart of the story, the protagonists were portrayed sympathetically as three-dimensional human beings fighting for their freedom.

A different *Times* narrative approach to Palestinian protest was on display in the front-page, 1,958-word report by Jerusalem bureau chief Jodi Rudoren published on August 5, 2013, under the headline "My Hobby Is Throwing Stones."[89] The piece was notable not only for its prominent play in print and online but also because there was virtually no news in it. Here the venerable *Times* was reporting that "youths hurling stones has long been an indelible icon—some call it a caricature—of Palestinian pushback against Israel." The story included precise data on stone-throwing from UN and Israeli military sources, but the Palestinian context was reduced to literary descriptions and clichéd quotes, such as one from ten-year-old Abdullah: "I feel happy when I throw stones on [*sic*] the soldiers. They occupy us."

The piece did allude to reasons behind the stone-throwing in terms that *Times* readers might relate to: "They throw because there is little else to do in Beit Ommar—no pool or cinema, no music lessons after school, no part-time jobs other than peddling produce along the road. They do it because their brothers and fathers did." However, this superficial reasoning is entirely devoid of the causal contexts of the Israeli occupation—political, social, historical, and economic, found in other *Times* reporting[90]—and of alternative nonviolent Palestinian responses. The net effect of such incomplete, decontextualized reporting—by no means unique to the *Times* but a common phenomenon in the American mainstream media landscape[91]—reduces Palestinians to one-dimensional caricatures, the very word used to describe them at the outset of the piece—a kind of self-fulfilling journalistic prophecy, even if unintended.

As compelling as what appeared in these two *Times* reports is what did not: If the *Times* saw fit to devote such considerable resources to publishing not one but two long-form stories about Palestinian resistance within a five-month span when intercommunal violence was relatively low, then why not a story about expressions of constructive Palestinian initiative and agency outside that frame? Why not delve into what boys in Beit Ommar do when they are *not* throwing stones—which is, presumably, most of the time?

The past two decades have witnessed the proliferation of so-called alternative-media outlets, most operating as digital platforms, that present deeper and broader views of Palestinian society in both news reports and opinion pieces—and in the process challenge the limited framing that so often characterizes mainstream media coverage. In English, these include the *Electronic Intifada, Mondoweiss,* and *Al Jazeera.*[92] Such outlets spur and inform networks of Palestinians and their supporters in civil societies around the world, providing important alternative framing of the conflict. However, the global audience as a whole for news and information about the conflict is significantly larger than the subset within it that turns to alternative outlets, and this larger audience may not be inclined to seek broader perspectives and progressive voices beyond the mainstream.

Parallel to media coverage, if less accessible to the public, the most recent generation of social science research on Palestine and Palestinians has favored qualitative, narrative approaches to their history, culture, and society. The value of storytelling as a focal point of narrative has been noted as a counterpoint to quantitative research, if not an antidote: "If quantitative research foregrounded dominant trends, stories were to theorize the particular. The post-modern suspicion of authoritative, professional, scientific and institutional truths legitimated the search for new voices."[93]

The use of narrative in social science research came to the fore in the 1980s, a "narrative turn" away from quantitative methods focusing on statistical data. This turn stressed "a general anti-positivist and often humanist approach to the study of human psychology and culture" and at the same time created new theoretical constructs—"a new kind of concept of narrative" known as narratology.[94] By the early 1990s it was observed that, "mourning the devaluation of narratives as sources of knowledge, and emphasizing the moral force, healing power, and emancipatory thrust of stories, scholars across the disciplines have (re) discovered the narrative nature of human beings."[95]

On a continuum whose tone and emphasis became more urgent as physical encounters between Israel and the Palestinians became more violent and extreme at the turn of the twenty-first century during the second Palestinian *intifada,* or uprising, and beyond, many scholarly narratives have increasingly situated Palestinians squarely in opposition to Israel, characterizing them—as does much mainstream media coverage—as victims, strugglers, protesters, and fighters. Exploring mechanisms of oppression and resistance—the causes of Palestinian loss and Palestinian reactions to it—is a salient trend in social science works of the past generation. These works tend to focus on Palestinian responses organized around broad political, economic, and military principles and activities (e.g., political parties, protest demonstrations, economic self-sufficiency campaigns and boycotts of Israeli products, forms of armed resistance) that are organized, formal, and for the most part collective.

Such studies include *Palestinians: The Making of a People* (Kimmerling and Migdal, 1993); *Palestinian Identity: The Construction of Modern National Consciousness* (Khalidi, 1997); *The Iron Cage: The Story of the Palestinian Struggle for Statehood* (Khalidi, 2006); *The Ethnic Cleansing of Palestine* (Pappé, 2006); *Israel's Occupation* (Gordon, 2008); and *The Plight of the Palestinians: A Long History of Destruction* (Cook, 2010). Recent critical works include *The Battle for Justice in Palestine* (Abunimah, 2014); *Popular Protest in Palestine: The Uncertain Future of Unarmed Resistance* (Darweish and Rigby, 2015); *Apartheid in Palestine: Hard Laws and Harder Experiences* (Ageel, 2016); *Inter/nationalism: Decolonizing Native America and Palestine* (Salaita, 2016); and *The Dynamics of Exclusionary Constitutionalism: Israel as a Jewish and Democratic State* (Masri, 2017).[96] A subgenre of literature on Palestine amplifies Palestinian voices in long-form, first-person narratives and oral-history collections while addressing broad historical and political contexts in less detail, including *Palestine Speaks: Narratives of Life under Occupation* (Hoke and Malek, 2014).[97]

The themes of dispossession and struggle that tend to imbue scholarly works provide important historical and political context for Israeli policies and Palestinian responses, while oral histories provide invaluable outlets for unmediated Palestinian voices. At the same time, there is room for an inclusive hybrid of the two: deeply contextualized narratives that allow for consideration of Palestinians exercising their human agency creatively and productively, in ways that are informal, individual, and instinctive. The narratives in *Stories from Palestine* demonstrate that even as Palestinians are impacted by the conflict, they are not subordinate to it as they move forward in their everyday lives.

Why do such stories remain largely untold in favor of arcs that are shaped by conflict, emphasize oppression, and often culminate in violence? Clues might be gleaned from perspectives of media and communications theorists.[98]

Herbert Gans has written that journalists do more than observe reality and report events. By selecting topics and sources and by framing issues, they construct reality and go even further: "The news does not limit itself to reality judgments; it also contains values, or preference statements."[99] In deciding what to include and what to omit from their reports, journalists are guided by normative values they share with their audiences. This may be done consciously or otherwise. "The values in news are rarely explicit and must be found between the lines—in what actors and activities are reported and ignored, and in how they are described," Gans says. "If a news story deals with activities which are generally undesirable and whose descriptions contain negative connotations, then the story implicitly expresses a value about what is desirable."[100]

So what is found, and not found, in the chronicling of Palestinians—existing as they do in a landscape of conflict and violence but also as human beings with aspirations that they channel into creative and productive endeavors—can be understood to fall within certain boundaries, as Todd Gitlin describes: "News involves the novel event, not the underlying, enduring condition; the person, not the group; the visible conflict, not the deep consensus; the fact that 'advances the story,' not the one that explains or enlarges it."[101]

It is arguably more logical, if not preferable, to reason that journalists and scholars do not intentionally and/or methodically pursue agendas in order to create hegemonic discourse, which focuses on ideas within a sphere of consensus and shuns ideas situated beyond the pale in a sphere of deviance,[102] or to reinforce the status quo via dominant discourse while either minimizing oppositional and alternative discourses or omitting them altogether.[103] Karim H. Karim suggests that there is not "a deliberate plan by the mass media to portray certain issues in particular ways, but a 'naturalized' hegemonic process through which they adhere to a common field of meanings." As media outlets do so, their process "does not involve the aggressive presentation of specific views but a more subtle and ubiquitous mode which operates within dominant discourses."[104]

Gitlin also finds that media framing is not conscious, and journalists who reproduce and reinforce media frames do not think of them as hegemonic: "Hegemony operates effectively . . . yet outside consciousness; it is exercised by self-conceived professionals working with a great deal of autonomy within institutions that proclaim the neutral goal of informing the public."[105] At the same time, limited framing and constricted discourse can be unintended results. Media frames, he says, are "principles of selection, emphasis, and presentation composed of little tacit theories about what exists, what happens and what matters."[106] By virtue of their pervasiveness and accessibility, the media "name the world's parts, they certify reality *as* reality."[107]

On the other hand, perhaps more darkly, Edward S. Herman and Noam Chomsky have asserted that consent is effectively and purposefully manufactured by the media, which assume a propaganda function geared to a specific social purpose—"but not that of enabling the public to assert meaningful control over the political process by providing them with the information needed for the intelligent discharge of political responsibilities." On the contrary, Herman and Chomsky argue that the intended social purpose is to preserve the status quo, to "inculcate and defend the economic, social, and political agenda of privileged groups that dominate the society and the state."[108]

While there is much to ponder in this array of ideas, journalists do not operate in the realm of theory. And whether or to what degree scholars see themselves and their work as reflecting or reinforcing the social norms that surround them is an open question. But that, perhaps, is key when trying to assess why Palestinians are so often reduced, even in sympathetic and factual terms, to victims of oppression and/or perpetrators of violence within a nearly all-encompassing realm of conflict.

Consider Emad Burnat, a Palestinian farmer turned filmmaker who recorded protests against Israel's separation barrier, which cuts deeply into the West Bank for long stretches, blocking access to agricultural cultivation in Burnat's village of Bil'in and many other Palestinian communities. His footage became the basis for the internationally acclaimed *5 Broken Cameras*,[109] whose title reflects Burnat's persistence in continuing to shoot his documentary despite the Israeli army's repeated attempts to stop him.

The backstory of the film, which attracted the media spotlight when it was nominated for an Oscar in the Best Documentary Feature category for 2012, is essentially *why* Burnat chose to wield a camera in response to the challenges he faced as a Palestinian farmer. What in his lived experience, character, and aspirations propelled him to turn to film as a vehicle of nonviolent protest? Conceivably and most probably, these details could be understood if not shared by Western audiences: the desire to be productive, the freedom to pursue one's livelihood unhindered, the ability to seek recourse in the face of injustice.

But in the main, media accounts that brought Burnat international attention did not focus on the linear narrative of his story. Instead, as his film documents, the reporting revolved around his serial encounters with Israeli soldiers. In this framing, based on a type of conflict that most Western audiences have not experienced, Burnat emerges heroic and determined to persevere, but it does not render him "like us" in his motivations and chosen course of action.

The inimitable Palestinian scholar Edward Said, in his landmark work *Orientalism*, took up the question of why Western academic literature, well into the twentieth century, persisted in presenting Arabs and Muslims as "the Other." Said defined Orientalism in part as "a *distribution* of geopolitical awareness into aesthetic, scholarly, economic, sociological, historical, and philological texts" and posited that "Orientalism is—and does not simply represent—a considerable dimension of modern political-intellectual culture, and as such has less to do with the Orient than it does with 'our' world."[110]

Perhaps, then, a subconscious notion that underlies prevailing scholarly and media depictions of Palestinians—even when viewed with sensitivity and their cause depicted as just—is that they are "Others." In essence, their conflict-ridden experiences are, for most

Westerners, not "like ours," rendering Palestinians and their society not "like us." The result of such exposure is to "Other" them, even unintentionally.

But what impact does "Othering" have on making policy and making peace?

What if opening a new window on Palestinian society could contribute to a recalculation of the elusive equation for resolving the conflict?

What if reflection of the presence of Palestinians as creators and producers endeavoring within the context of their predicament were to stir reconsideration of how to alleviate if not eliminate that predicament?

What if contextualized narratives of constructive Palestinian agency were to expand understanding of the conflict such that those who shape public opinion and form policy might develop new ways of seeing approaches to resolving it?

What if those who already hold such a people-centered view—which not only recognizes but also *insists* on the immense human potential of Palestinians as a sine qua non for peace—could be further empowered?

If Palestinians in the West Bank, east Jerusalem, and Gaza Strip, whose collective society is ripe to be liberated from the schizophrenic mix of Palestinian protogovernments[111] and Israeli occupation, were to find new opportunities to achieve independence, self-determination, and freedom, then the salutary effects of their gains could radiate to their neighbors and throughout the region.

Forty years after Palestine disappeared from maps of the world in 1948, the Palestine Liberation Organization declared a Palestinian state in 1988 during the first intifada. A generation later, in 2012 Palestine was granted nonmember observer status at the United Nations. Yet Palestine remains enmeshed in contradictions: It is neither sovereign nor free, but it maintains national identity, culture, and territory and receives international recognition. It remains under Israeli military occupation—with the West Bank divided into three virtual cantons by a system of checkpoints and settler bypass roads, and with the borders of the Gaza Strip virtually sealed—yet its people have created institutions and spurred grassroots initiatives that are distinctly Palestinian in mission and character.

These are exemplified by the ten universities established in the West Bank and Gaza Strip, nine of them since the Israeli occupation began in 1967.[112] They are evident in the Palestinian Non-Governmental Organizations Network, an umbrella association of a reported 135 grassroots organizations that receive international recognition and funding for their work on issues of women's, children's, and youth welfare and culture; democracy and human rights; and health, law, and societal development.[113]

Palestinians do not yet have a democracy or full-fledged government required to channel it—and these will emerge only as the result of sustained structural change. But Palestinians' resourcefulness and constructive agency will be indispensable in effecting this change, as *Stories from Palestine* attempts to show.

It must be acknowledged that the conflict also exacts its toll on Israelis, albeit to a different degree. Israel is a sovereign state, and its citizens enjoy freedoms, opportunities, and other measures of stability that are beyond the reach of Palestinians as long as they remain under occupation. This work does not compare the two societies, and it does not present narratives suggesting that Palestinians' needs and rights are paramount to those of Israelis. But the kinds of Palestinian perspectives, aspirations, and achievements reflected in these stories lack the ready outlets that their Israeli counterparts often find in many mainstream media and scholarly representations, as well as in U.S. policy considerations of the conflict.

Existing somewhere between the first and third worlds, Palestinian society is awaiting rebirth, at once mired in political and economic stagnation[114] while maintaining a thriving national identity and a resolute, collective sense of purpose. Among the five million Palestinians living in the West Bank, east Jerusalem, and Gaza Strip, there are fascinating and important stories of constructive human agency to be told.

The narratives presented in *Stories from Palestine* are based on interviews begun in late 2015–mid-2016 for the first chapter, on Palestinian agriculture, and continued in 2018–19 for the remainder of the work. The narratives reflect the activities, perspectives, and conditions of sources at the times they were interviewed, with some data and other background information updated subsequently.

Measurements of distance and area are expressed in local metric and other terms: kilometers (1 kilometer = approximately .62 miles), square kilometers (1 square kilometer = approximately .386 square miles), square meters (1 square meter = approximately 10.7 square feet), and dunams (1 dunam = approximately .25 acres).

Chapter 1 presents a story of Palestinian agriculture in the West Bank, with farmers determined to continue cultivating their land even as the landscape in which they do so is shrinking.

Chapter 2 presents a story of Palestinian education in the West Bank, with teachers, professors, and officials paving the way for youth and producing knowledge.

Chapter 3 presents a story of Palestinians in the West Bank pursuing the arts, recreation, and other cultural pleasures in life, such as those offered up by Madees Khoury and her family at the Taybeh Brewing Company.

Chapter 4 presents a story of Palestinians maintaining their presence in east Jerusalem, often a focal point of conflict but always a locus of Palestinian identity.

Chapter 5 presents a story of Palestinians persevering amid the harsh conditions and uncertainties of daily life in the Gaza Strip.

These five stories and the narratives that support them are meant to impart a sense-making of meanings imbedded in the lived experiences of Palestinians—so that we may consider new ways to interact with them.

CHAPTER 1

Made in Palestine

Adnan Massad receives visitors who have come to talk to him about why he farms and how he does it—and especially to see his tractor, which runs on recycled vegetable oil that was used in restaurants to fry falafel.

Here in Faqqu'a, a Palestinian village in the northern West Bank, the early afternoon is awash in mid-May sunshine, the cloudless sky a brilliant blue, the breeze persistent—a whisper, perhaps, from the Mediterranean coast forty kilometers or so to the west.

Massad, a spry sixty-two, is known as Abu Nur ("father of Nur," his eldest son). He sits relaxed, his knees folded under his lanky frame on brown furrowed soil in the shade of an olive tree. He wears a white baseball cap brim-backward over his thick white hair, which is matched by a full white mustache and beard. Clad in a light-green zip hoodie and jeans, he takes a drag on a cigarette as he describes his thirty acres: on just under half, he cultivates olive trees; on the rest, he grows almond trees, wheat, beans, peas, and animal-feed crops.

Massad works up to ten hours a day on this land, inherited from his father, Abd as-Salaam, who inherited it from his father, Mahmoud. The family has lived in Faqqu'a, about three kilometers east of Jenin, for at least six generations—"maybe more," Massad says, "hundreds of years."[1] His ancestors migrated from what is today Syria.

As a boy Massad helped his family raise wheat, barley, and lentils. After finishing high school in Jenin, from age twenty he worked in construction, three years in the West Bank and twenty-two in Israel. He found the work boring, but it supported his wife, four sons, and a daughter. By age forty-five, though, Massad had had enough and decided to farm his land full-time. He earns less farming than he did in construction; he says the choice to trade higher income for greater freedom was difficult but right.

"I am free to decide how to manage my time," he says. "I work for myself, not others." Like farmers around the world, he starts work early in the morning, returning to eat with his family at midday and rest before returning to the fields. To the original grain and vegetable crops he added olive and almond trees fifteen years ago.

Today Massad's children are grown; his sons all work construction in the West Bank. The family works the land together at harvest time, but Massad does the year-round maintenance himself. He plows, fertilizes, and weeds his fields alone, riding high atop the red Massey Ferguson 185 tractor he bought used in 1981 and refurbished.

In 2016, with the help of the Center for Organic Research and Extension, a local Palestinian NGO that promotes organic farming and marketing of fruit, vegetables, and grains grown by small family farmers, Massad converted the tractor to run on used falafel oil, replacing diesel. CORE paid the initial $5,000 cost of the German-made peripheral converter and its installation. The move cut his tractor-fuel expenses by more than half, saving him nearly $2,000 a year. Reducing farmers' use of fossil fuel and enhancing restaurants' waste management are also good for the environment, which is referenced on the CORE placard affixed to the converter proclaiming in Arabic and English that the red iron horse is an "eco-friendly tractor."

Running tractors on used vegetable oil is not new—"you can see it on YouTube," Massad says. CORE adopted the method as a focal point of its Green Track Palestine project and has also enabled other Jenin-area farmers to convert their tractors. CORE recruits restaurants in Jenin—including the Kentucky Fried Chicken franchise there—and in surrounding towns and villages to save the oil they fry falafel in for two or three days and then sell it for a token price to the farmers, who pick it up. Massad gets most of his oil from two eateries in Faqqu'a and extra supply from restaurants in Jenin during the harvest.

He says the benefits of working with CORE extend beyond the oil to additional agricultural extension support including supply of beehives, which he uses to pollinate his almond trees and produce honey for market. He has also bought almond and jojoba seedlings from CORE at a deeply discounted price.

Although the Palestinian market for organic produce is relatively new, it does command higher prices, he says, even though fertilizing and weeding crops by hand, without chemicals, is more difficult than in conventional farming. Then there is the challenge of water, faced by all Palestinian farmers. With rainfall insufficient to sustain most crops and with working wells in short supply, he must buy water, adding significantly to his costs.

Nur stops by the grove to drop off refreshments for his father and the guests: cold bottled lemonade, sweet pastries, and thick Arab coffee. Massad chuckles as he pours it, considering the question of why farming is important to him.

"If I weren't a farmer—if we didn't farm—where would we bring farmers from?" he grins. "Pakistan? China?" Farming is instinctive, "something that comes from inside, telling you that you have to maintain your land," he says.

The visit ends on a light note with Massad recalling his visit to kin in the U.S., where he toured Chicago, Washington, DC, and Las Vegas. He bids his guests farewell in typical Arab fashion after they thank him for his time and hospitality.

Ahla wasahla, Adnan Massad says. "You are welcome."

Land is the ultimate prize in the Israeli-Palestinian conflict—but Palestinians are continually confronted by harsh realities of the Israeli occupation that makes cultivating their land difficult and in some cases impossible.

Like Adnan Massad, though, they continue to farm, a steadfast expression of their presence and heritage.

In many other parts of the world, their stories would be ordinary. In Palestine, prevailing circumstances render them remarkable.

The toll of land confiscation under Israeli occupation has been constant and consistent. Palestinian agricultural lands shrank from 2.4 million dunams (approximately 593,000 acres) in 1980 to 1.03 million dunams in 2010—a loss of 57 percent, according to UNCTAD, the United Nations Conference on Trade and Development.[2] Before Israel occupied the West Bank and Gaza Strip in 1967 after the Six-Day War, agriculture constituted more than half of the Palestinian GDP. By 2012 it accounted for only 6 percent.[3]

Expansion of Israeli settlements—including confiscation of Palestinian land—and restricted access to water are chief causes for decline in Palestinian land use, the UN agency reported[4]—contributing in significant measure to Palestinian dependence on Israel. By 2018 the Palestinian economy in the West Bank and Gaza Strip was running a $2.65 billion trade deficit with Israel, according to the Palestinian Central Bureau of Statistics—accounting for 49 percent of its overall trade deficit of $5.4 billion, with a population of just under five million. In food and livestock alone, the Palestinian trade deficit for 2018 was $1.27 billion, or 23.5 percent of the overall deficit.[5]

This is not what was intended in the now-defunct Oslo Accords of 1993, a plan for a permanent settlement of the conflict by 1999 based on the land-for-peace principle contained in UN Security Council Resolutions 242 (1967) and 338 (1973). The accords implicitly envisioned the establishment of an independent, demilitarized Palestinian state coexisting side by side with a secure Israel. While Israeli military forces withdrew from Palestinian population centers in the West Bank as a result of Oslo, the major issues of the conflict remained unresolved and became more complex, with Israeli settlement and land confiscation unabated.

In the generation that has passed since the iconic Rabin-Clinton-Arafat handshake on the White House lawn at the signing of the accords in September 1993, population and land ratios have continually shifted in Israel's favor, adding a distinct economic overlay to a conflict marked by violence and political stalemate. The number of Israeli settlers in the West Bank has more than tripled since 1993: according to the Israeli NGO Peace Now, by 2019 the number had reached approximately 430,000 (accounting for 13 percent among a Palestinian population of approximately 2.9 million), with another 215,000 settlers in east Jerusalem (among a Palestinian population of approximately 340,000); media reports in 2019–20 put the overall settler total at 700,000.[6]

Although the rate of settler growth has slowed, at 3.4 percent in 2017 it was still more than one and a half times greater than population growth in Israel proper.[7] While the number of West Bank settlements officially recognized by Israel has remained fairly constant, from 126 to 130 (and about 100 smaller "outposts"),[8] the settlements have continued to grow in population and area, sanctioned and subsidized by a succession of Israeli governments despite having been deemed illegal in UN Security Council Resolutions 446, 452 (1979), and 465 (1980).

In the face of these circumstances, though, Palestinians continue to work the soil, innovating as they go to overcome short supplies of land and water. Most are small family farmers like Reja-e and Musaab Fayyad, who in 2016 were growing organic strawberries, juicy and sweet, on a three-dunam patch of land—three-quarters of an acre—in the village of Zababdeh, just south of Jenin. The brothers box their red fruit in pint-size plastic containers labeled "The Brothers Farm, Zababdeh Palestine"; the stickers echo the motif and colors of the Palestinian flag.

"We are local producers," says Musaab, twenty-six, who has a degree in finance and a family line of farmers at least three generations long. "Our customers come here to pick the berries themselves—and they feel good about it."[9] The cartons that the Fayyads use to pack their produce bear slogans in Hebrew such as "from the peaks of Galilee-Golan," a region roughly seventy-five to one hundred kilometers north of Zababdeh, across the Green Line, the internationally recognized demarcation separating Israel from the territories it occupied in 1967. Such Palestinian-made containers are in short supply, says Reja-e, forty-one, so the brothers use Israeli ones.

To overcome limited access to water, the Fayyads built an eighty-thousand-gallon rainwater catchment basin to irrigate their crops, and they stocked it with *musht*, otherwise known as tilapia or St. Peter's fish. The brothers pipe the water into their greenhouse to irrigate the plants and feed them with fish waste, saving 90 percent on fertilizer costs.

The Fayyads' ingenuity is also on display underneath the hanging strawberry crop in the greenhouse, where ripening red fruit dangles above rows of greens planted in the ground, including arugula, string beans, broccoli, celery, scallions, parsley, and hot peppers. Not only does combined above- and below-ground cultivation maximize the small growing space, but the in-ground crops also divert disease-carrying insects from the strawberries, increasing the yield of the brothers' cash crop. "Each plant attracts specific insects and diseases," Reja-e says. Varietal intercropping serves to confuse insects, decreasing the diseases they carry up to fivefold. To this cornucopia the brothers later added tomatoes and pineapples.

The Fayyads' agricultural techniques are born of necessity and, perhaps, pedigree. Their paternal grandfather, Assad, originally from Haifa, grew corn, wheat, lentils, and beans. In 1948—when the State of Israel was established and military campaigns displaced approximately 55 percent of the indigenous 1.3 million Palestinian Arabs to clear the way for a Jewish majority within the borders of the Jewish state drawn by the 1947 UN partition of Palestine[10]—Assad was among thousands of Arab refugees who migrated to the West Bank. There his son Abdullah, a schoolteacher, continued to farm in Zababdeh on rented land, raising wheat, corn, watermelon, and beans.

Reja-e and Musaab farm that same land, which Abdullah eventually came to own. After growing strawberries in the ground for five years, they invested $20,000 to build the greenhouse and buy another 18,000 strawberry seedlings to plant above ground. Musaab, a graduate of the Arab American University just up the road in Jenin, turned to agriculture for lack of available finance jobs; Reja-e has supplemented his income working as a security officer for the Palestinian Authority. The brothers have averaged about $2,300 a month during the seven-month strawberry season but took little profit early on, reinvesting the proceeds to pay down loans and build their business, realizing small but increasing gains from economies of using rainwater and fish-waste fertilizer.

In season, they have sold up to three hundred and twenty kilograms of organic strawberries a month, about a third to vendors in Ramallah, about sixty kilometers south, and the rest to local customers. Strawberries grown in Israeli settlements in the West Bank are also available in local Palestinian markets but spoil faster, Musaab says, because Israeli growers use chemical pesticides and fertilizers to get a higher yield. "Not many of our customers are aware of the health benefits of organic food," he notes, "but they like the taste of our strawberries. They are sweeter and won't liquefy after a few days." In the meantime, the Brothers Farm contributes to the small but growing Palestinian market for organic produce. "For us," Reja-e says, "it's a way to spread awareness."

For Palestinians, the very act of cultivation and its resulting harvests spread another kind of awareness, in the view of Nasser Abufarha, who has built a business rooted in sustaining Palestinian agriculture and exporting its produce. "Many people around the world see injustice in the conflict," he says, "but they don't know what Palestinians have to offer to them." Reducing Palestinians to victims of oppression is an unfair characterization, he maintains; keeping Palestinians visible as cultivators of the land is crucial.

"We're still producing some of the best treasures the earth has to give. It's important that the world sees this, including Israelis," Abufarha maintains. When people around the world consume Palestinian produce, he says, they bond with Palestinians. "And in this bonding, Palestinians become relevant, and are not dismissed as bad news."[11]

Images of young women bearing harvest baskets and water jugs are iconic in Palestinian folk art. Young male balladeers declare their love for the land at Palestinian weddings. *Sanābil*, or wheat stalks, adorn Palestinian embroidery. And so, the continuity of Palestinian farming, Abufarha reasons, is a cultural imperative.

After earning a doctorate in international development and cultural anthropology from the University of Wisconsin—Madison, Abufarha, born in 1964, returned home to immerse himself in the landscape of activism and development. In 2004 he established Canaan Fair Trade[12] based on the idea that the link between the people and their land not only binds Palestinians to their history and culture but also sustains their future.

Abufarha's light and airy second-floor office in the Canaan factory overlooks dunams of olive groves in Burqin, the small town five kilometers west of Jenin where his mother is from; Abufarha was born and raised in his father's native Jalamah, about five kilometers north, where the family grew oranges, eggplants, tomatoes, cucumbers, watermelon, and cantaloupe. The distance between these points is short, but Abufarha's worldview is broad and deeply rooted in the certainty of the once and continuing centrality of agriculture in Palestinian life.

"The traditional life of making a living off the land—that's a culture. And we have that culture," he says. "But it lacks support and investment for its sustainability. The main thing is to sustain it and benefit from it, to carve a space for it in modern society, in modern economy."

Canaan aims to bolster Palestinian agriculture by retooling traditional farming methods to answer modern demands for organic foods, fair trade, and environmental accountability. "We are not separate from the world," Abufarha notes. "There is an influx of modern manufactured foods, and there is an acceleration of agribusiness versus agriculture." The five-thousand-square-meter Canaan factory opened in 2008; by early 2020 it was producing for export an average of twelve hundred metric tons—approximately 346,300 gallons—of olive oil a year as well as packaged almonds and grains, all organic and grown by a network of small family farmers. Forty Palestinians work at Canaan year-round; in the fall olive-harvest season, the number swells to seventy.

Palestinian farmers work under conflict-zone conditions and face challenges that are politically motivated by the occupation, Abufarha says, such as constraints on land, water, and movement. In this context, he believes, preserving the nexus between Palestinians and their land is paramount. "The conflict is about land. Israelis know that the relationship between the Palestinian and the land is at the core of the representation and configuration of the place," he says.

Not mere anthropological theory, this notion materialized in January 2016, when the European Union rejected Israel's labeling of export products made in the occupied West Bank, east Jerusalem, and Golan Heights as "Made in Israel"[13]—trade estimated to be worth at least $300 million per year.[14] The EU position mirrors international law and consensus that the territories occupied by Israel since 1967 are not within its internationally recognized borders, and it echoes three-decades-old UN Security Council resolutions that Israeli settlements have "no legal validity."[15]

In the wake of the EU declaration, the U.S. Customs and Border Protection agency reiterated a 1997 Treasury Department decision ruling that Israeli-produced goods from the West Bank and Gaza Strip must be labeled as such: "It is not acceptable to mark [such] goods with the words 'Israel,' 'Made in Israel,' 'Occupied Territories-Israel' or any variation thereof."[16] Coincidentally or otherwise, two months later U.S.-based Airbnb received a petition with 140,000 signatures calling on the online lodging marketplace to stop listing properties in West Bank settlements, many of them described as being located in Israel.[17]

Canaan's agricultural products are made in Palestine. They are sold in bulk and as finished and packaged goods to markets in Europe, North America, Asia, and the Middle East. By early 2020 exports were averaging $11 million a year, up to $8 million in olive oil and $3 million in almonds and grains including *freekeh* and *maftoul*. Sixty percent of the olive oil is sold in the U.S., 20 percent in Europe, and the remainder in Canada and Asia. Bulk sales of olive and almond oil account for half of all revenues, with Canaan the chief olive oil supplier to Dr. Bronner's Magic Soaps in the United States. American outlets Whole Foods and Williams-Sonoma carry Canaan-branded items, which comprise 35 percent of sales. Private-label partners account for the remaining 15 percent.

His entrepreneurship buoyed by international demand for Palestinian products, Abufarha pushes forward in his campaign to nurture Palestinian agriculture, even as Israel continues to confiscate Palestinian land in the West Bank. "It's not only about how much confiscation takes place," he says. "It's what we do about it that matters—because what defines ownership is the social relationship with the land and how sustainable that relationship is."

Abufarha's roadmap for sustainability points in many directions. Canaan is the food-processing link in its sustainable crop value chain; he established the Palestine Fair Trade Association as the marketing vehicle to export farmers' crops for above-market prices according to international fair trade standards. Canaan's tuition scholarship fund for children of farmers has supported forty-four young Palestinians attending local four-year universities from 2007 to early 2020.

CORE, the organic farming research, extension, and training arm, is staffed by Palestinian agronomists who earned PhD and master's degrees in Palestine and Europe. They work with farmers to transfer regenerative farming methods that renew soil health, including use of organic fertilizers and intercropping, and to bolster small-farming sustainability through programs such as tractor conversion that swaps diesel fuel for used falafel oil. CORE also partners with the PA Ministry of Agriculture, cooperating and coordinating on research and extension projects. From 2015 to 2019, CORE raised $564,800 from sources including The Land of Canaan Foundation, the European Union's Horizon 2020 research and innovation program, U.S.-based ice cream giant Ben & Jerry's, Christian Aid, and World Vision.

Areen Shaar holds a master's degree in civil engineering she earned in the U.S. and worked fifteen years outside the field of agriculture before serving as CORE program manager in 2017–18, but she didn't hesitate to accept the position. "Agriculture is a main sector for us here in Palestine," she says. "With agriculture we own the land, the history, our existence as Palestinians. So, the land is part of us."[18]

Shaar, born in 1974 in Anabta, a small town next to Tulkarm, says Palestinian farmers are vulnerable and Palestinian agriculture is fragile. "We need to support it as much as we can in order for the farmers to sustain their living. I take this as a kind of humanitarian work—on a human level, not only on an economic level."

Given the intrusion of land confiscation by Israel, as much as Palestinians can cultivate their land, "we can continue with our resistance and our existence as Palestinians here," she says, evoking the olive tree as testament to the continuity of her people. "For us it's not just a holy tree. It's about history, about existing on our land. It's amazing to stand in front of a tree that is thousands of years old and imagine our ancestors working on this piece of land.

"They were standing where I stand," she says. "What were their dreams for us? What was their thinking when they planted this tree? It was watered with our ancestors' sweat, not only water."

The passion that has driven Shaar in her work is of a piece with Abufarha's vision. He recounts having met, some years ago, a German woman who expressed concern for Palestinians' welfare. "Don't worry too much," he recalls telling her. "We are integrated in the ecosystem of the land of Palestine, and we are organic in it. As long as we sustain this relationship, we will remain."

From a rise overlooking the olive groves of Faris Hussein and his cousin Rafiq in Ti'inik, a hamlet thirteen kilometers northwest of Jenin in the northern tip of the West Bank, the plains of Afula and mountains of Nazareth appear in the middle distance, inside Israel, beyond the Green Line. Together the Husseins farm eighty-six dunams in their village, just over half planted with olive trees, the rest with melons, alfalfa, wheat, and soft-shell almonds. Their cultivation is bound by kinship, but they are part of a larger family as well.

The cousins belong to the local Palestine Fair Trade Association cooperative, which has attracted twenty members and been headed by Rafiq. Earning above-market prices for their crops is a key draw. "The association organizes the farmers, and its marketing program sustains good prices, better than we could get in the local market on our own," Faris explains.[19]

By early 2020, across the northern and central West Bank, 1,217 Palestinian farmers were participating in the PFTA network and CORE programs, comprising fifty-two cooperatives and six women's collectives and cultivating approximately 63,700 dunams. With the average family size at seven, nearly 8,500 people were supported by this agriculture, mainly in the north between Jenin and Nablus but also in and around Salfit, Ramallah, Tulkarm, Qalqilia, and Tubas. Another six hundred farming families have benefited from the PFTA network since 2004.

The association trains members in fair trade standards and regulations as well as organic-farming methods; external audits for fair trade and organic certifications are conducted by Fairtrade International, based in Germany, and the Institute for Marketecology in Switzerland. The PFTA is also overseen by the Palestinian Authority's Interior and National Economy ministries. Says Abufarha: "We are working according to our own needs and philosophy but also according to internationally recognized standards."

A nine-member elected governing board runs the association, and delegates represent their co-ops and collectives in a general assembly. The PFTA pricing committee maintains contact with local and international markets, according to Mohammed Al-Ruzzi, who has served as manager of the association's office in Jenin and negotiates rates for virgin and extra-virgin olive oil.[20] Depending on sales volume, PFTA co-ops and collectives can also receive a fair trade premium each season in addition to fair trade market prices for their crops. Each group decides how to invest the premium, from buying farm equipment to giving back to the community. In 2014 the Ti'inik cooperative donated its bonus to establish a local health clinic.

Since 2006 the association's Trees for Life program, funded by PFTA olive oil buyers and Palestinian solidarity groups in Europe, the United States, and Canada, has distributed approximately 156,000 olive and almond saplings to Palestinian farmers, in some cases to replace trees uprooted or burned by Israeli settlers. "We pay a symbolic amount of two shekels per olive tree," Faris says. "The market price is ten shekels."

The Husseins trace their roots in Ti'inik back two hundred years, and like most Palestinians their family has worked the land for just as long. Faris, born in 1949, recalls the animals his family used to farm when he was a boy; now a red, four-cylinder Massey Ferguson 165 sits parked outside his house. His father was a full-time farmer; Faris graduated from the University of Jordan in 1974 with a degree in Islamic studies, returned to Ti'inik to become headmaster of a local school, and farmed on the side. Now retired, he continues to cultivate the land, but not without difficulties that Palestinian farmers face routinely in the West Bank.

Chief among them is water, Faris says. "Israelis have as much water as they want. We have a problem digging new wells." In November 2015 the Israeli army bulldozed three small wells that Ti'inik farmers dug without permits, which are routinely denied.[21] Without wells, farmers cannot irrigate their crops, but without permits such wells are considered illegal, and the army routinely destroys them.

"Land without water has very little value," says Ciro Fiorillo, who has served as head of office for the Food and Agriculture Organization (FAO) of the United Nations in Jerusalem, which supports agricultural aid projects in the West Bank and Gaza Strip.[22] Israeli restrictions on water, including diversion of water resources to Jewish settlements, allow for irrigation of less than 5 percent of Palestinian cultivated land, severely limiting agricultural productivity. Irrigated land produces on average fifteen times the yield of rain-fed land;[23]

even though Israel, Jordan, and the Palestinian territories share the same climate, the average yield per dunam in the West Bank and Gaza Strip is half that of Jordan and 43 percent of the yield in Israel.[24]

"If you cannot irrigate, the best you can do is dry cropping—olives, low-intensity cereals," Fiorillo says. "But with irrigation you can shift from cereals to vegetables." Vegetable farming is more labor intensive, raising employment, and more profitable, raising income. "Then you build an irrigation system, and then you build a greenhouse, and you produce much more value," he notes. "With a two-dunam greenhouse, a family can live a reasonable life."

But Palestinian farmers are blocked not only from digging new wells to irrigate their crops but also from repairing existing ones, for which they must also obtain Israeli permission. The Israeli-Palestinian Joint Water Committee, which issues permits, had all but ceased to function beginning in 2010. Palestinian participants were asked to legalize wells constructed in Israeli settlements—but all settlements and any related infrastructure are considered illegal under international law. Palestinian committee members refused, stalemate ensued, and few permits have been issued to Palestinians since. Israeli settlements continue to use irrigation systems built without permits; Palestinian wells dug without permits continue to be destroyed and maintenance of old ones hampered.

"There are hundreds of wells, and these wells have been established thirty, forty, fifty, one hundred years ago," Fiorillo says, adding that most Palestinian water-carrier networks also need repairs, with rust and holes causing leakage and water loss of up to 40 percent. For wells, "the committee has to authorize the maintenance; otherwise the civil administration can stop the work." Fiorillo says the military confiscated replacement pipes—which do not require permits—that the FAO donated to Palestinian farmers in 2015 to repair leaking networks. After an appeal to Israeli authorities that went through the Dutch parliament, he says, the majority of the pipes were returned and installed.

Israel's intent behind these policies, Faris Hussein says, "is to occupy the land. If there's no water, there's no productivity. This increases our dependency on their food products." It also displaces Palestinian labor. "Our young people won't be farmers but will go to work in Israel" as unskilled laborers, mainly in construction, he says. "They earn better wages [there] than doctors, teachers, and government workers. This also makes it difficult to find enough workers to harvest our crops."

Tens of thousands of young West Bank Palestinians work in Israel and Israeli settlements. In 2019 the Bank of Israel reported that more than one-third of the eighty-one thousand Palestinians working in Israel were forced to purchase their work permits;[25] and approximately thirty-six thousand Palestinians were also reported to be working in West Bank settlements, mainly in construction, earning up to three times the average Palestinian wage.[26] But in Israeli settlement agriculture jobs, Human Rights Watch reported in 2016, daily wages were as low as $17.50—around one-third of the Israeli minimum wage, with no benefits.[27]

For Palestinians not alienated from their land, holding on to and accessing it in areas densely populated with Israeli settlements or near the Israeli separation barrier can be daunting. Israel began building the barrier in 2002 during the second Palestinian uprising, ostensibly for security reasons. The Israeli human-rights organization B'Tselem has characterized the structure—which takes the form of a concrete wall in Palestinian urban areas, including east Jerusalem and Bethlehem, and electronic and barbed-wire fencing in rural areas throughout the West Bank—as "a major political instrument for furthering Israeli annexationist goals." Approximately 85 percent of the barrier route zigzags beyond Israel proper east of the Green Line, cutting into the West Bank and separating Palestinian farmers from their lands.[28]

In the village of 'Anin, a few kilometers west of Ti'inik, the Israeli military confiscated farmland to build the fence, the PFTA's Al-Ruzzi says. Scores of Palestinian communities have been similarly affected, with an estimated 9.4 percent of the West Bank, including thousands of dunams of Palestinian farmland, to be partitioned west of the planned barrier route under Israeli control when its entire 712-kilometer length—more than double that of the Green Line—is completed. As of September 2017, 65 percent of the barrier had been built.[29]

The section of the separation barrier near Ariel—a large settlement city in the central West Bank that by August 2018 boasted a population approaching twenty thousand, an Israeli-accredited university, a hospital with its own medical school under construction, and a forty-five-plant industrial zone[30]—has separated Palestinian landowners in the nearby town of Salfit and six surrounding villages from nine thousand dunams of their farm and grazing land, according to Human Rights Watch.[31] One Palestinian landowner in the area who had grazed ten thousand head of livestock was left with no more than one hundred; another landowner who planted fifteen dunams with root vegetables had the land confiscated outright, and when the military imposed restrictions on access, equipment, and planting in another of his thirty-five dunams, he stopped cultivating them entirely.[32]

When the military does grant access, "permits are given to old people, not young people," Al-Ruzzi says. "But we need strong people to harvest and transport crops. Access often depends on the officer at the checkpoint." In addition, he says, PFTA purchasing officers driving to olive presses in the West Bank during harvest season in some years have faced risky and difficult passage imposed by Israeli military forces on roads in "hot zones" in and around Ramallah and Salfit due to violent unrest stemming from clashes at holy sites in Jerusalem.

Despite the obstacles, olive tree cultivation—ongoing in Palestine for more than two thousand years—remains the staple of its agriculture, accounting for 54 percent. Half the oil is produced for home consumption; the other half is sold domestically and abroad, Al-Ruzzi says. Canaan has an 80 percent share of the exports. In good years he estimates that overall olive oil yield in the West Bank averages twenty-six thousand metric tons. In 2017 the yield was nineteen thousand five hundred metric tons; in 2019 it reached thirty-seven thousand metric tons.[33]

"The olive tree," Faris Hussein says, "is a blessing. It gives us food, medicine, and heating." Healers use olive-leaf extracts to lower blood-sugar levels and blood pressure. Artisans carve handicrafts from its wood. In Palestine and beyond, olive oil is eaten with hummus, both scooped up in pita bread.

Faris sighs. "We live on this land. We'll die on this land. We'll be buried inside this land."

Then he brightens. "It is our mother. It is our homeland. It is everything."

Farmers in and around Jenin live in the breadbasket of Palestine. The city and its environs lie on the southern edge of Marj ibn 'Amr—the Jezreel Valley, a great fertile plain extending north beyond the Green Line almost to Haifa. With an estimated population by early 2020 of 52,000, the city of Jenin is the seat of the Jenin governorate and the center for an estimated regional population of 328,600.[34] Of eleven administrative districts in the West Bank, Jenin governorate is the only one in which the Palestinian Authority controls the majority of the land, a peculiarity linked to the relatively small number of Israeli settlers in the area, some two thousand.

For all the challenges that Jenin-area farmers face, including water and access to land near the separation barrier, conditions become more difficult further south in the West Bank, where the verdant, flat topography of Marj ibn 'Amr gradually gives way to peaks and valleys and then, to the east and further south, the amber-brown Judean desert, where the bulk of the Israeli settler population lives.

In 1995 the interim agreement of the Oslo process divided the West Bank into three zones. The PA has sole control over Area A, constituting the built-up areas around Palestinian cities and about 18 percent of the territory. Israel and the PA jointly control Area B, about 21 percent. Israel has sole control over Area C, which accounts for 61 percent of the West Bank, including the Jordan Valley and 63 percent of West Bank agricultural land.

By 2018 approximately 365,000 or 90 percent of the 405,000 Israeli settlers in the West Bank were living in Area C among 393,000 Palestinians.[35] Despite this virtual population parity, Israel has designated 68 percent of Area C for settlements (including future expansion) but less than 1 percent for Palestinian use.[36] In 2013 the World Bank estimated that alleviating restrictions on access to land and water and other aspects of Palestinian production in Area C could add as much as $3.4 billion a year to the Palestinian economy, up to one-third of its GDP.[37]

Throughout the West Bank, Israel has claimed approximately 166,650 dunams—approximately 41,000 acres—for direct settlement activity (excluding extended jurisdictional areas of settlements, road networks, and military facilities), according to Human Rights Watch—with 64 percent of this land designated for agriculture and industrial zones.[38] Privately owned Palestinian land is expropriated both outright and by being declared "state land"—either way becoming inaccessible.

For lack of other employment opportunities outside of Israel and Israeli settlements, the number of Palestinians working in agriculture increases even as the productivity of the sector continues to decline. "People have no other place to work," Fiorillo of the FAO says. "So more people cultivate the same or even less land. Declining productivity per person means declining value in salaries, profits, or any other form of income." According to UNCTAD, while agriculture accounted for 15 percent of total Palestinian employment in 2011 and 20 percent of exports, only 6 percent of 292,000 agricultural workers earned income, with 94 percent working as unpaid family members.[39]

Displacement and disruption caused by the occupation ripple through the Palestinian economy, in agriculture and beyond—to the extent that UNCTAD has characterized achieving sustainable development in the West Bank and Gaza Strip as "nearly impossible."[40] Palestinian productivity is hampered by restrictions on movement and access to land and water; these in turn not only increase uncertainty about property rights and inhibit private investment, but they also tie Palestinian labor and consumption into a knot of dependency.

However, factors not directly related to the occupation also impact Palestinian agriculture, according to Fiorillo. "The weaknesses of public services and of private services that depend on public regulation is not a matter of occupation," he says, citing the Palestinian Authority's limited capacity to provide quality control, extension, and research services for agriculture. In addition, Palestinian banks do not have loan products for small farmers who lack acceptable collateral, even as annual demand has reached $150 million. "This is an effect of the slow process of building the Palestinian state. It is related to the history of the country," he says, "but it's not just the occupation."

Since the PA was established in 1994, it has allocated little more than 1 percent of its total annual budget to agriculture, with 85 percent of that going to Ministry of Agriculture salaries.[41] In 2013 the ministry charted a three-year development plan for new projects and service improvements, projecting allocations of approximately $543 million for 2014 to 2016.[42] However, "recurrent economic, political, and humanitarian crises," such as the 2014 Gaza war and its aftermath, "have claimed much of [the PA's] scarce resources, energy, and policy attention," UNCTAD reported.[43]

Whatever the relative weights of the causes, the impoverishing effects of these factors are apparent, to the point that Palestinians face "forced dependence" on the Israeli economy, according to the UN agency.[44] They have become a captive market, not only as laborers in Israel and Israeli settlements but also as consumers of Israeli products, with Israel sending a steady flow of below-export-quality goods to Palestinian markets at prices with which local producers cannot compete. The overall Palestinian trade deficit of $5.4 billion in 2018— $2.65 billion or 49 percent of it with Israel[45]—equaled 37 percent of the $14.6 billion Palestinian GDP.[46]

Palestinians also experience food insecurity, which is distinct from malnutrition or lack of food. "Palestinians don't have enough income to access in a stable and predictable manner food in adequate quantity and quality," Fiorillo says. The FAO reported in 2019 that over one-third of Palestinian households in the West Bank and Gaza Strip, numbering 1.7 million people, were food insecure in 2018, with 11.6 percent in the West Bank and 68.5 percent in the Gaza Strip.[47] This phenomenon is not natural but manmade, Fiorillo says. It results from factors including dramatic dips in food supply due to periodic wars in Gaza, chronic displacement of Bedouin communities in the West Bank by the Israeli military, and consistently low levels of Palestinian income. The 2019 FAO report also cited Israeli restrictions on the movement of people and goods, limited access to essential services, and continuing energy shortages since 2017 as having significant and severe effects on Palestinian livelihoods, including agriculture.[48]

By contrast, food security is not even classified in Israel. "Essentially," Fiorillo says, "you have to equate it to a European country."

Back in Zababdeh, Basma Qablawi, forty-three, was cultivating her home garden in 2016 not far from where the Fayyad brothers were growing their strawberries. With support coming from as far away as Tokyo, Imm Qaisar, as she is called, planted a four-hundred-square-meter garden outside her back door in 2013 with aid from the Nippon International Cooperation for Community Development (NICCOD), an NGO supported by the Japanese government. For three years Qablawi grew more than a dozen varieties of vegetables and herbs, her backyard blooming with lettuce, cabbage, radishes, fennel, lemongrass, za'atar, and garlic.

The yield supplemented her family's savings and income, with the bulk going to home consumption and the rest generating modest sales of $50 to $75 a month. "I trust what I eat when I plant it myself," she says of the home-grown, organic jute mallow she has grown to cook *mulukhiyah* and cauliflower for *makloubeh*. When the NICCOD grant ended, Qablawi reduced her home cultivation to okra and thyme.[49]

International aid for Palestinians extends to agriculture, but this support has been relatively scant. From 2000 to 2006 it amounted to $30 million, or less than 1 percent of $4 billion in total foreign aid received by the Palestinian Authority.[50] From 2013 to 2016, NICCOD provided $450,000 for the Zababdeh organic farming project, consisting of a sixty-dunam "big farm" collective, the home-gardening initiative, and processed-food production. Twenty women including Qablawi grew home gardens; other local women produced and sold organic herbal teas, barley cookies, and za'atar mixes.

Land for the farm was rented from local owners, and sixteen local men worked the soil with stock, equipment, and expertise provided by NICCOD. Local food markets in Jenin and cooperatives elsewhere in the West Bank bought the yield. The farm sprouted rows and rows of over two dozen types of grains, vegetables, fruits, and herbs: wheat and barley; chick peas, hot and sweet peppers, onions, potatoes, and kale; watermelon and yellow melon; basil and cilantro. The main goal was income generation, according to NICCOD country representative Naoko Inagaki, with revenues reaching $20,000 in 2015.[51]

For compost, the farmers used straw, manure, and vegetable residue to produce organic carbon- and nitrogen-based fertilizers, according to project agricultural engineer Majdi Abu Na'eem, thirty-six, an agronomist and graduate of Al-Quds Open University. Straw was used in place of plastic sheeting to reduce weeds, increase soil humidity, and protect against insects; mesh was used instead of plastic in the greenhouse. Crops were rotated and interplanted. "Planting different types of vegetables next to each other misleads insects and reduces disease," says Abu Na'eem, echoing the technique the Fayyads use to increase their yield.[52]

Palestinians are slowly becoming aware of the benefits of farming and eating organic, says Safaa Jarbou, thirty, who served as local coordinator for the Zababdeh organic farming project and earned her degree in biology and biotechnology at the Arab American University. "We are trying to affect farmers' thinking. It will take time, but it will bring great benefits. People will pay more for healthy food."[53]

The home-gardening and food-processing initiatives were also aimed at boosting women's empowerment. "Arab society is patriarchal," Inagaki notes. "We wanted to provide opportunities for women to work outside their homes, even if it's right next to their houses."

Qablawi tended her big garden each day for an hour and a half to two hours. She and her husband, an accountant for the Palestinian Authority, have three sons and three daughters ranging in age from children to young adults. "It's better to work at home so I can be available for my family's needs any time," she says.

Like so many Palestinian farmers, Qablawi says water is the main challenge of cultivation. During the project, NICCOD covered half of her family's $60 monthly water bill, which paid for irrigation of her crops.

"Farming is our heritage and culture," Imm Qaisar says. "It's the main address for the Palestinian people. It's like a crown on our heads." And so, the collective-farm and home-garden projects have continued, supported on a smaller scale by local Palestinian organizations.

"We are staying," Jarbou says. "We will work. We will be as productive as we can."

The current generation of young Palestinians is the third to grow up under occupation. Israeli governments have moved progressively to the Right. Peace talks ground to a halt in 2014. The Trump administration, while granting major concessions to Israel in the absence of negotiations, has withdrawn aid to the Palestinian Authority as a cudgel to force the Palestinians back to the bargaining table. Periodic episodes of gut-wrenching violence still erupt between Israelis and Palestinians, briefly making headlines around the world.

Throughout, Israeli settlement expansion and land confiscation continue. In March 2016, during a state visit to Israel by then U.S. vice president Joseph Biden, Israeli military authorities in the West Bank appropriated 2,350 dunams south of Jericho, declaring them to be state land.[54]

Kibbutz Almog is about eight kilometers south of Jericho at the southern tip of the agriculturally rich Jordan Valley. Around the time of the land seizure, a large sign along the kibbutz access road depicted a young Israeli girl hugging a white dog. The sign's Hebrew message translated: "Now's the time to make a good life decision / The expansion of Kibbutz Almog / Come live in your own home on a half dunam in the enchanting north of the Dead Sea."[55]

Against this backdrop, amid this landscape, though, Nasser Abufarha remains optimistic. He remains inspired by his people's determination to persevere and live vibrant lives. He is driven by his own sense of the *longue durée*.

"In farming, every field has flowers and thorns," he says. "You can either see the thorns and put your hands up [in surrender] or see the flowers and weed your way through.

"I see a lot of flowers in Palestine. That generates a lot of promise. The fact that I can trace this through the landscape to millennia gives me hope—that we will still have a future."

CHAPTER 2

Lessons in Liberation

The road to winning a $1 million teaching prize began for Hanan Al-Hroub during her childhood in a refugee camp, pivoted when her husband and children were shot at by Israeli soldiers during the second Palestinian uprising, and crystallized as she worked to create a learning sanctuary for her second-grade pupils.

In March 2016 Al-Hroub sat on a stage in Dubai, one of ten finalists awaiting the result of the second annual Global Teacher Prize competition, sponsored by the UK-based Varkey Foundation. Al-Hroub had been among eight thousand entrants worldwide from whom the finalists—from Australia, Finland, India, Japan, Kenya, Pakistan, Palestine, the United Kingdom, and the United States—had been chosen. In a live video announcing the winner, Pope Francis began by praising teachers as "artisans of humanity, builders of peace and unity."[1]

A week earlier, Al-Hroub had celebrated her forty-fourth birthday. Born in 1972, she grew up in the Dheisheh refugee camp, just south of Bethlehem, the sixth of eleven children and first daughter among seven brothers and four sisters.[2] Her family had originated in nearby Al-Qabu, twelve kilometers southwest of Jerusalem—one of hundreds of Arab villages throughout Palestine that were occupied, depopulated, and destroyed by Israeli military forces during and in the wake of the 1948 Arab-Israeli war. A mountaintop hamlet with a population of approximately three hundred and less than two thousand

51

cultivable dunams planted mostly with grains and olive trees, Al-Qabu was one of a string of small villages in the southern Jerusalem corridor near the railway line between the city and the coast.[3]

When Israeli forces occupied Al-Qabu on October 22–23, 1948, its inhabitants were expelled or fled eastward toward Bethlehem and the Hebron hills;[4] in March 1949 Israeli troops mounted an operation to take the strategically situated lands of Al-Qabu and three nearby villages. In May troops again raided Al-Qabu, evicting returnees and blowing up their houses.[5] In 1950 the cooperative village of Mevo Betar was established for Jewish Israelis on the lands of Al-Qabu, and state forests were planted on its surrounding lands.[6] Not far away, the Dheisheh refugee camp had been established in 1949 on one-third of a square kilometer by UNRWA, the UN agency that supports Palestinian refugees across the region. By 1967 the camp had a population of approximately eight thousand residents with roots in forty-five Palestinian villages west of Jerusalem and Hebron.[7]

Despite the proliferation of Israeli settlements built in the area surrounding Bethlehem following Israel's occupation of the West Bank in the 1967 Arab-Israeli war, Al-Hroub's father, Hamed Muhammad Obeidallah, supported the family by farming. He reclaimed barren and fallow lands in the village of Wadi Fukin, west of Bethlehem, near the lands that the family was forced to leave behind in Al-Qabu in 1948. He cultivated olive trees and grew vegetables, including tomatoes and eggplants, winning recognition from the Palestinian Agricultural Relief Committees in 1986. Al-Hroub recalls that her father persevered despite harassment from Israeli settlers who would uproot his newly planted seedlings, one scenario of conflict in a landscape of many.

"I was raised in an environment that was full of violence," Al-Hroub would recount as the media spotlight focused on her leading up to and following her Global Teacher Prize win in 2016. "I didn't have much of a childhood. A child will mature quickly here."[8] She has said growing up in Dheisheh "imbued me with the persistence and resilience I needed to face challenges. Children elsewhere can enjoy their childhood, but not Palestinian children. You grow up aware and informed about politics and what's happening around you."[9] The early education she received in the camp's UNRWA-run elementary school for girls was a positive imprint and an early cue for the professional course she would later follow. "I never forgot the quality of my education there or my teachers," she would recall. "We had plenty of games, and the girls from my school would participate in the sporting competitions that took place in our districts. We also had many activities that stimulated our minds, challenged us mentally."[10]

At age eighteen, immediately after finishing high school during the first Palestinian intifada, she got married but did not continue with her education because Palestinian universities were being routinely shut down by the Israeli military during the uprising. By the time Al-Hroub was twenty-five, she and her husband, Omar, had five children: twin girls, two boys, and another girl. In early 2000 she began to take courses at Al-Quds Open University. In October 2000, at the beginning of the second intifada, her husband was driving their nine-year-old daughters home from school when Israeli soldiers shot at their car from a military checkpoint at the entrance to the village of Al-Khader near Bethlehem when no other disturbances were occurring in the area, she says. Omar was lightly wounded in the shoulder. The children were traumatized.

Al-Hroub withdrew from her studies for a year to address her family's ordeal. "My children saw their father wounded, and five soldiers were standing in front of them, staring at them and talking among themselves," Al-Hroub says. "When they left, they were laughing."

Her husband's wound was not serious, but she says her children's reaction was very difficult: "A hatred of school and a fear of going back and having the same thing happen again. The fear of losing their father and the dread that began to haunt them. Isolating themselves from others. The hatred for studying and the decline in their achievements in school. And the violence that started to erupt between them and other siblings, as well as their becoming alienated from me, their mother, and violence toward me as well."

Every day Al-Hroub had to persuade her children to go to school. Confronted with the absence of support from the educational system and the lack of specialists trained to deal with such situations, Al-Hroub recalls, "I found myself in a situation where I had to help my children, to free them, to help them get over that trauma so they could return to school like the other kids. I wanted to save my children from the spiral of violence that they experienced." She began to create special activities for them to do at home, setting up a corner of their house with art supplies and games to engage her children and recapture their interest in learning. "I was able, little by little, to free them from fear, little by little to free them from the violence they experienced, from isolation from me and others—to reintegrate them gradually with their environment."

At the same time, Al-Hroub knew that her children's experience was not unique. "Every Palestinian child is exposed, directly or indirectly, to violence, maybe in his immediate environment, and through TV, websites, and social media he sees the violence of the Israeli occupation," she says. "The images of violence affect his behavior, his way of thinking, feelings, outlook, and choices. If he doesn't find help, his whole life will be changed. His choices for the future will be determined by these forces that surround him."

Al-Hroub's experience and conclusions are echoed in reports by humanitarian agencies that document violence confronting Palestinian children in and near their schools. In January 2019 officials of three UN agencies including UNICEF issued a statement asserting that "incidents of interference in schools by Israeli forces, demolitions, threats of demolition, clashes on the way to school between students and security forces, teachers stopped at checkpoints, and the violent actions of Israeli forces and settlers on some occasions are impacting access to a safe learning environment and the right to quality education for thousands of Palestinian children."[11] Among 111 documented incidents affecting 19,196 children in the West Bank in 2018, more than half involved "live ammunition, tear gas, and stun grenades fired into or near schools by Israeli forces, impacting the delivery of education or injuring students." The statement also cited some fifty schools in the West Bank and east Jerusalem as being under threat of demolition, and five schools as having been "demolished or seized by Israeli authorities."[12]

In 2013 the World Council of Churches (WCC) reported on impacts of Palestinian children's and youths' encounters with Israeli soldiers and settlers in the West Bank and east Jerusalem. In the village of Tuquʻ, south of Bethlehem, approximately twelve hundred students were attending an elementary school and two secondary schools, the latter near a main road traveled by villagers and Israeli settlers from Teqoa and Noqedim, built on lands belonging to the village. "On most school days, Israeli soldiers station themselves next to the schools during students' daily commutes," the WCC reported. "Schoolchildren are taught about not allowing themselves to be provoked by settlers or the military, and not reacting by throwing stones."[13]

A counselor at one of the schools said: "Children are stressed and afraid when the army is outside the school, which affects their concentration. They keep looking out the window to see if the soldiers are there. Their grades drop and some leave the school early."[14] Mohammed, a father of two, said: "I am worried every day. You never know if your children will return from school. The military affects the children in different ways. Psychologically many children have nightmares and are afraid. Soldiers often put up checkpoints to examine students' IDs on their way to school, and they often threaten the faculty that they will shut down the schools completely."[15] A teacher noted: "They (soldiers) throw tear gas into the classrooms. . . . Last year they did this and the principal went out to the entrance of the school to talk to them, but they did not care. We put the children inside the classrooms, but we can't protect them from the soldiers."[16]

In a 2019 report on children and armed conflict around the world, the United Nations cited the deaths of 59 Palestinian children in 2018, 56 of them killed by Israeli forces—the highest number since the 2014 war in the Gaza Strip. Another 2,756 children had been injured, 2,674 by Israeli forces "in the context of demonstrations, clashes, and search and arrest operations."[17]

As she was helping her children regain their equilibrium, Al-Hroub says, "I thought that if they went through this trauma and didn't get any [outside] help, then most if not all Palestinian children who experience similar traumas didn't get any help to overcome those kinds of traumas. So I decided to become a classroom teacher." She reenrolled at university and in 2005 completed her bachelor's degree in elementary education. She began teaching in 2007, continuing to develop the methods she had devised at home for her own children so that her pupils might overcome, at least during their school day, the environment of conflict and violence that confronted them elsewhere.

Dressed as a clown named Zarifa, wearing a colorful rainbow wig and red ball nose, Al-Hroub enters her second-grade classroom at the Samiha Khalil school in Al-Bireh with a monkey puppet named Saadoon gently tapping a tambourine. All eyes are fixed on Zarifa and Saadoon as they lead a counting game. Then Al-Hroub, out of costume in a flowered hijab and dark, long fitted coat and pants, propels a yellow balloon marked with the numeral nine into the air and asks what number pairs yield its sum. "Two and seven, four and five!" come the replies. Then she divides her charges into teams that compete to find clothespins and socks marked with the same numbers and be the first to clip them to a clothesline she has hung in the classroom. The learning day continues as the children move among different corners of the room that Al-Hroub has dedicated to reading, drawing, math, and singing.[18] The props for these activities come from her salvaging a supply of empty egg and grocery cartons, popsicle sticks, clothes hangers, laundry lines, old tires, and toys and games other children have outgrown—which she collects and gathers from her home, family, neighbors, local shops, and even trash bins.

In her transition to classroom teaching, Al-Hroub scoured the internet for scholarly literature and, in the virtual absence of specialists within the Palestinian educational system, consulted outside experts, including mental health professionals, in order to deal with the range of behaviors she encountered among her pupils. "We are talking about a child who already has been exposed to difficulties before he gets to school," she says, citing frequent inspections and interrogations by soldiers at checkpoints and extended distances some children must walk to their schools to circumvent the Israeli separation barrier and roads that can be used only by settlers.

"Every day, children arrive late to their schools. Imagine a child who arrives in the middle of the first lesson. When you ask him for the reason, he answers: 'The army jeep or the soldiers detained us.' Imagine a child enters your class crying, and when you ask him why he tells you that they had arrested his father last night, or he lost his cousin or his brother or somebody else was killed. A seven-year-old child is crying in your classroom. How will this child be able to concentrate? How can he study or learn? There will be no learning goal, because what dominates him and his thinking are the events that occurred before his arrival to school."

These events often spur a range of negative and sometimes violent behaviors, Al-Hroub says, such as aggression, domination, self-imposed isolation, and a lack of concentration and desire to learn. "The situation is not normal, the child is not normal, the environment is not normal," Al-Hroub says. "The occupation does not discriminate, does not respect either old people or children, does not distinguish between old or young.

"Our students come to our classrooms, they look at us and hear us—and we think they are learning. But we are mistaken. Their eyes are with us but their minds are not. We must create readiness among them for learning—behaviorally, psychologically, and cognitively. Even at their young age I can see the tears, sadness, and grief in their eyes. They cannot cry, but I feel that their hearts are crying.

"They do not suffer from any cognitive problem," she asserts. "The reasons behind their declining educational accomplishments are the events and incidents they have been exposed to outside the classroom, which continue to occupy their minds and distract them from focusing. The minute I shut the door behind me, I seclude my students from what is happening outside."

In striving to create an alternative universe in which her pupils may regain some of what has been taken away from them, she uses an activities-based "play and learn" approach to teaching a broad range of subjects that incorporates games, drama, dancing, and music— "anything," she says, "that can liberate the pupil from the vortex of violence surrounding him in order to transform the classroom into a place that has peace, security, and joy. As he plays, he thinks he is playing, but he is learning and studying. The child realizes that his mind is respected in my classroom, his humanity is respected in my classroom. He lives his genuine childhood inside this classroom."

The right to education is recognized the world over. The Universal Declaration of Human Rights and the International Covenant on Economic, Social and Cultural Rights state that education "shall be directed to the full development of the human personality" and link it to dignity, human rights, and basic freedoms.[19] Al-Hroub asks:

"When you deprive a child of his right to study, then what do you leave for him?"

Describing her mission to counter such interference, she speaks intently, punctuating her measured phrases with small but precise hand gestures. She is soft-spoken but forceful, her cadences alternately evoking poetry and homily. She is a wellspring of concern—if not passion—not only for the welfare of Palestinian children but also for how their futures will shape Palestinian society.

"I do not focus only on transmitting knowledge. In essence, I want to change their behavior," she says of her pupils, "to integrate them with my own imprint, with my spirit, inculcate myself into them." As with her own children's experience of being shot at and seeing their father wounded, she maintains: "I do not want that violence used against them to be transformed into their behavior against each other and against their society. I want to send them into society with positive behavior, with patterns of behavior that society needs, with values and ethics.

"As I enter the classroom, I want to talk about peace. How can I talk about peace inside the classroom when there is no peace outside? But we have to do that. I provide my Palestinian children peace inside the classroom. I provide them an environment void of violence, an environment full of respect and love," she says.

Since winning what is often referred to as the Nobel Prize of teaching, Al-Hroub has been invited to dozens of conferences and speaking engagements around the world. She has met with Catholic high school teachers and university students in Luxembourg; she has lectured at the Harvard Graduate School of Education. She is also in demand at home, conducting workshops and meetings with teachers, counselors, and university students. Her toughest audience, however, may be Palestinian children themselves—her greatest challenge to encourage them to find hope and maintain it in a harsh and often discouraging landscape.

On a visit to the Am'ari refugee camp, east of Ramallah, Al-Hroub encountered a group of third- and fourth-graders playing in the street during a period of midterm exams. She asked the eight- and nine-year-olds why they weren't at home studying. When one child said he didn't want to study, she told him that studying is a path to university education, employment, and success in life. The boy replied that he believed there was nothing worth living for.

"I told that child and that group of children: 'We must live for the sake of Palestine!'" Al-Hroub says. "Then the child replied: 'For the sake of Palestine I want to be a martyr, I want to give my life for the sake of Palestine!'"

She answered: "'Let us assume that you were killed and became a martyr and they bury you in the ground. Can you serve Palestine after you are in the ground?' He answered no. I asked him: 'What is better, to shorten your life, or to prolong your life and stay above the ground and to build Palestine brick by brick?'

"And he said to me: 'You are the only person we see who smiles despite the absence of anything beautiful or sweet around us. Look around you, there is nothing beautiful here. The houses are not beautiful. The school is not good. Neither the father nor the mother is good. Our friends are not good. There is nothing good or beautiful in this world! Then why should we live? Live for what?'"

Al-Hroub replied: "It is enough that *you* are beautiful and good. You are the most beautiful thing in this life. For the sake of yourself you need to live! Didn't you say that you love Palestine? Then please live for the sake of Palestine, and Palestine will be happy that you are alive!"

The task of Palestinian teachers is complicated. Like many teachers around the world, they often face large class sizes and low pay; Al-Hroub says teachers are among the lowest-paid employees of the Palestinian Authority. The educational system as a whole, she believes, needs to put more emphasis on teaching decision-making skills so young Palestinians can ultimately protect themselves.

"As teachers, are we asking ourselves what is our key goal? Is it to build a free human being, a thinking person who applies his mind to reasoning and solving problems he faces in his life? Our goal should be that students should have skills to face the problems they encounter," she says. "Our responsibility as Palestinian teachers is more difficult than that of other teachers, because we must teach our students how to live under occupation. A teacher must remain strong enough in order to stand before her students as a brave person, to radiate bravery and courageousness, to convince them that they have the capabilities to change tomorrow and the future."

Al-Hroub's methods and message resonate. In her own family, the five children she has raised with Omar, a legal consultant who earned a PhD in intellectual property, have all continued with their postsecondary education, studying law, business, civil engineering, culinary arts, and physical education.

In announcing Al-Hroub as the winner of the Global Teacher Prize, Pope Francis said: "A child has the right to play. Part of education is to teach children how to play, because you learn how to be social through games, and you learn the joy of life. I would like to congratulate the teacher Hanan Al-Hroub for winning this prestigious prize."[20]

On stage in Dubai, Al-Hroub, wearing a traditional embroidered Palestinian *gallabiyyah*, leans forward and momentarily covers her mouth in surprise, then rises with arms outstretched at shoulder level in a gesture of victory. Beaming broadly, she greets the nine finalists one by one, embracing the women and shaking hands with the men. On a large screen behind them is projected a live feed from Manara Square in the heart of Al-Hroub's hometown of Ramallah, where the crowd watching her win on a giant video screen there erupts in cheers and waves Palestinian flags.

Joyfully, she accepts her trophy. In Arabic, she says: "Thank you, thank you all. God bless you." In English, she says: "I did it! I won! Palestine won! Congratulations to all of you. You are amazing teachers." She moves across the stage to the finalists, declaring in Arabic: "Teachers are the real forces on Earth, and they can bring change. My colleagues, join hands."

Hanan Al-Hroub takes her place with them, arms upraised.

The Global Teacher Prize certificate of accreditation presented to Palestine hangs in the Ministry of Education and Higher Education in Ramallah, where Minister Sabri Saidam describes the challenges of Palestinian education and of innovation challenging tradition in a landscape challenged by conflict.[21]

His phrasing is lyrical and his message deliberate, punctuated by frequent vibrating of his mobile phone. "People around the world learn and study to liberate minds," says Saidam, who became the Palestinian Authority minister of education and higher education in August 2015 and served through April 2019. "In Palestine there is a dual mission: to liberate minds and geography. And that makes education in a nation that lives under the circumstances we're in the platform for the liberation of geography. We have schools like anybody and everybody else in the world. We have universities like everybody else in the world. But we have a more emotional, moral, and national commitment and mission that goes beyond the work of standard education and education-based society."

Trained as a scientist who earned a bachelor's degree in applied physics and electronics and a PhD in electrical engineering in the United Kingdom,[22] Saidam evokes a timeless creation metaphor to locate the predicament of Palestinian education under Israeli occupation within modern times. "We are told that God created the universe in six days and rested on the seventh," the minister says. "Humanity finds it difficult to believe that a land that was occupied in six days cannot witness the emergence of the seventh day. So education is not about teaching only. It's about liberating a country and a people. It is the most effective weapon in combatting occupation."

That Palestinian classrooms—where children, youth, and young adults learn not only to persevere in a society with limited freedom but also to prepare for a future in which independence will eventually be won—are battlegrounds for liberation is also a metaphor. However, successive Israeli governments have repeatedly alleged that the Palestinian educational system, in particular through its textbooks, has served as a breeding ground for incitement.

Numerous studies have contradicted such assertions, in particular a 2013 academic study funded by the U.S. State Department that examined textbooks issued by the Palestinian Ministry of Education and used in the West Bank and Gaza Strip, as well as books from Israel's state secular and religious school systems. The *New York Times* reported that while the study found "extreme examples of dehumanization and demonization were 'very rare' on both sides," Israeli and Palestinian textbooks alike provided "unilateral national narratives that presented the other side as an enemy," "a lack of information about each other's religions, culture and daily life," and "the failure even to mark the existence of the other side on most maps."[23]

Studies conducted by research institutes in Israel and Europe in 2003 and 2004—spurred by persistent Israeli claims of Palestinian incitement that culminated in congressional and parliamentary committee hearings in the U.S. and Europe—concluded that the allegations were based in large part on Jordanian and Egyptian textbooks that had been in use in the West Bank and Gaza, respectively, before being phased out by the Palestinian Authority in the wake of Oslo, as well as being based on incorrect translations.[24] The studies found the new textbooks issued by the PA to be free of incitement and the overall orientation of the curriculum to be peaceful.[25] In 2011 the Israeli professor who conducted a study of textbooks used in Israeli schools and authorized by the Israeli Ministry of Education told the *Guardian* that the books consistently represented Palestinians "as refugees, primitive farmers, and terrorists. You never see a Palestinian child or doctor or teacher or engineer or modern farmer."[26]

At the helm of Palestinian education, Saidam takes these factors into account. "Israelis say that we are inciting against occupation and we are a bunch of terrorists. But they fail to realize that we have children, we have families, we have a nation that aspires to prove to the world that we are not the children of a lesser god." By 2018 the illiteracy rate among the Palestinian population aged fifteen years and above in the West Bank and Gaza Strip had dropped to 2.8 percent from 13.9 percent in 1997; comparatively, UNESCO statistics for illiteracy rates among persons fifteen years and above in 2016 were 24.8 percent in Arab states and 13.8 percent worldwide.[27] In 2018, among an overall population of approximately five million, 21.3 percent of the Palestinian population had completed secondary school, 5.6 percent had earned intermediate (community college–level) diplomas, and 15 percent had earned bachelor's degrees and above.[28] From 2014 to 2017, Palestinian colleges and universities graduated an average of 41,461 students per year and community colleges an average of 3,658 students per year.[29]

"We are here," Saidam says, "to bring life to the State of Palestine, where the prosperity of our children and the freedom to exist and to move become the endeavor of the entire society."

Saidam was born in 1971 in Damascus, his family origins in 'Aqir, a village on the outskirts of Ramla, in the Palestinian coastal plain about twenty kilometers due east of the Mediterranean coast; 'Aqir was depopulated by Jewish military forces prior to the outbreak of the 1948 Arab-Israeli war.[30] His father, Mamdouh, was a member of the Fatah Central Committee of the Palestine Liberation Organization in Syria; his mother, Jamila, was one of five women elected in 1996 to the first Palestinian Legislative Council, the legislature of the Palestinian Authority in the West Bank and Gaza Strip. Upon completing his PhD in 2000, Saidam moved to Palestine and continued his family's political pedigree within the Fatah party, the largest political faction of the PLO, serving as a member of its legislative Revolutionary Council until becoming telecommunications minister in 2005. After becoming education minister, he was elected to the Fatah executive Central Committee in December 2016.

In the face of circumstances unique to Palestinians living under occupation, Saidam has undertaken a campaign of educational reforms to address a broad range of needs and challenges common to educational systems across the globe. As minister, he says the top three priorities for Palestinian education are "to see technical education as the way forward, to see entrepreneurship as the platform for the development of the Palestinian economy, and a landslide interest in preschools." In the 2017–18 academic year, 1.25 million students attended 2,203 government-run primary and secondary schools out of a total 2,998 including UNRWA and private schools;[31] and 211,294 students were enrolled at fourteen universities and colleges with another 11,480 attending community colleges.[32]

During Saidam's tenure as education minister, in April 2017 the Palestinian Authority ratified the first Palestinian Law for Education and Higher Education, a thoroughgoing revision of practical aspects of the educational process. The beginning of compulsory education, which extends to tenth grade, was revised to include kindergarten. Preparation for the *tawjihi*, or general secondary education matriculation exam, was revised to replace rote memorization with reading comprehension, critical thinking, and interactive learning. The higher-education preparatory process was streamlined for compatibility with

European and American A-level, international baccalaureate, and SAT systems, with grading and testing systems automated. The new law also outlined clear educational objectives, specified the functions of the education ministry, and codified requirements for hiring teachers.[33]

Saidam has played the role of captain rather than champion, working with a core team of approximately one hundred ministry staff, some of whom have also served on the Education Reform Committee—what he calls "the backbone of change"—along with representatives of Palestinian society from the private sector, members of various public commissions, and former teachers and school principals. "If I did not find a team conducive to reform, I would have been impeded big time," Saidam says.

Working collaboratively, Saidam and the ministry introduced a digitization initiative to include computers in fifth- and sixth-grade classrooms; "open-education Saturdays" that paired one hundred schools in the West Bank with the private sector to provide extracurricular opportunities in fields including robotics, computer programming, sports, drama, and poetry; and "accomplishment portfolios" of mandatory and elective coursework in specific subject areas that secondary-school students compile for two years before being proficiency tested in the twelfth grade. Saidam has overseen the creation of outreach programs for special-needs communities, with the ministry opening nine "challenge schools" in Bedouin and other remote areas and four "determination schools" run in hospitals so children with critical illnesses can continue their education.

Saidam has also worked to guide social expectations about education to jibe with the needs of the marketplace. Since 2007 a rise in Palestinian educational levels has been accompanied by increased unemployment rates, particularly among university graduates.[34] By mid-2019 the percentage of youth ages eighteen to twenty-nine in the West Bank and Gaza Strip accounted for 23 percent of the overall Palestinian population; those who earned a bachelor's degree or higher increased to 17 percent in 2018 from 12 percent in 2007 (with female youth degree holders increasing to 22 percent from 11 percent and males to 13 percent from 11 percent).[35] While 52 percent of Palestinian youth participated in the labor force in 2018 (an increase from 44 percent in 2008), overall unemployment reached 45 percent (27 percent in the West Bank and 69 percent in the Gaza Strip) and 58 percent among graduates of universities, colleges, and community colleges.[36]

Accordingly, the Ministry of Education has placed high priority on merging technical education into standard curricula and has identified nine principal fields of vocational and technical education, including agriculture, preeminent in the northern West Bank; stone masonry, salient in the southern West Bank in and around Hebron; and core specific skills of electrical wiring, basic cement work, carpentry, and mobile-phone maintenance. "We are trying to combat the stigma associated with technical education," Saidam says. "We are trying to utilize the capacity of children now influencing their parents vis-à-vis technology to convince them that technical education does not push you into social degradation." In addition, higher-education programs leading to degrees in overcrowded professional specializations including law, dentistry, and certain engineering and humanities disciplines have been subject to what Saidam refers to as "specialization rationing" in order to eliminate redundancy and curb unemployment. "It's purely an issue of social classification," he says. "People would like to see their kids graduate as engineers but not physicists."

The ministry has also introduced clean energy into schools via the use of solar panels to produce electricity. Schools use some of the power they generate, sell the excess to their local communities, and channel part of the income back to support school programs and other costs. The initiative not only enhances environmental awareness by promoting clean energy but also contributes to a measure of independent Palestinian spirit. "It's a self-sustainable kind of energy production," Saidam says, "since our main energy source is Israel."

The Al-Asrar school for young Palestinian cancer and dialysis patients in the Augusta Victoria Hospital on the Mount of Olives in east Jerusalem is one of the four "determination schools" run by the education ministry. On June 4, 2018, Saidam arrived to attend a graduation ceremony for the children attending school at the east Jerusalem hospital when he was stopped at the entrance gates by Israeli security agents. Detained for forty-five minutes, Saidam says he was told that despite holding a permit that allows him to travel in Israel, he was not allowed to enter Jerusalem without prior permission. Soldiers put up a temporary "flying checkpoint" at the hospital to check all cars that passed, he says, then escorted him out of Jerusalem across the Hizma military checkpoint.

Saidam had visited the city the week before to meet with Palestinian educators. In late February 2018, Israeli Public Security Minister Gilad Erdan rejected a request by Saidam and other Palestinian officials to visit the Terra Sancta School in east Jerusalem,[37] based on a broad interpretation of a provision in the Oslo Accords that prohibits official PA activity in Israel.[38] Given the contested status of east Jerusalem, which Israel occupied and incorporated much of within the city's municipal boundaries following the Six-Day War of 1967 in contravention of international law, an uptick in visits by Palestinian officials to the eastern part of the city reportedly occurred in the wake of the Trump administration's recognition of Jerusalem as the capital of Israel in December 2017.[39] In the statement banning Saidam's planned February 2018 visit, Erdan said, "The battle for our sovereignty in Jerusalem isn't over. The PA, together with additional elements, are trying to undermine it and to harm and eat away at it every day, and I will continue to act with all my strength to prevent this and demonstrate our sovereignty in every part of our capital."[40]

The tussle over sovereignty has implications for what educational curricula hold sway over the minds of Palestinian primary and secondary students in Jerusalem, estimated to number approximately 109,400 in 2016.[41] Forty-one percent were attending municipal schools whose curricula are determined by the Israeli Ministry of Education; 19 percent were attending schools run by UNRWA and the Waqf, or Islamic trust, that teach an independent Palestinian curriculum; and the remaining 40 percent were attending schools that are affiliated with churches and other associations and are formally recognized and partially funded by the Palestinian Ministry of Education.[42] Among the priorities of the ministry—which is not allowed to operate in east Jerusalem—Saidam says, is "upholding Palestinian education in Jerusalem and increasing its share," which in 2018 amounted to approximately $30 million of the Palestinian Authority's developmental budget for education.

Given the range of challenges facing Palestinian education, Saidam says education is the most visible of all sectors in Palestinian society, reflected by recent increases in the share allotted for educational development overall. In 2018 the Palestinian Authority allocated $1.2 billion, accounting for 27 percent of its overall budget, to develop preschool through higher education (excluding ongoing expenses such as salaries and energy costs), up from 21 percent in 2017 and 16 percent in 2015, Saidam notes. In addition to allocations for education directly from the PA, whose overall budget is largely dependent on support from donor countries, Palestinian education is supported by the Joint Financing Arrangement consortium comprising Belgium, Finland, Germany, Ireland, and Norway, which have allocated approximately € 159 million for educational development from 2010 to 2019.[43] Support for school construction, expansion, and equipment also comes from international and local NGOs as well as the Palestinian community at large, he says.

Ultimately, in Saidam's view, it is the community itself that must generate the will to advance education in Palestine, not as an island but as part of the ever-evolving world. "Almost every sector in our lives as humans, not only as Palestinians, has changed," he says. "Look at the way we deal with technology, look at the way we deal with communications, look at the way we deal with clothing—even fashion has changed.

"But schooling has not changed. It still remains the desks lined up facing the board, the teacher teaching in a vertical way with no horizontal, critical thinking. But resolving such impediments cannot come with the press of a button. You have to prepare society for acceptance. I have been through change, and I know that people celebrate change in principle. But when it comes to practice, you burn your fingers. And I have burned my fingers many times." Saidam recites refrains of resistance he has encountered in revising the *tawjihi* curriculum to emphasize interactive learning over memorization. "People want short cuts. They don't want you to give them experiments. Just give us the exam," they say. "Give us the answers and forget us."

Bucking tradition, Saidam converted fifty-four primary and secondary schools in the West Bank into "smart-learning schools" with no books, homework, and exams. "These schools are yielding extremely positive results," he says. "We introduce the philosophy of engaging children in education by virtue of loving the thing rather than by being led into accepting the thing. The teachers use technology, but most importantly they use drama, music, *debke* folk dance, and short trips outside school, and they also welcome speakers from the local community. The role of the community is what counts in the modernization of the entire system."

Once again, he points to initiatives that blend technical education into standard school curricula in order to answer the need for an increased supply of skilled workers. "We do not have enough teachers to do that. So for the first time, we killed the taboo of not allowing strangers through the doors of the school. We go for the parents. We ask the kids: If your dad is a carpenter, please invite him to come.

"The children become so proud that their parents are standing before their friends and schoolmates, teaching them. And that specific parent will realize that his skill is appreciated, and that he's transferring knowledge to kids.

"The philosophy is engagement," Sabri Saidam says. "Engagement."

When Reham Khalaf decided on a career in medicine, she did so with a double focus: "I always said I want to be a doctor who is aware of the community's needs but who responds to these needs with scientific answers."[44]

Born in 1981, Khalaf grew up in the town of Jenin in the northern West Bank with two brothers and two sisters, the second of five siblings. Her parents were high school teachers, her father teaching geography, her mother English. "There was a special emphasis on education," she says. "I had this sense of the world, countries, and their capitals, but also knowing how English can help you communicate with the world and have a better future." Her parents encouraged her to study medicine. "Every parent wants his or her child to be a doctor," Khalaf says, "but we still don't say, 'I want my child to be a scientist in Palestine, I want my child to be a researcher in Palestine.' Investment in science is really very new here. To raise a child to love science and to work as a scientist in Palestine is really challenging. It requires a long-term investment."

Khalaf's educational and career path bespeaks such a long view and her eye toward the future. She earned her medical degree in general medicine and surgery from Al-Quds University in Jerusalem in 2005, then worked two years in Nablus, first at a hospital and then teaching at An-Najah University. "I started to focus on evidence-based medicine," she says. "I didn't want to go directly to specialization. I wanted to do scientific research; I wanted to be a doctor and a scientist at the same time." But she found local research opportunities to be limited.

"If we want to improve the healthcare system in Palestine, it would be by improving the buildings, increasing the number of staff, training the staff in clinical procedures," Khalaf says. "This is something that is already being worked on. But if you truly want to make a long-term improvement, you need to study the particularities of Palestinians, their health status. You need to understand the particular healthcare challenges of the population and then design a targeted treatment plan."

Her early medical work in Nablus coincided with the beginning of a rapid rise in use of mobile phones and computers by the Palestinian population in the West Bank—"attachment to the smart life," as she calls it. She and her colleagues began to sense that communities and the society as a whole were changing based on the types of medical issues that were arising among children.

Coupled with changes in technology, the political economy was shifting in the central West Bank, which was experiencing accelerating urbanization and vertical growth with construction of high-rise apartment complexes. Burgeoning employment opportunities linked to the development of Ramallah as the center of government, economy, and trade—buoyed by the Palestinian Authority and its many ministries, as well as the proliferation of Palestinian and international NGOs—also resulted in more women entering the workforce and diminishing reliance on extended-family child rearing, common in rural areas. Young families began to flock to urban environments and live in apartments with limited green spaces and play areas.

"At that time we had lots of people from Jenin, Nablus, and the other cities in the West Bank pouring into Ramallah, establishing their families away from their parents, from their family homes," Khalaf says. "Children were in less contact with their grandparents and were cared for in day-care centers." This, too, generated presentation of new and different medical issues in children, including learning difficulties, memory problems, hyperactivity, and sleep disturbances, she notes.

Khalaf knew that in addition to changing environmental factors, Palestinian children's genetic makeup was also key to understanding how nervous-system disorders were becoming increasingly prevalent. But research opportunities within higher education were few. "We had almost no chance to do research at that time in the Palestinian territories," she says. "Master's programs had just started, there were no PhD programs, no strong emphasis on research. Even for medical specialties there were very few centers in the West Bank. The only option for higher education at that time was abroad. It's very different from the current situation," Khalaf says. She won a French government scholarship in conjunction with Paris-Sorbonne University designed to help develop Palestinian medical schools by training researchers. From 2008 to 2012, she attended the Université Pierre et Marie Curie, as it was known then, completing master's studies in integrative biology and physiology and earning her PhD in developmental neurosciences and neurogenetics.

Khalaf arrived in Paris newly married; she and her husband, Mahmoud, planned on his getting a scholarship to study there for a master's degree in information technology. After making applications for a year, he was accepted to a university in Paris but twice refused a visa in Jerusalem. With his encouragement, Khalaf continued on her own in Paris. Studying in English and speaking it fluently, she had to learn French from scratch in order to manage aspects of daily life. Attempting to make arrangements for her husband's arrival that was not to be, she recalls, "I had a big motivation to learn French, and I did it within six months," taking courses and learning independently by going on outings with French acquaintances.

"I got a bike, and we would go out for hours and hours biking and talking and expressing myself and communicating with people in French," she says. On her way to becoming a PhD, the Palestinian medical doctor from Jenin would cycle through all of Paris, from north to south.

"It was wonderful," Khalaf says.

Back in Jenin, she turned her attention as a clinician and researcher to consanguineous marriages, deciphering molecular and genetic causes of rare diseases among Palestinian families with married cousins. Although reliable statistics on the rate of such marriages in the West Bank and Gaza Strip are lacking, Khalaf says, the rate is likely consistent with that of cousin marriages among Palestinian Arab citizens in Israel and Arabs in the Gulf countries, which studies have approximated at 30 to 40 percent.

She began to focus on developing evidence-based strategies to improve healthcare delivery to her Palestinian community by identifying genetic and hereditary diseases occurring in the population that present symptoms of hyperactivity; epilepsy; developmental delays in motor skills, language, and social and cognitive skills; and features of dysmorphism (disproportionate sizes of the head, facial features, and limbs as well as height). Common genetic diseases related to consanguinity include thalassemia, a type of anemia; cystic fibrosis; and those related to musculoskeletal development, such as osteogenesis imperfecta, or fragile bone disorder.

"It's a huge burden," Khalaf says, citing an additional risk factor related to genetics and heredity in Palestinian communities that is not linked to consanguinity. Men who take second wives in polygamous marriages and father children at advanced ages may have de novo genetic mutations that cause genetic changes in their offspring that tend to affect children with neurodevelopmental disorders and may cause other diseases, including certain cancers, among adults. Such manifestations may be less severe than in cousin marriages, because offspring born in such late second marriages inherit gene mutations only from the father rather than from both parents. With her background in neurodevelopment, Khalaf focuses on disorders related to children including autism, hyperactivity, intellectual disability, and language underdevelopment.

Determined to achieve double competency as both a clinician and a researcher, upon returning from France Khalaf had planned to join a residency program in pediatrics and then specialize in clinical genetics. "I wanted medicine, but I also wanted science," she says. But back in Palestine, her only option was to take an academic position at An-Najah rather than a clinical position. "Double positions do not exist in our universities," she notes. "An MD/PhD path is available in Western countries today because they value the fact of having a physician, a clinician, and a scientist at the same time." Lacking such an option at home, Khalaf began to search for alternatives and considered going to the United Kingdom for her specialization. But she and her husband decided against further family separation as they became parents of three children, two sons and a daughter, within five years.

In October 2017 Khalaf joined the faculty at the Arab American University in Jenin, where she is an assistant professor of physiology and human genetics. Flexible scheduling allows her to teach and do research three or four days a week. However, because Palestinian universities at present have no formal ties to Israeli institutions due to a policy of not normalizing relations with the occupying power, Khalaf has postponed training in clinical genetics at a hospital over the Green Line in nearby Afula, where genetic issues that arise among Palestinian patients in Israel are the same as those in the West Bank. Even if she were eventually to obtain permission from her university for the training, in order to do so she would also have to apply for a medical license to practice medicine in Israel and obtain a permit from Israeli military authorities to travel back and forth through the Jalamah checkpoint. The effort this would require is matched by her pragmatism; such an opportunity would be the best option to maintain her research work at the university, remain with her family, and train as a clinician.

Meanwhile, Khalaf maintains a full research roster along with her teaching duties at the Arab American University. With partners from Exeter University, which funds their research, she studies the genetics of a group of rare diseases, enrolling children from eighty Palestinian families from consanguineous marriages in the West Bank who have twenty different symptoms tied to genetic disorders, including intellectual disability development, motor and language delays, and dysmorphism. On the local level, Khalaf is part of a group of Palestinian researchers including a pathology colleague from the Arab American University, researchers from An-Najah, and pathologists and other specialists from seven hospitals across the West Bank who are studying the genetic causes of hereditary colon cancer among Palestinians. "We wanted the first set of data to come from Palestine before starting contact outside. For me this is the project of pride because it's only Palestinians who are working on this," she says. The funding is from An-Najah, where ten students and ten faculty have reviewed data from one thousand colon cancer patients.

Khalaf has also received funding from her university to study genetic mutation occurring in Alström syndrome, a rare disease where children have diabetes, obesity, and blindness, all caused by a single genetic abnormality. Although the condition is rare and exists in the West Bank in only one village near Jenin, there are many cases there.

Social and geopolitical challenges run parallel to Khalaf's scientific expertise and empathetic acuity toward the needs of her community. The human drive for knowledge and need for healthcare are universal; modalities of achieving them differ according to specific conditions of venue. "Science in its most glorious aspects fills an internal need of a scientist to discover, but it also has an important impact on societies in terms of their development," Khalaf says. "For a society that has more needs and challenges, the need for science is even more urgent."

She points to the local colon cancer study as an example. Because the disease affects younger people and is occurring at higher-than-average rates, there is a tendency among the population to attribute the causes to use of tear gas against Palestinians by Israeli soldiers and water polluted by chemical by-products from factories in Israeli settlements draining into Palestinian lands. "People say that the occupation is a reason for having higher rates of colon cancer," Khalaf says, but adds a cautionary note based on science.

"But we also have lifestyle practices by Palestinians—diets that are changing from typical Mediterranean dishes to fast food, sleep disturbances in the population, general exposure to urbanism, the higher number of cars—all of this impacts the general health. So studying a disease, finding answers to what the individual has in terms of genetic makeup, and how this genetic makeup impacts the development of cancer in that patient was an idea to explore." In addition, she says, another desired outcome of the study is to establish screening protocols that can guide families with colon cancer patients toward genetic testing. "We cannot change the occupation," she says, "but we can change the factors in our healthcare system to deliver better services for the population."

Khalaf also cites social factors behind cousin marriages, which increase the risk of neurodevelopmental disorders and can affect multiple members within the same family. "Usually these are poor families," she says. "The father is working as a laborer; they have very limited resources. Usually they do not have the possibility to adapt their life to the severe burden created by diseases in their children. When you have one child with a handicap, you will go to do physical therapy, occupational therapy, speech therapy. But when you have three, you will give up. You will keep them at home." Furthermore, Khalaf notes, in some communities young women feel more comfortable marrying someone they know well, such as a cousin, rather than someone whom they do not know as much about.

Resulting consanguineous marriages and the health disorders associated with them put severe strains on the limited resources of the Palestinian healthcare system. "It has to deal with a huge number of children coming from these families in terms of diagnoses requiring lots of imaging, lots of tests," Khalaf says. "There are quite frequently respiratory diseases, pneumonias, epilepsies. This is very costly. Now parents want to do prenatal screening. And you would do family counseling. You could ask them to stop marrying cousins, but I am always thinking, shall we really deliver this message?

"If you look at the map today, and you see the Palestinian villages, the Palestinian cities, we are only Palestinians in the West Bank," she says, noting that over the last two decades, Israeli authorities have dramatically reduced the number of residency permits issued to foreign women who marry Palestinian men from the West Bank. "So your only chance is to marry a Palestinian. Within a certain time, the Palestinian genetic makeup will become extremely, extremely pure. Now you may be able to say, don't marry your cousin. But in a hundred years' time, you cannot say, do not marry a Palestinian. Maybe we can tell people to stop marrying cousins in open communities like Dubai and Qatar. But in Palestine, the number of choices you have are really limited. And if you decide to marry a foreigner, you have to stay outside. You cannot come back to live in your place."

Khalaf also points to the need for a recalibration of institutional thinking at Palestinian universities, which depend to an extensive degree on student tuition for revenue, increasing teaching demands on faculty and reducing time and funding available for research. At present, she says, "to play a research and a clinical role is not an option. This type of job does not exist in Palestinian universities. There is no one who can have only a research job and keep up to date, teaching very few courses." Unlike Western academic institutions that receive government grants for research, Palestinian universities require full teaching loads of four hundred hours per year, essentially double; and Palestinian researchers depend mainly on international funding.

Still, Khalaf is at home, moving forward with her work in her country and in her community, combining teaching, research, and clinical work with family life and rearing three young children. "I love this place," she says. "I want my children to grow up in this place. My first idea during my medical training was that I was from the first generation trained to do medicine in Palestine."

Khalaf finds inspiration in her students. "Being with young people is empowering," she says. "You can see the future in these students. I'm always happy to find second-year or third-year students who have very advanced scientific skills. They give me lots of hope." She finds fulfillment in helping Palestinian families. "Finding an answer, a diagnosis for a family that has suffered a genetic disease for the past thirty or forty years is something that gives you hope. When you can tell them, we found the gene, we can help you, has always been a strong motivating factor to keep me going. I'm happy to be at the university and also have contact with patients. Both are very rewarding. Either one is good. But doing both is a source of double power."

And Reham Khalaf derives another source of power that propels her toward the future when she hears her older two children express happiness seeing her on her way to work—and understanding, intuitively, that she is doing something important.

She laughs as she quotes them in Arabic: *Mama rayha al-mus-tashfa jibi ayanat id-dam!* Mama, they say, is going to the hospital to bring blood samples.

CHAPTER 3

Beautiful Resistance

First, there is the key, a giant metal sculpture perched atop a two-story, keyhole-shaped arch that is the virtual doorway to the Aida refugee camp, situated next to Bethlehem and the southern reaches of Jerusalem. For Palestinians the key symbolizes the homes their refugees have left behind since 1948—and the promise of return.

On the left just up the curving Elias Bandak Street at the entrance to Aida is the services office of UNRWA, the UN agency that by late 2020 was serving 5.6 million Palestinian refugees across the region,[1] including the more than 6,000 who live here.[2] The small building's signage and façade are painted in United Nations blue. Several hundred meters further up the road on the right is a short section of the Israeli separation barrier, much of its length a concrete wall that cuts a swath hundreds of kilometers long through the West Bank, confining Aida camp to the north and east. But here the barrier has been made into a canvas bearing a mural of the Dome of the Rock mosque in Jerusalem, challenging the Israeli guard tower hovering above.

The walls of the entrance to Aida talk, their inscriptions and images telling a story of Palestinians' displacement, of their resistance, and of their knowledge that struggles like theirs are known to other peoples around the world. The names of thirty-three martyrs from Aida—the Arabic word *shahīd* precedes men's names and *shahīda* appears before those of women—flank a map of Palestine and likeness of Palestinian leader Yasser Arafat. Renderings of twelve of the camp's young men—some former political prisoners, others still imprisoned—surround an emblem denoting UN General Assembly Resolution 194, which in December 1948 resolved that Palestinian refugees have the right of return.[3] Inscribed in Arabic nearby is the message that article 13 of the Universal Declaration of Human Rights—which the General Assembly adopted the day before Resolution 194—affords everyone the right to leave any country, including their own, and to return.[4]

Illustrations on Aida's walls depict young Palestinian men and women hurling stones by hand and slingshot; slogans proclaim that Palestinians will achieve victory and return. There is testament to the forty-one-day hunger strike that Palestinian prisoners staged in April and May 2017 to demand better conditions in Israeli jails. A small inscription in Italian of "Palestina Libera" denotes the message of a free Palestine; a giant graffito painted on another section of the separation barrier calls up a parallel to Basque liberation, proclaiming "Gernika 1937, Palestina 1948!" Another of Aida's walls echoes, in English, the exhortation of American civil rights leader Martin Luther King Jr. in April 1967 that "we must rapidly begin the shift from a thing-oriented society to a person-oriented society."

On an overcast Sunday afternoon, the drab dullness of the sky and the weathered façades of buildings in Aida camp are countered by the energy emanating from a multipurpose room in the Alrowwad Cultural and Arts Society. Fourteen children ages six to nine, all but three of them girls, have gathered for a beginning theater class. Their trainer, Issa Abusrour, guides them in movement exercises and challenges them to imagine different moods and scenarios as they follow his cues.

They drop to the floor. "Change!" he says, and some of the children stand; others right themselves to a kneel. "Change," he repeats, "quickly, quickly!" and they run across the room. "Freeze!" he commands, and they hold their positions in place. He gathers them in a circle and asks them to guide each other to assume poses, then create stories about what the poses mean. "He's praying!" they say of a boy kneeling with his head bowed; "She's angry!" they say about a girl holding her head between her hands. Each set piece ends with applause for the one who held the pose. After a water break, Issa gathers the children in a tighter circle, asking for one volunteer, then another to stand in the middle with eyes closed and then fall back into his waiting grasp, then tilt forward to be supported by the other children. The volunteers are rewarded with applause for their bravery and trust. Then the group plays a game of tag resembling duck, duck, goose.

These are children whose fathers' and brothers' and uncles' names and likenesses have been etched on the walls outside, at the entrance to Aida; whose sisters and cousins have created from those walls a canvas of struggle. These children are the fourth generation of Palestinian refugees, the fourth generation to live in the Aida refugee camp.

But for now, at Alrowwad, they are laughing.

Abdelfattah Abusrour, who founded Alrowwad in 1998, was born in Aida in 1963. His father, Abdelkarim, was from Bayt Nattif; his mother, Fatema, was from Zakariyya. For centuries, their families had lived in the two villages located about twenty kilometers southwest of Jerusalem and an equal distance northwest of Hebron.[5] From 1948 to 1950 the residents of Bayt Nattif and Zakariyya became refugees along with approximately 725,000 other Palestinians, over half of the country's indigenous Arab population of 1.3 million.

In 1948 the Abusrour family was among the more than two thousand inhabitants of Bayt Nattif and, like most residents there, earned their living cultivating cereal crops and raising livestock[6] while also selling fabrics in the village. There are competing narratives of the circumstances under which Bayt Nattif originally came under attack by Jewish military forces in January 1948;[7] however, on October 19 of that year inhabitants fled in panic following bombing of the area by the Israel Air Force.[8] On October 21–22, during Operation Ha-Har, Israeli military forces occupied the village, the conquest of which enabled them to assume control of a key transit artery used by Egyptian troops buttressing the largely unarmed Palestinian towns and villages in the southern desert and coastal regions during the 1948 Israeli-Arab war.[9] With Bayt Nattif in the hands of the Harel Brigade of the Israeli army's elite Palmach unit, the Arab inhabitants reportedly fled for their lives, after which the Palmach blew up the village.[10]

Nearby, the smaller village of Zakariyya[11] was conquered on October 23, with Israeli soldiers finding it almost empty and executing two remaining inhabitants. In December military forces swept the village and expelled approximately forty elderly men and women, but other villagers found their way back. In January 1950 Israeli prime minister David Ben-Gurion decided to evict, "without coercion," the Arabs of Zakariyya—the "longest lasting" of multitudinous Palestinian communities to be cleared from the southern Jerusalem corridor area; on June 9 of that year they were evicted.[12] Zakariyya—along with what remained of more than one hundred other abandoned Palestinian villages—was demolished in a campaign initiated in the spring of 1965 by the Israel Land Administration "to 'level' the abandoned villages with the aim of 'clearing' the country."[13]

The notion of expelling Palestinians, demolishing their villages, and resettling Israelis in their place—thus precluding the refugees' return—had been articulated before the war between Israel and Arab forces from surrounding countries began in May 1948. As early as December 1947—immediately following the UN General Assembly's adoption on November 29 of Resolution 181, which partitioned Palestine into an Arab state and a Jewish state—military advisers to Jewish leaders including Ben-Gurion asserted that in response to fighting that had erupted between Arabs and Jews, the latter should "be prepared to reply with a decisive blow, destruction of the place or chasing out the inhabitants and taking their place."[14] In late January 1948, the Jerusalem district headquarters of the Haganah, the prestate Jewish army, proposed operations to bolster security including "the destruction of villages or objects dominating our settlements or threatening our lines of transportation," including "the destruction of the southern bloc of Beit Nattif."[15] Through the second half of 1948, according to Israeli historian Benny Morris, "the IDF [Israel Defense Forces], under Ben-Gurion's tutelage, continued to destroy Arab villages, usually during or just after battle, occasionally, weeks and months after. The ministerial committee [of the Defense Ministry] was not usually approached for permission. The destruction stemmed from immediate military needs . . . and from long-term political considerations."[16]

Four *moshavim*, cooperative agricultural communities, were established for exclusive habitation by Jewish Israelis on the lands of Bayt Nattif: Netiv HaLamed-Heh in 1949 and Aviezer, Roglit, and Neve Mikhael in 1958.[17] On the lands of Zakariyya, the moshav Zekharia was established in 1950.[18]

In the first two months after becoming refugees in 1948, the Abus-rour clan was dispersed, some living in the fields of Beit Ummar and Surif in the Hebron region, others migrating to Jordan, Syria, and Lebanon. Abdelkarim rented a room for his immediate family in Beit Sahour, east of Bethlehem, for eighteen months. When UNRWA opened Aida in 1950, the family registered as refugees and moved to the camp, living in tents there for the first six or seven years among families who originated in thirty-five villages around Jerusalem and west of Hebron.[19] By the time Abdelfattah Abusrour was born in 1963, six sons and four daughters born to his parents had died, leaving him the youngest of four surviving brothers. At age fifty-five, he remembers the public toilets located in the four corners of the camp in its—and his—early years before housing structures were built to replace the tents. He remembers his fellow refugees carrying containers to fill at the camp's water-distribution points. He remembers with a laugh that Aida camp got its first television set in 1968, and it belonged to his neighbor Jawdat, "who used it as a cinema, with people paying to enter."

From age eleven, Abusrour began to explore different modes of artistic expression. He found outlets in painting—mostly symbols of resistance—as well as sculpture, writing, theater, and photography throughout his youth. He attended an UNRWA-run elementary school and an Israeli-run high school whose classes were held in rented houses in Beit Jala, the town west of Bethlehem's main road. After school he took art classes at the Paley Center in east Jerusalem and via the Arab Women's Union in Bethlehem. At the same time, his fascination with nature and science also took him into the fields surrounding Aida to spot snakes and photograph the variety of plant life.

As he grew up, his artistic tendencies were more internal than influenced by others, he says, but notes that his mother, "if she had been in another country, probably would have been a great actress and storyteller." Instead, she became a self-taught midwife, known widely for her skills from Bethlehem to Hebron. His father made a living as a merchant, opening a fabric and clothing shop in the Bethlehem marketplace. "But I could see his heart wasn't in it," Abusrour recalls. "He was selling things for almost the same price as he would buy them for, sometimes even less. It was a place that people could come and chat, a social place."

When Abusrour talked to his parents about studying art at university, they encouraged him to pursue a field in which he could earn his living first and then think about other things. So he majored in biology and minored in chemistry at Bethlehem University in the early 1980s while continuing his artistic pursuits and joining the Palestinian Union of Artists. In 1984 he won a French government scholarship to a summer language program in France, but Israeli authorities denied him an exit visa. After reapplying six times, he got the permit and in 1985 went to France on a different government scholarship that enabled him to earn a master's degree and PhD in biological and medical engineering from Université Paris Nord.

Abusrour's years in France also enriched his artistic work, and he continued to paint and exhibit. He nurtured his avocation as a playwright, actor, and director—which continues to this day—by cofounding a theater group in which he cowrote plays; in one he performed a monologue about being a Palestinian refugee.[20] "I saw the impact of arts," he says. "When you see a play or film or dance show or photo or painting exhibition, stereotypes disappear. This is where we are on equal ground, and these are the bridges of pure humanity that we can build together."

Abusrour arrived in France on a laissez-passer travel document issued by Israel that identified his nationality as Jordanian. French authorities issued him a residency card with his nationality identified as "Jordanian refugee under Israeli mandate."

He protested. "I said: 'I am not a Jordanian who fled to be in Israel. I am a Palestinian refugee under Israeli occupation.'" After four hours of discussion, he was instructed to return the next day, only to find that he had prevailed. "They gave me a residency card saying nationality 'to be determined,'" he says. The following year, when his residency card was renewed, French authorities left the line for nationality blank.

"That was the starting point for me of thinking of how we can show this other image of Palestine," Abusrour says. "That we are human beings. We reclaim and defend our humanity. That we are not born with genes of hatred or violence. Nobody is born with that." Coupled with his art, this awareness signaled that something new was taking root. Eventually he would put a name to it: beautiful resistance.

Abusrour returned to Aida in 1994 to serve his country. "I thought that Palestine was waiting for me to save it," he says a generation later, wry humor on display in his office at Alrowwad, which bustles with activity. Colleagues knock on the door and enter for brief consultations; children's voices echo in the halls.

Coming back was for him an act of resistance, he says, "because if everybody who is educated would leave the country, who would build this country? The Israelis want us to leave. They made me suffer to get out and gave me despair so I would never come back. I would not give them what they wanted." With his degrees, he went to work doing product testing for a pharmaceutical company in Beit Jala. He also began to teach biology part-time at Bethlehem University and at the UNRWA teachers college in Ramallah. At the same time, he volunteered to teach theater at the university and in Aida, armed with the belief that "theater is one of the most amazing, powerful, thoughtful ways to express yourself, to shout as loud as you want and hopefully build a peace within."

In 1998, serving on the board of Aida's youth center, Abusrour directed the camp's theater troupe there, at the entrance near the iconic key sculpture, an area highly exposed to shooting and Israeli military incursions. One day he was rehearsing with about sixty children ages seven to thirteen a play in which they related details of their family backgrounds when Israeli soldiers in pursuit of youths from the camp began firing tear gas canisters. "I contacted UNRWA to call the Israelis to stop shooting so that we could evacuate the children," he recalls. "It took about two hours." In need of a safer space, he relocated the theater group to his brother's house inside the camp, and with a group of friends from Aida officially started the Alrowwad Cultural and Theatre Training Center—choosing "Alrowwad" for its meaning in Arabic: the pioneers.

The organization caught on and grew, gradually expanding beyond theater to be renamed the Alrowwad Cultural and Arts Society and include dance, music, photography, and video—"whatever it takes to get our young people to see their potential living for Palestine rather than dying for Palestine," Abusrour recounts. He is at once matter-of-fact and philosophical about how Alrowwad works to combat the dangers of life in the conflict zone of Aida, where Abusrour has witnessed daily life under occupation become increasingly restricted during the course of his lifetime.

"When I was growing up here, it was still open spaces. We had space to move around. We were doing our theater plays in the fields, on terraced lands, a natural stage, beyond where the wall is today," he says of the Israeli separation barrier that began around Aida as a barbed-wire fence in 2002 and culminated as a concrete wall eight meters high in 2005. "But our childhood spaces beyond the wall have disappeared."[21] Before the Oslo peace process began in the early 1990s, he recalls, "we would go to the sea, it was accessible. There were usually no checkpoints that required permits, except to Eilat and the airport. Otherwise we could go all over: to Ras al-Naqoura, Netanya, Haifa, Acre, Nazareth." But Oslo restricted the mobility of Palestinians, effectively relegating them to enclaves in the West Bank and Gaza Strip. "The supposed-to-be peace process enclosed every-thing into Bantustans, even between Palestinian cities," Abusrour says. "The need for permits to cross checkpoints became official be-cause we started talking about two states."

Within the parameters of Aida, which at .071 square kilometers has an estimated population density of at least 77,464 persons per square kilometer and a population that has nearly tripled since 1967,[22] residents experience severe overcrowding, according to UNRWA.[23] "There were four open play spaces in the camp in my childhood," Abusrour recalls. "Now there is no space at all. It's all taken up with buildings with many floors, with no possibility to expand horizon-tally." Aida's very location is a tinderbox of potential danger, with some of its periphery, including the main road alongside the barrier, under Israeli military control. According to UNRWA, the camp

is partially surrounded by the West Bank Barrier and near to Har Homa and Gilo, two large Israeli settlements that are illegal under international law. These factors, along with the constant military presence and the camp's proximity to the main checkpoint be-tween Jerusalem and Bethlehem, have made the camp vulnerable to a number of protection concerns. These include regular incur-sions by Israeli Security Forces (ISF), clashes involving camp residents, many of whom are children, and an increasing number of injuries as a result of excessive force by the ISF.[24]

In 2017, of 236 Aida residents ages ten and up who were interviewed for a study on the use of tear gas by Israeli forces in and around Aida and the nearby Dheisheh refugee camp, 100 percent of respondents reported being exposed to tear gas that year, including 84.3 percent in their own homes.[25] Researchers from the Human Rights Center of the University of California Berkeley School of Law concluded:

The use of tear gas, particularly in the past 12 months, appears to be excessive. In Aida camp . . . people are being exposed to tear gas in their homes, schools, and other locations when they are not posing any obvious or immediate threat to public safety. . . .

. . . Especially in Aida camp, it is not possible to utilize tear gas in a targeted manner. The tear gas necessarily spreads throughout the camp, such that most—if not all—residents are exposed.

One underlying sentiment that all the residents stressed was that there was no safe space where [sic] residents could find. Homes, schools, and mosques, indoors and outdoors, were all at risk, both deep inside the camp and toward the main roads.[26]

Abusrour says that due to the volatile mix of confinement and violence, "now there are children who are eight and nine years old, who come to you and say, 'I want to die because nobody cares.' Because when the Israelis come in the middle of the night, they're breaking your door or humiliating your parents in front of you, nobody is there to protect you. Because there's a Palestinian Authority that has no real authority to protect its citizens in these kinds of cases." He sighs deeply. "Who is caring about the children? Who is caring about giving hope in those times of despair?"

At its core, Alrowwad is about what Abusrour calls "beautiful resistance"—*al-muqawama al-jamīla* in Arabic, a term that he originated. "I want to see people think about living rather than dying," he says. Through cultural and artistic engagement, beautiful resistance provides young people—two-thirds of Aida residents are under the age of twenty-four—with possibilities, he says, "that they can grow up, that they can change the world and create miracles without thinking that the only way is to shoot or blow themselves up." A father of five, Abusrour asserts: "No parents in the world want to see the day where they bury their children. So the aim is to celebrate their lives and their successes and hope that when the time comes, they will be walking in our funerals and not the other way around."

Nonetheless, Abusrour is adamant about Palestinians' right to resist occupation. "It is a legitimate right recognized by the international community. Palestinians have every right to resist the occupation by all means, whether it's armed or nonarmed."[27] However, he says, "99 percent of Palestinians have never carried a gun in their lives. Palestinians celebrate nonarmed struggle, they celebrate life." On numerous occasions he has seen parents hitting their children for throwing stones, "not because we don't want to resist, but because parents understand the consequences. We do not teach our children to hate. Beautiful resistance is not to replace this kind of resistance or that kind of resistance. But the majority of people choose nonarmed ways of struggle: existing, keeping their identity, their culture, and their humanity. Despite all the dehumanization of Palestinians, you do not see ISIS rising from Palestine."

The young people of Aida, as all Palestinians, are free to choose. "I am not here to dictate to children what they can do and what they cannot do. I am here to give them possibilities. If they want to come, *ahlan wasahlan*," Abusrour says, invoking the traditional welcome greeting in Arabic. "If they don't want, and go throw stones in the streets, OK.

"But if someone sends them to throw stones, then his war is with me, because he has no right to send children." And when people do choose to resist with arms, he says, "they lose part of their humanity. We don't want to build Palestine as a country based on weapons, because we care about the future."

In 2005 Abusrour left his work as a PhD biologist to devote himself to Alrowwad full time. "Little by little I discovered that maybe I can do better for Palestine and the world with theater and art much more than with biology," he says. When he took the Alrowwad theater troupe on the road, he saw its impact—not only on audiences but on the young performers themselves.

"I wanted the children to be the heroes. I wanted them to express themselves, not to be told what they can say. To give them the possibility to do what they want, to be what they want, and to express it." But this is not art therapy, he says; Palestinians are not sick people in need of treatment.

"I am talking," he says, "about the creative process."

Starting with core arts programs focused on theater, music, dance, and photography, over the course of two decades Alrowwad has broadened the scope of its engagement with Palestinians in Aida and neighboring communities as well as throughout the West Bank.

Alrowwad has added the Images for Life video program, a camp radio station, and educational programs focusing on health and the environment. The center offers after-school supplemental instruction for elementary-school children as well as a program supporting women's mental health. All programs are open to the children, youth, and women of Aida camp as well as residents of nearby Palestinian communities from east Jerusalem and the Bethlehem area to Hebron. Alrowwad presents "mobile beautiful resistance" theater, dance, video, and photography programs throughout the West Bank, its staff traveling by bus to offer up to four hundred programs in over two hundred fifty locations each year.

In Aida construction began in 2014 on a five-story, eighteen-hundred-square-meter complex to supplement Alrowwad's original three-story quarters; by late 2019 three floors had been completed to include a revenue-generating carpentry workshop that produces Palestinian-themed games and puzzles as well as a fourteen-room guesthouse and small health clinic. Media and robotics labs, recording and sewing studios, a restaurant and instructional Palestinian-cuisine kitchen, and a solar-paneled rooftop stage are also planned, with the expectation of creating a total of forty-five to fifty jobs at the complex and making Alrowwad 50 to 60 percent independent for the resources it needs to fuel its burgeoning landscape.

"When we started Alrowwad, I said with or without money we do it, because we didn't think it would grow in such a way," Abusrour says, noting that for the first ten years, the organization was run almost entirely by volunteers. By 2018 it had twenty-one employees and an annual target budget of $600,000–$700,000. "It's ups and downs," he says. "Every year we don't know what we will have to work with. Unfortunately, arts and culture are not a priority in funding."

To maintain Alrowwad's independence, Abusrour does not solicit support from international governmental and nongovernmental sources whose funding criteria are conditioned on "certain things that we cannot identify with," including definitions of terrorism linked to resistance and framing Palestinian needs as a humanitarian cause. "The humanitarian tragedy is because of the political context, not because of lack of resources," he asserts. "We are not poor because we don't have resources. We are put into poverty by this illegal occupation, which deprives us of the right to circulate freely, to import, to export, to manufacture; and then by donor countries which dictate to us what we should do rather than consult with us and help us do what we need to do: build infrastructures, create jobs, help people keep their dignity." He does not have direct ties with or take funding from Palestinian political parties: "I work with everybody but not under the umbrella of anybody." Support from the Palestinian Authority, which is largely funded by donor countries, has been limited to collaborative workshops run through the education, culture, and media ministries.

Funding for Alrowwad has developed slowly and somewhat randomly. In 2000 international visitors began to offer to volunteer and support small projects. In 2002 a Friends of Alrowwad group in France registered as a charitable organization and began to help raise funds to buy land and construct the original building, which was completed with support from German funding channeled through the United Nations Development Programme to the popular committee of the Aida camp as well as contributions from France, Belgium, and the U.S. From 2008 to 2013 students from seven high schools in and around Stavanger, Norway, raised more than $500,000 for Alrowwad; in 2009 a Friends of Alrowwad group was established in the U.S. Word spread to the philanthropic Stein-Sharpe family and Dusky Foundation, both based in Massachusetts, which have supported Alrowwad programs and contributed a combined additional $600,000 for the new complex by 2018. In 2011 the Luxembourg-based Action Solidarité Tiers Monde began to support the mobile beautiful resistance program; by 2019 additional Friends of Alrowwad groups had been established in the UK and Australia.

Abusrour has been recognized by the U.S.-based Ashoka and Synergos nonprofits,[28] which extend financial, training, and networking support—not only for the promise of his work as a social entrepreneur using the creative approach of beautiful resistance but also for Alrowwad's scope and impacts. Abusrour says all children who have grown up in Aida, including him, have thrown stones at a certain time in their lives—but he estimates that 95 to 98 percent of those who have participated in Alrowwad programs have not been killed, injured, or imprisoned. "Half of the team who work here are children of Alrowwad who were six or seven years old when Alrowwad started," he says; among them they run the organization's IT operation and teach dance, photography, and video.

Since 2008 an average of seven thousand children, youth, and women from Aida and nearby Palestinian communities have participated in Alrowwad programs at the camp each year; mobile programs throughout the West Bank reach another twenty thousand to sixty thousand Palestinians each year depending on funding. Beyond Palestine, young people from Alrowwad have performed theater works in Sweden, Denmark, France, Belgium, Austria, Luxembourg, Egypt, the UK, and the U.S. and have participated in arts festivals in Scotland, France, and the Netherlands.

One of the greatest successes of Alrowwad, Abusrour says, is that it reflects Palestinian culture and identity and has been created by Palestinians themselves on their own terms. At the same time, he sees a universal quality in beautiful resistance that makes it relevant "wherever there is oppression and injustice, to give space for people to be changemakers."

"Everybody is important, and everybody is a changemaker. If others join and help us, that's great. But if they don't, it is not an excuse to close our doors and go home.

"I don't believe that miracles will just happen," Abdelfattah Abusrour says.

"We need to provoke them."

Three thousand kilometers from her home in Ramallah, on the campus of the Mines Nancy *grande école* in northeastern France, Shyrine Ziadeh takes the stage in a full auditorium before an audience of about five hundred to talk about dance, about freedom, and about her cause.

It is May 2017, and Ziadeh, founder of the Ramallah Ballet Center, is presenting a TEDx talk, "Empower through Movement."[29] Her dark hair is pulled back in a low ponytail, setting off her expressive face. She wears an all-black outfit above her white sneakers: tights, skirt, top, and a short cape embroidered in a traditional Palestinian floral pattern of red cross-stitch. In French, she tells her audience: *"With your permission, I will continue in English."*

She begins in a slow but steady cadence, unspooling her topic with the long-ago and the universal. *"Let's go back to ancient history,"* she says. *"Humans always used their body movements to express and to reflect their inner feelings. They used their movements to share joy and happiness. That's the meaning of the word* dance. *Dance has had a major influence on culture throughout history."*

Ziadeh then shifts to the present, the particular, and the personal. *"Today, in a besieged country like Palestine, dance can empower people,"* just as it can empower people who live in free, developed countries, she notes. Palestinians perform *debke*, the dance pillar of their folk culture, at weddings and other celebrations not only to express joy and happiness, she says, but also *"to express our very existence."*

Ziadeh confides to her audience: *"Dance saved me a million times, mainly because I grew up in a country that is under occupation, where you need a permit to move from one place to another, where it has checkpoints all over the cities, and where we are surrounded by a wall, and our prisoners are on hunger strike at this moment. It has saved me,"* she says, *"and it made me feel safe.*

"Dancing in my own little room—disconnected from the world outside, where it is dangerous and not safe, and my life was threatened— I felt happy, dancing in my own little room. And I felt a sense of freedom." She adds: *"It also saved me as a woman in an Arab society where women's rights are not very equal and systematically trampled. Dance was my only weapon to achieve freedom."*

She recounts details of the journey that brought her to this stage: the after-school dance classes that helped shape her identity; the lack of dance and art academies in Palestine that led her to major in business administration; the volunteer dance teaching that led her to establish the Ramallah Ballet Center in 2011, the year after she graduated from Birzeit University.

"This is how I launched my project to give children a space to move and feel free in a country where freedom does not exist," she says. *"RBC is a space for everyone. It gives them power, and we teach them how dance could be a tool to empower them and give them this sense of freedom."*

The auditorium goes dark as Ziadeh cues up a video of her teaching a ballet class to girls ages four to six. Some wear pink ballet slippers, many others are in their stocking feet, all of them stretch and assume the five basic ballet positions as they laugh and smile. Then the video cuts to a different scene, of Palestinian young men doing street and break dancing in the same studio, gyrating and rotating gymnastically on axes of feet, hips, hands, and heads, their energy exploding in positions from upright to nearly prone.

The lights back on, Ziadeh relates the flip side of the early years of the center as word about it spread in local and international media coverage. She was confronted with a wave of negative local reaction posted on social media by conservative onlookers for whom RBC represented an unwelcome innovation. But family, friends, and observers from afar whom Ziadeh had never met expressed their support, and she pushed forward, eventually extending the center's offerings to adults with weekly salsa nights and welcoming local dance troupes into the space. *"It's amazing, this informal community that we are doing together, to develop our country through art,"* she tells her audience.

She does not hold back the lower notes of her narrative. *"Sometimes I wanted to give up. I didn't want to continue, because it's not easy to go through this alone,"* she recalls. *"I wanted to quit everything. Because sometimes I didn't have volunteers, and I didn't have anyone to help me. But thanks to the support of my mother, she didn't allow me to stop. She said, 'Look at the girls. They are smiling. They are happy.' And my mother, who is my role model, is a very strong woman herself. She taught us how to give and give but never give up.*

"So I didn't, and I won't, and here I am, in front of you today."

The audience applauds.

She tells them that she has found a master's-degree program in dance here in the EU, but mustering the necessary financial resources is another challenge she must overcome. *"It's not easy for individuals in my country who want to develop themselves to proceed for help,"* she relates. But she is undeterred in her vision to build on the foundation of the Ramallah Ballet Center and establish an international dance academy in Palestine one day, so that *"people from all around the world can come and dance.*

"Movement is for everyone," she says. *"Not only for underprivileged people or refugees or people coming out from war, but also for any employee or manager in a tech company. Because movement can help to improve our well-being.*

"When you move, you feel happy. And when you are happy, you want to do more. You want to produce and you want to create."

And then she challenges the people who have come to listen to her here in Nancy to embark on movement of their own.

"Using dance as a tool to express will never end, as there are always cases to represent and to defend. Till we have our equal rights and [a] more civilized world. Till we accept and get accepted by humans and different cultures living together on this Earth.

"And you are all here tonight," Ziadeh says, gesturing to her listeners. *"What cases would you like to make? What causes would you like to defend? What ideas would you like to spread?*

"Isn't it time to start to move for it?"

Born in 1988, Ziadeh grew up in Ramallah and started dancing when she was five or six years old, the same age as her young pupils in the video. At the time, ballet instruction was new to Palestinians, but her father was the first to encourage her. She studied with Russian and American teachers in the city, later expanding her scope to include belly dancing and jazz. By the time she reached her early teens, the second intifada, or uprising, hit home with full force in March 2002, when the Israeli army invaded Ramallah and laid siege to the head-quarters of Palestinian leader Yasser Arafat for thirty-four days.[30]

As an adult at age thirty-one, Ziadeh remembers the fear she felt living amid Israeli tanks, Palestinian stone throwers, and stray bullets shattering the windows of the apartment building on Dar Ibrahim Street where she lived with her parents, two brothers, and two sisters.[31] Her father, Asaad, worked in currency exchange; her mother, Aida, worked with widows and wives of prisoners in a women's empowerment project at the Palestinian Melkite Center. During the invasion, other relatives who lived in the building would often huddle with Ziadeh's family in their apartment. Taking refuge alone in her room, seeking calm with music and movement, and finding another world away from the surrounding fright, she decided that dance would become her life's pursuit.

Ziadeh continued to study dance throughout her teens and during her university years taught dance as a volunteer in schools, summer camps, and the Am'ari refugee camp. She became aware that dance is not only about moving the body but also enables dancers to build their confidence and feel free. "It makes people stronger, helps them overcome traumas," she says. "It makes them love their bodies, love themselves so they want to fight for their lives."

Both of these notions—on the one hand the overall physicality of dance and in particular that of female dancers and on the other the potential of art to be a liberating force in society—stoked local push-back against the Ramallah Ballet Center in its formative years. In local and international reports about the center, critics saw girls and young women dancing, assuming ballet poses with legs parted, and pronounced the initiative to be against religious and cultural norms. "What we were doing represented a change in mentality," Ziadeh says.

Many comments echoed themes of "let's defend Al-Aqsa, not dancing," and "we should feel sad, not happy, because we are under occupation," she recalls. Still others suggested that the center was really a belly-dance club, prompting her to leave the doors of the studio open so that anyone could come in and see what was really going on.

Financing the center was another challenge. Ziadeh stretched seed money she received from her parents and fees parents paid for classes to cover costs. The Holy Family Catholic Church donated a small space for the center's first year; then she rented a larger space with room for a full-fledged studio from the local Orthodox church. Often going without a salary, Ziadeh used her business degree to pick up part-time work elsewhere as a project coordinator and adviser to youth start-ups while running the RBC and insisting that it remain independent. She decided not to turn it into an NGO in order to raise funds from international agencies and governments, which through their support of hundreds of Palestinian cultural and other grassroots organizations can and sometimes do influence their mission and structure. "The idea of establishing the studio was to be free," Ziadeh says. "The idea was not to be controlled by other people."

But she could not handle the teaching load alone, and with many local Palestinian dancers engaged in touring abroad, Ziadeh has relied heavily on international volunteers, tailoring the type and frequency of classes offered at RBC to volunteer teachers' availability. "Salsa, tango, *debke*—it depends on the teacher," she says. "If there is a teacher here for one month, we do workshops; if there is a teacher for one year, we do regular classes twice a week." In RBC's second through fifth years, an NGO in Estonia with a connection to a university dance program there sent Ziadeh a new teacher every three months, expenses paid. RBC has had other volunteer instructors from countries including Finland, France, Germany, and the U.S.

Throughout, Ziadeh has considered herself as a movement specialist rather than a dancer, a term that connotes a trained stage performer. To encourage others to develop freedom of movement and expression is to spark change, but she sets modest boundaries in defining her role.

"If I say I'm a changemaker, it means I have reached my goal. But I am still in the process, still evolving."

Ballet evokes images of a sea of pink tutus, of graceful, precise pirouettes *en pointe*. As RBC caught on and attracted international media attention, Ziadeh told Agence France-Presse in 2014 that "teaching ballet and its philosophy is a way of showing the world that something beautiful comes from Palestine" and is, at the same time, "a good way to revolutionize Palestinian culture."[32]

Ziadeh has shaped the Ramallah Ballet Center to mesh with its local context. She focuses on developing the methods of ballet as a means to self-expression rather than as tools to train professional dancers. Rather than offering classical instruction, RBC instead has focused on ballet techniques—balance, extension, centering of the core, synchronized movement—to empower dancers' bodies and minds. "We are working more on contemporary expressive movements of the body," Ziadeh says. "The styles we give to the kids are freer and more modern so they can express their feelings." With this ethos in mind, RBC teachers have designed their own class content. "We don't follow any particular school. We take some techniques from here and there, and we create choreography in the studio. But we start with ballet techniques."

Palestinian girls who take classes at the Ramallah Ballet Center have the same eagerness to dance as their counterparts do in Los Angeles, Paris, and Beirut, Ziadeh says, but their opportunities to progress differ. "We don't have ballerinas in Palestine. In Egypt, they have brought teachers from Russia; in Turkey, professional teachers are funded by the government. We don't have those resources," she says, noting that RBC, like most other independent grassroots Palestinian cultural organizations, does not receive funding from the Palestinian Ministry of Culture. The absence of Palestinian dance and other art academies is also the result of prevailing social and political conditions. "People in Palestine believe in other kinds of education that are applied and business-related," Ziadeh says. "For us, dance is a hobby."

In addition to two levels of ballet classes for girls, RBC has also offered a weekly salsa class for adults, and the Istiqlal *debke* troupe sponsored by the Palestinian Authority has rehearsed in the studio and conducted classes for girls and boys. The center has also functioned as an occasional hub for Palestinian dancers from across the West Bank and inside Israel, and it has hosted break-dance and hip-hop "battle" exhibitions.

However, with ballet technique at the core, developing expressive body movement has been Ziadeh's pivotal aim for her students. Three years after creating RBC, she staged the full-length production *The Princess behind the Wall* at the Ramallah Cultural Palace in May 2014.[33] Sixty students ages four to sixteen presented a montage of dance scenes imparting defiance of the Israeli separation barrier, which stretches for approximately fifteen kilometers southwest, south, and southeast of Ramallah.[34] To strains of classical ballet music, Western pop, and Arabic *taqāsim* instrumental improvisations, performers in pink and burgundy tutus, leotards, and jazz pants filled the stage with movement evoking freedom and imagined possibility, eliciting cheers and applause from the audience before and after toppling a prop representing the barrier.

"We dance it in our way, we tell our own stories," Ziadeh says. "We're not dancing *Swan Lake* but *The Princess behind the Wall*. We're not changing the concept of ballet but adding to it, something from our history, from what we are living."

Shortly after Ziadeh gave her talk in Nancy, she returned to Europe in August 2017 to embark on the two-year Erasmus Mundus program to pursue an international master's degree from Choreomundus, a program in "dance knowledge, practice, and heritage." Offered by a consortium of four universities in France, Norway, Hungary, and the United Kingdom, the interdisciplinary Choreomundus program focuses on cross-cultural aspects of dance and other movement systems within heritage frameworks.[35] As a non-EU applicant, she was accepted to the master's program without funding but declined. A month later she was awarded a full scholarship by the Erasmus consortium, which is linked to UNESCO. During her studies she managed the continued operation of RBC remotely and on a reduced schedule, depending on her mother to steer the course in her absence.

While taking courses at all four universities, Ziadeh researched and wrote her thesis on the role that *debke* plays in reconstructing Syrian refugees' identities in refugee camps, transit countries, and countries of resettlement. In her fieldwork in two camps on the Greek island of Lesbos, she found a near-absence of the dance as refugees absorbed the shocks of their arrival; among Syrian immigrants who had resettled in Trondheim, Norway, she found relaxed and informal *debke* dancing at their weekly social gatherings. It was in the Syrian immigrant transit community in Athens that she found refugees' strongest identification with *debke*, the most popular of their organized weekly activities. The folk dance helped the immigrants maintain their connection to their homeland while strengthening their motivation to integrate into their new European surroundings.

In July 2019 Ziadeh was awarded her master's diploma at the University of Roehampton in London. "I feel like I'm reborn in this field," she says. "It gives me motivation to do something, to ask for more, because now I have something proven with me." Beyond learning theories that weave dance and heritage, in addition to documenting restorative effects that dance can have for those who experience traumas of war, she has joined an international network of academics and professionals with a common cause.

"I don't want to be alone anymore, and this is what I learned in those two years," Ziadeh says. "I went out and met many people who are like-minded, and now they are ready to help." After completing the master's program with her, a Finnish classmate traveled to Ramallah to teach at RBC.

From the calm sanctuary of her room amid the frights of war in Ramallah, to the fledgling dance studio she created in the face of local resistance and meager resources, across Europe to master the theories and practices of movement, she has come to better understand how to combine her passion for dance with her people's need for freedom.

"I understand now that whatever is happening, people want to dance," Shyrine Ziadeh says. "They are excited about that. That was something I was scared about when I started. Many people told me: *No one will put their kids in the dance school because we're under occupation. No one needs dance.* But now I know that the thing they need most is dance.

"Whatever happens, they like to have fun. They want to live."

Narratives of living assertions of Palestinian culture amid the landscape of life under occupation are of a piece with analytical frameworks that assign to culture qualities of dynamism, agency, and struggle. "Popular culture is one of the sites where this struggle for and against a culture of the powerful is engaged," Stuart Hall, a preeminent cultural theorist of the mid-twentieth century, has argued. "It is also the stake to be won or lost in that struggle. It is the area of consent and resistance."[36]

Raymond Williams, a theorist of equal stature writing in the same era, has posited that "the idea of culture is a general reaction to a general and major change in the conditions of our common life. . . . The working-out of the idea of culture is a slow reach again for control."[37] Further, Williams observed, "To take a meaning from experience, and to try to make it active, is in fact our process of growth."[38] Similarly, culture has been variously construed both as "shared knowledge and schemes created by a set of people for perceiving, interpreting, expressing, and responding to the social realities around them"[39] and as "a dynamic process of cognition, communication, and co-operation that produces meaningful structures that signify a whole way of life and struggle."[40]

Beyond living manifestations of these concepts as seen in loci of Palestinian culture including Alrowwad in the Aida camp and the Ramallah Ballet Center, Palestinians have also struggled for—and won—the right to assert their culture on the broader world stage, but not without pushback from the powerful. In October 2011, UNESCO voted to admit Palestine as a full member of the United Nations agency, which "seeks to build peace through international cooperation in education, the sciences, and culture."[41]

Despite lacking sovereignty nearly two decades after the Oslo peace accords were signed in 1993 and more than a decade after Oslo was to have resulted in a lasting peace between a newly independent Palestinian state and a secure state of Israel by 1999, Palestinians were nonetheless fully engaged in state-building at the time of their UNESCO victory. Admission to the organization had been preceded by a United Nations report in April 2011 concluding that the functions of the Palestinian Authority—the Palestinian protogovernment based in Ramallah—were "now sufficient for a functioning government of state" in six areas of primary UN engagement: governance, rule of law, and human rights; livelihoods and productive sectors; education and culture; health; social protection; and infrastructure and water.[42]

The International Monetary Fund and World Bank had issued similar endorsements. Ahead of a donors' conference in Brussels that April, the IMF, in a report on the economies of the West Bank and Gaza Strip, concluded that for the first time, it viewed the Palestinian Authority as "now able to conduct the sound economic policies expected of a future well-functioning Palestinian state, given its solid track record in reforms and institution-building in the public finance and financial areas."[43] The World Bank had concluded in September 2010: "If the Palestinian Authority maintains its performance in institution-building and delivery of public services, it is well positioned for the establishment of a state at any point in the near future."[44]

When it came to the vote on admitting Palestine to UNESCO, however, the United States was arguably the first among equals of 14 countries to vote no; 107 nations voted yes, and 52 abstained.[45] The vote epitomized a clash between geopolitics and international recognition of cultural identity. Since Oslo, U.S. policy has insisted that UN agencies should wait for a political resolution of the Israel-Palestine conflict based on bilateral negotiations, which would pave the way for full Palestinian membership in the UN as a whole, rather than UN agencies or other international groups acting to recognize Palestine beforehand.[46] Nevertheless, on November 29, 2012, the UN General Assembly voted to recognize Palestine as a nonmember observer state by a vote of 138 in favor (including China, France, India, Italy, the Russian Federation, and Spain), 9 opposed (including the United States, Canada, the Czech Republic, Israel, and the United Kingdom), and 41 abstaining.[47]

Following the UNESCO vote, the *New York Times* reported that cheers filled the hall at the agency's Paris headquarters, "with one delegate shouting, 'Long live Palestine!' in French." The paper also reported that Ghassan Khatib, a Palestinian spokesman in the West Bank, called Palestine's admission to the organization "'a vote of confidence from the international community' and said it was 'especially important because part of our battle with the Israeli occupation' involves defining history and heritage."[48]

The U.S. "no" vote also triggered a cutoff of funding to UNESCO based on laws mandating "a complete cutoff of American financing to any United Nations agency that accepts the Palestinians as a full member."[49] Passed prior to Oslo in the early 1990s, when the Palestine Liberation Organization (PLO) was still considered by the U.S. to be a terrorist organization and before the PLO recognized Israel, the U.S. laws remained in effect even after the PLO recognized Israel and became its cosignatory to the U.S.-brokered Oslo Accords.[50]

At about $70 million, U.S. funding to UNESCO totaled 22 percent of its yearly budget; the agency lost another 3 percent contributed by Israel in the wake of the vote to admit Palestine.[51] By October 2012 UNESCO had secured $70 million in pledges to offset roughly half the total $144 million in dues withheld by the U.S., compelling the agency to undertake massive program reductions and cost-cutting measures. The *Times* reported that efforts by U.S. ambassador to UNESCO David Killion and the Obama administration to get the funds restored had failed. Every single program of the agency was affected, according to UNESCO director-general Irina Bokova—including many benefiting the U.S., such as programs for the Afghan police, early-warning systems for tsunamis, and journalism and democracy training in Egypt and Iraq.[52]

U.S. strong-arming of UNESCO did not, however, deter the agency from acceding to Palestinian bids in 2016 and 2017 for recognition of the need to protect and identify cultural-heritage sites. In mid-October 2016, UNESCO passed a draft resolution supporting Palestinian complaints over Israeli actions in and around the Old City of Jerusalem, where the Temple Mount/Haram Al-Sharif complex housing the Western Wall, holy to Jews, and the Al-Aqsa and Dome of the Rock mosques, holy to Muslims, are located. The complaints alleged invasive Israeli archaeological excavations, damage to buildings, and lack of access to the Muslim holy sites for worshipers and officials of the Waqf, the Islamic trust that administers the sites. The draft resolution also cited Israel's repeated refusals to allow UNESCO to send a technical mission to Jerusalem to report on conservation issues.[53]

In response, Israel suspended cooperation with the agency, and U.S. officials and American Jewish leaders condemned the resolution. The crux of the protest was not the substantive issues raised in the resolution per se but its language. The draft text referred to the Old City and east Jerusalem as a whole as being occupied by Israel, as acknowledged by UN Security Council resolutions and international law; referred to the site of the holy shrines using the terms "Al-Aqsa Mosque/Al-Haram Al-Sharif" with no mention of "the Temple Mount" or "Western Wall"; and affirmed "the importance of the Old City of Jerusalem and its Walls for the three monotheistic religions"—Judaism, Christianity, and Islam—without specifically mentioning the religious significance for Jews of the site, where two ancient Jewish temples are believed to have stood.[54] On October 26, 2016, UNESCO passed a final version of the resolution with toned-down and more inclusive language but retaining the essence of the substantive issues.[55]

On July 7, 2017, despite a diplomatic campaign by Israel and the U.S., UNESCO declared the ancient center of the southern West Bank city of Hebron as an endangered Palestinian World Heritage site. The enclave around its core is under full Israeli military control and inhabited by hundreds of militant Israeli settlers; two hundred thousand Palestinians live in the city, most of which is administered by the Palestinian Authority. The ancient quarter includes the Cave of the Patriarchs, a shrine holy for Jews, Muslims, and Christians as the burial place of biblical patriarchs and matriarchs.[56]

On October 12, 2017, the Trump administration announced that the U.S. would withdraw from UNESCO due to the agency's "anti-Israel bias" and also cited arrears due the agency totaling approximately $550 million.[57] Prior to recognizing Palestinian claims regarding Muslim holy sites in the Old City of Jerusalem and the ancient quarter of Hebron, the agency in 2012 had recognized the Church of the Nativity in the Palestinian city of Bethlehem as a World Heritage site; and in 2015 UNESCO had adopted a resolution criticizing Israel for mishandling heritage sites in Jerusalem and preventing freedom of worship.[58] On January 1, 2019, the U.S. and Israel officially quit UNESCO at the stroke of midnight, American unpaid dues having mounted to $600 million and Israel owing an estimated $10 million.[59]

By 2019 in the wider world, 137 states, most in Asia, Africa, and Latin America, had recognized the State of Palestine—including China, the Russian Federation, and India.[60]

And as Palestine held its ground via UNESCO in culture wars with the United States and Israel over holy sites from Jerusalem to Bethlehem to Hebron, the Khoury family was waging a campaign of its own a bit further north in the West Bank hamlet of Taybeh, bringing Palestinian culture to beer aficionados far and wide.

Madees Khoury takes a break from managing operations at her family's Taybeh Brewing Company to talk about the path that led her from the United States to her life and work in the Palestinian countryside of the West Bank.[61] Inside the family home opposite the brewery, she escorts a visitor past a large salon that can accommodate a dozen guests easily—reflecting the importance of hospitality in Arab culture—to sit at the big wooden table in the spacious adjacent dining room.

Born in Boston in 1985, Khoury was ten years old when her family returned to their ancestral Christian village of Taybeh, fifteen minutes or so from Ramallah and twenty from Jerusalem. Among a wave of Palestinian returnees who had high hopes in the wake of the Oslo peace accords and the establishment of the Palestinian Authority, her father, Nadim, and uncle David had returned in 1994 from nearly two decades in the United States to found the first microbrewery in the Middle East. Their families joined them in Taybeh the following year. A fifth-grader, Khoury regretted having to leave her school friends behind and not being able to participate on the cheerleading squad for which she had been chosen, so she joined the gymnastics team at her new school in Ramallah instead.

Her paternal grandfather, Canaan, tried to ease the transition for her, her brother, two sisters, and cousins by building them a pool and a treehouse. "He spoiled us," Khoury recalls at age thirty-two. "He tried to make it easy for us to adapt and adjust to the culture and to living here." The relatively open environs of Ramallah for school and extracurricular activities helped. When the second intifada broke out in 2000, it brought more culture shocks and fears that her grandfather aimed to quell.

"He kept encouraging and calming us," she says, recalling his reassurances: *You're not any better than any other Palestinian here. Everything's going to be fine. This is just a phase, and you are going to overcome it.* "And he was right," Khoury says, flashing back to twohour treks through the mountains to reach Ramallah, seven and a half kilometers and, under different circumstances, a fifteen-minute car ride away. "We had to walk through checkpoints; sometimes we weren't able to come home after school. It was a really hard time. But it made us stronger as Palestinians."

After finishing high school, Khoury went back to the Boston area to earn a bachelor's degree in business management and leadership in 2007 from Hellenic College in Brookline, the alma mater of her father, uncle, and several other family members. She then returned to her life in Taybeh to begin working at the brewery and studying for a master's in business administration, which she earned from Birzeit University in 2010. But her second transition from life in the States to life in Palestine was more challenging. Relaxed American campus life gave way to a more guarded Palestinian university environment where "everyone's all dressed up and careful how they talk, careful how they sit, careful how they deal with people," she says. "The teaching techniques are very different too. Here you have to memorize everything; there you have to think out of the box." She also found that many friends from high school had married or moved away.

Khoury focused on her studies and work, in the process reacclimating herself to Palestinian culture. She worked her way up in the family business from assistant brewer to operations manager in an industry with few women and forged ahead to become her own person in a patriarchal society. "I'm not just the beer lady, the daughter of the owner," she says of her rites of passage.

"I have grown. I have established my reputation. I have established myself."

Nadim Khoury, who began to experiment with brewing beer and worked in a liquor store when he was a university student in the U.S., has told more than one interviewer probing the success if not the novelty of the Taybeh Brewing Company that brewing beer in Palestine is not like brewing beer anywhere else in the world.[62]

Madees Khoury has learned the lesson of this maxim by following in her father's footsteps and working at his side. Water is a primary challenge. Ninety-five percent of beer consists of water, she says, and the Taybeh brewery uses Palestinian spring water, the source of which is three kilometers from the village. However, despite Palestinians accounting for 86 to 88 percent of the West Bank population, Israel restricts their water supply to approximately 20 percent of the potential yield of the major aquifer in the West Bank.[63] Further, the water supply designated in the mid-1990s Oslo Accords for the Palestinian population in the West Bank, which has since tripled,[64] has not kept pace but has instead diminished.[65]

"All the [Israeli] settlements around us have running water 24 hours a day," Khoury says, recounting that in the summer of 2017, "once every eighteen days we would get running water from the spring," sometimes for a whole day, sometimes for less. "The year before that it was once every fourteen days; the year before that it was once every ten days. They give you just enough water to fill up your tanks on the roof. In the summertime it's not enough. We try to avoid exporting during the summer because water restrictions are greater then."

The Khourys have added rooftop tanks and use a well to collect rainwater for cleaning the brewery. They also buy extra water as needed at prices inflated up to tenfold, Khoury says. "The Israelis limit the amount of water we get, so the Palestinian water company has to keep buying more and more water from them. It's one way to keep controlling the Palestinian people's resources and basic human rights—and water is one of them."

Despite the main ingredient being in short and expensive supply, Taybeh Brewing Company produces on average six hundred thousand liters of beer per year, totaling close to two million bottles in six varieties: the best-selling golden—a crisp German-style lager lighter on malt and hops—dark, amber, nonalcoholic, India pale ale, and white beer, which is made with Taybeh-grown wheat and spiced with orange peel from Jericho and locally grown coriander. There is also a specialty winter lager brewed seasonally with a relatively higher alcohol content and spiced with cinnamon, honey, nutmeg, cloves, and ginger. Half of the company's sales are in the West Bank, where due to the prohibition in Islam of the consumption of alcohol by Muslims, it can be sold only in localities where Christians, estimated to number less than 2 percent of the population,[66] live: east Jerusalem, Ramallah, Bethlehem, Beit Jala, Beit Sahour, Birzeit, Jifna, Zababdeh, Jericho, and Taybeh. In order to broaden market share, in 2010 Taybeh Brewing introduced its nonalcoholic beer in locales where the West Bank's majority Muslim population lives, accounting for 5 percent of domestic sales.

Of the 50 percent export sales, a third is sold in Israel, including west Jerusalem, with the remainder in Japan, fourteen countries in Europe, Chile, Canada, and the U.S., which accounts for 4 percent of sales. Taybeh beer sold in the States must be labeled "product of the West Bank"; other exports, including to Israel, are labeled "product of Palestine." The brewery imports its malt from France and Belgium and hops from Germany and the Czech Republic and uses no additives or preservatives.

In 2013 the Khourys expanded their enterprise, opening a boutique winery under the Taybeh label to produce twenty-five thousand bottles a year, all made from grapes grown in Palestine, 90 percent red and 10 percent white. Taybeh exports its wine to Denmark, France, the UK, and U.S. but concentrates on the local market. "We are educating the Palestinian consumer on varieties of local grapes and how to enjoy a glass of wine with food pairings," Khoury says of Taybeh's Cabernet Sauvignon, Merlot, Syrah, and Cabernet Sauvignon Grand Reserve, aged in French oak barrels for two years, as well as Bitouni, made from an indigenous Palestinian grape.

"Winemaking has been going on for hundreds of years in this country. Mothers and grandmothers take whatever grapes they have in their backyards and make it into wine, but they don't know what kind of grape it is," she says. Her brother, Canaan—who completed the Master Brewers Certificate Program at the University of California at Davis, as their father had, after earning an undergraduate degree in mechanical engineering from Harvard University—conducted a study of local grape varieties. He found twenty-one that are unique to Palestine, including the Bitouni red and Zaineh white, both native to the Hebron region of the southern West Bank.

Beyond local markets, though, Palestinian businesses such as the Khourys' that depend on imports and exports are challenged by conditions of life under occupation that slow movement of goods and increase costs, thereby putting Palestinian entrepreneurs at distinct disadvantages. Khoury relates the saga of the waylaid shipment to a 2018 beer festival in Copenhagen as a case in point. Taybeh Brewing's attempt to ship a forty-foot container of nineteen pallets of beer and one pallet of wine by sea, beginning on May 1, a full month before the festival opened, was dashed by security-checkpoint delays at Sha'ar Ephraim near Tulkarm, a commercial crossing point for Palestinian laborers and goods from the northwestern West Bank into Israel; political turbulence in the Gaza Strip that caused the shipping vessel to be rerouted from the port of Ashdod north to Haifa; and further security checks and delays at Haifa port that ate up another week and a half during which Taybeh's twenty pallets of product sat idle.

Khoury ticks off the odyssey of trying to move the shipment northward up the Mediterranean coast: "We had to send the beer from Ashdod to Haifa. And then *because* we are Palestinians, we had to go through security check all over again in Ashdod, and we had to get a permit to move the beer from Ashdod to Haifa, and we had to get approval from Haifa port to bring beer there. You can't do that in one day. Everything takes time, and the more time it takes, the more money you end up paying the Israelis. We missed the vessel that was supposed to leave on the 4th from Haifa, we missed the vessel leaving the 8th, and then it was scheduled to leave on the 13th of May. After we got to Haifa, it was done, papers all set. May 13th there was a strike at the port for five days. On the 19th they started to work on our container; it left on May 20. It takes sixteen days to get to Copenhagen, so it was definitely not going to get to the festival by the 31st."

With her goods en route by sea, Khoury decided to send 40 cases of beer by air. Having secured another permit, she got the shipment to Ben-Gurion Airport on May 16, where it was not loaded for departure until May 22, but it arrived in Denmark in time for the festival. Total air and sea shipping fees, ground transit to the ports, and permit and inspection fees resulted in a net loss for Taybeh Brewing on the deal—a blow to the bottom line but one that Khoury, nonetheless, takes in stride. That her company's beer was enjoyed a continent away from where it was made with no drama apparent to those who drank it is what made it a win, she says, in spite of the bottom line.

"I don't think of it as a loss because I got the beer there before the festival," she says. "To have our beer in Europe, in Denmark, anywhere in the world at a beer festival under a Palestinian label, people don't know how much it took to get it into their hands. I consider the beer not just beer. It's an image of Palestine. When you go to the West, most people don't know what Taybeh is. And they're surprised: *Oh, it's a Palestinian beer. So there's beer in Palestine? When did that happen?*

"And they try to learn more about the beer, about Palestine, about Palestinians, the Palestinian-Israeli conflict, the whole situation. It creates a buzz about Palestine and Palestinians," she says.

"Who thinks that Palestinians drink alcohol, or make it? Because what they see on the news is completely different from reality."

Signs of normalcy—of fun and merrymaking, of revelers enjoying music, dancing, crafts, food, and beer at an outdoor festival—are not the usual images of Palestinian life that observers around the world see on their screens, as Khoury notes. Yet such scenes are the stuff of the Taybeh Oktoberfest celebration held every year since 2005, begun under the administration of then mayor David Khoury to boost the local economy—and at which the Taybeh Brewing Company has been a proud and prominent purveyor of liquid refreshment. For the 2017 festival, Madees's brother Canaan topped off Taybeh Brewery's standard offerings with five novelty beers created especially for the event: bitter mango, lemon-raspberry wheat beer, *shatta* ale made with chili peppers, sumac ale, and brett beer, aged in old wine barrels with spontaneous fermentation.

The early autumn, two-day Oktoberfest draws crowds averaging eight thousand to the village of Taybeh each year. "When you get thousands of people coming to a very small town, and they're walking in the streets, they're visiting the old city, visiting the old churches, and drinking Palestinian beer and eating Palestinian food, listening to Palestinian music," Madees says, "whatever your beliefs are, whatever your religious views are, whatever your political views, wherever you were born and whatever language you are speaking—everyone is just having a good time and celebrating life.

"We have thousands of Palestinians from all over Palestine coming, we have Palestinian Israelis who come, Palestinians from Nablus and Hebron who are conservative and don't drink but come because they enjoy the atmosphere and the music and the food. We have a lot of ex-pats, a lot of internationals, tourists, and a very few Israelis who do come, who are curious to learn more about Palestinians and how they're celebrating Oktoberfest," she says.

A Jewish Israeli attending the festival for the second consecutive year told an interviewer anonymously in 2016: "What I really appreciate about it is the opportunity to experience Palestinian society first-hand rather than through a screen. Just seeing Palestinians having a good time is an extremely valuable experience in itself."[67]

The intersection of the ordinary everydayness of drinking beer and running a business with the extraordinary conditions of life under occupation is hinted at in Taybeh Brewing's promotional poster depicting an outsize, brown bottle of its golden beer. The poster is headlined in Arabic—*shajje' al-sena'āt al-Falastīniyya* ("encourage Palestinian industries")—and carries two mottoes in English: "Drink Palestinian" and "Taste the Revolution."

While some interpret the reference to revolution in a political sense, Khoury says, it was meant to refer to the revolution of craft beer. Taybeh Brewing Company was the first of its kind in the region; since its establishment in 1994 a second Palestinian microbrewery has opened in nearby Birzeit, and Khoury counts a dozen craft-beer companies operating in Israel, three in Lebanon, and one in Jordan. "The craft industry is booming everywhere, so it's about time it grows on this side of the world," she says.

But the notion of revolution also relates to her family's perseverance and their determination to keep doing business. "It's a peaceful way of resistance to the occupation, of being here and overcoming all the challenges," she says. "When we produce a high-quality Palestinian product under the name Taybeh Palestine, and we sell our beer in Israel, and you have some Israelis who do drink the beer and enjoy it, that is both normalcy and resistance to the occupation.

"Because we're actually getting the beer to them, they're not coming here to get it. We have to go through the commercial checkpoints, we have to have the Hebrew sticker on every single bottle of beer, we have to get the permit to enter. We have to go the ten-mile step to get the beer into their hands."

Khoury believes that along with transforming spring water, hops, and malt into beer, the Taybeh Brewing Company is also transmitting understanding of her people and country in every bottle it produces. "Every city, every town has a different story, every person has a different story to tell, and Taybeh beer is a part of that. Not everyone understands conflict and being under occupation. But in order to get the sense of Palestinian people to other people who have never been under occupation, you have to reach them through something relatable—like music, food, beer. That is something people can understand," she says.

"Not a lot of people are going to understand the struggles that we go through. They don't understand that we need a permit to go to Jerusalem, just twenty minutes away, or that we have to go through security checks as individuals to go somewhere.

"But they understand that we are normal people, and we are living, and we need basic human rights like anyone else in the world," Madees Khoury says.

"And we drink beer and eat and dance, along with all the other enjoyments of life."

CHAPTER 4

Day by Day in Jerusalem

The mid-December sky is a clear, brilliant blue above the Old City on this Friday morning, the air chilly and crisp. At 10:30, the foot traffic is still light at Bab al-Zahra, also known as Herod's Gate,[1] opposite the post office and police station at the foot of Salah-Eddin Street, a main commercial corridor in east Jerusalem.

Worshipers on their way to *salat yawm al-jum'a*, the Muslim Friday noontime congregational prayer, begin to trickle through the gate, coming from as near as the Arab neighborhoods of the city and as far away as Galilee. Younger women in dark, mid-calf, tailored coats push children in strollers; older women wearing longer, looser cloth coats and embroidered *gallabiyyas* carry small shopping bundles. Most women cover their hair. Older men wear long *abaya* cloaks or sport coats and traditional white or red-checked *keffiyeh* headdresses. Some of the younger men in short leather and cloth jackets wear baseball and ski caps; others are bareheaded. Young and old, most of the men are not bearded; some have mustaches, others are clean-shaven.

The pedestrians are headed toward the compound of the two great mosques of Al-Haram al-Sharif, the Noble Sanctuary: the golden-domed Qubbat al-Sakhra, or Dome of the Rock, and the silver-capped Al-Aqsa. Many carry traditional *masbaha* prayer beads of polished stone, ceramic, or wood. All walk silently or talk with companions in low tones, their modest comportment and purposeful gait a fitting prelude to prayer.

By 10:50 a.m. three young Israeli soldiers, two men and a woman, take up their post outside the archway of the gate, their olive drab uniforms topped with military berets. Rifles slung over their shoulders, they talk among themselves as they observe but refrain from interacting with those passing through Bab al-Zahra.

Twenty minutes later, Imad Khatib arrives with his son, Afif, twenty-seven, who towers above his father by more than a head. The elder Khatib, fifty-eight, is president of the Palestine Polytechnic University in Hebron. Clean-shaven and without head covering, he is wearing a navy cloth jacket, grey knit polo pullover and corduroys, and black leather loafers. Khatib is in fine spirits. We pass through the gate, and he guides us through alleyways of the Muslim Quarter, yellow-white Jerusalem stones paving the way underfoot and embracing the surrounding space with low-rise interior walls.

Khatib comes every Friday to the Old City to walk its alleyways, pray, and meet friends, combining religious devotion with an assertion of presence. "You can breathe in the history and tradition," he says,[2] savoring the environs as we begin our short trek from the gate to the mosque compound. We pass the century-old open-air market, where plucked chickens and their livers are on orderly display. Fruits and vegetables paint the space with color: green parsley and scallions, deep-purple eggplants, bright orange *mandalinas* (as tangerines are known here), dappled red pomegranates, white cauliflower. Pots of spices and grains are set out near assorted small household goods; the aroma of fresh-baked pita bread and sesame-covered *ka'ak* rings wafts through.

Khatib's own family history and tradition are present in the Muslim Quarter too: his 104-year-old Aunt Shamma, on his mother's side, lives nearby; and his Uncle Anwar, on his father's side, a former governor of Jerusalem under Jordanian rule, lies at rest in a centuries-old cemetery.

As we enter the northern end of the great plaza of the mosques through a passageway known as King Faisal's gate, Khatib estimates that today, as on most Fridays that do not coincide with Muslim holidays, some thirty thousand to forty thousand worshipers will gather on these thirty-five acres. Women will pray in the Dome of the Rock, men in Al-Aqsa. Others of the faithful will remain outside, on the steps of the mosques and in the surrounding small olive groves.

At 11:20 the muezzin begins the solemn call to prayer, separating his phrases with softly inhaled breaths clearly audible over the loudspeaker system, at times clearing his throat. At 11:30 he recites the *fātiha*, the opening verse of the Qur'an. By 11:40 a steady stream of worshipers files through and fills the space, men and women carrying small, colorful prayer mats called *sujjad* and plastic sacks of goods bought in the market. Groups of women sit on the stone platforms of the plaza in the sunshine, others under the shade of olive trees on black soil softened but not muddied by early-winter rains.

By 11:45 a.m. a second voice is heard over the loudspeaker as the imam begins to recite the *khutbah*, or sermon. He begins by urging the faithful to pursue a path toward the spiritual and away from the material, even in these difficult times in which Arab Jerusalem, he says, is under a siege of high taxes, house demolitions, and the continual building of new neighborhoods for Israeli settlers—all meant, he says, to empty the city of its Arab inhabitants.

The believers must become educated and remain patient, and in this, release from their trials shall come soon. Al-Aqsa will remain for its people, he reassures them, despite their difficulties; the dawn is very near. After a brief pause, the imam continues, touching on strife elsewhere in the Arab world—with specific reference to the war in Yemen—as well as the fate of Palestinian detainees and prisoners.

After the sermon, each worshiper carries out a repeating sequence of movements: folding arms across the chest, bowing at the waist, kneeling upright with knees folded under, then prostrating with palms and forehead to the ground—all while softly uttering the supplications of prayer.

Then the faithful rise as one, Palestinian women and men in Jerusalem, in this noble sanctuary—built by humans and endowed with belief in the divine, a serene and sacred place of awe and communal renewal.

By 12:20 the Friday prayer has ended, and the worshipers stream out of the mosques and across the great plaza energized, speaking more animatedly and gesturing more freely than on their way in. They make their way back to the alleyways that wind through the Old City, leading in all directions to its eight great exterior gates, which channel them back into the rest of Jerusalem and beyond.

Imad and Afif Khatib have prayed in Al-Aqsa, a weekly ritual that holds dual meaning for the elder Khatib. The first is spiritual, he says, because the mosque and its environs constitute one of Islam's holiest shrines, past and present, since the late seventh century. "Being connected to this place is very important to me. I think about our ancestors who lived here, who built this place, who conveyed Muslim civilization to the world."

The second meaning, he says, is "patriotic."

"This place is very important to us all, because it symbolizes the Palestinian cause in all its means. Palestine and Arab history revolve around one very important place," Khatib says.

"Jerusalem."

In 1967 Jerusalem was the epicenter of Israel's victory in the Six-Day War. The Israeli government immediately expanded its control over and within Jerusalem, the eastern part of which, including its Arab population and the Old City, had been under Jordanian control since 1948.

Since 1968 the international community has consistently rejected the legitimacy of this de facto annexation in United Nations Security Council Resolutions, including 252, 267, 471, 476, and 478. Nonetheless, Israel pushed forward, radically transforming the landscape of Jerusalem by redrawing its municipal boundaries to encompass seventy square kilometers (twenty-seven square miles, equaling 17,000 acres) of land taken from the West Bank, including east Jerusalem and twenty-eight surrounding Palestinian villages.[3]

On this land, by the end of 2017 Israel had settled 215,067 Jewish citizens in a dozen urban settlements built in and around east Jerusalem exclusively for their habitation, in contravention of international law, according to the Israeli NGO Peace Now. The population of Jerusalem had reached 901,300—with 341,729 Arabs constituting 38 percent, a proportion equal to that of the settlers among Jerusalem's total Jewish population of 559,571.[4]

According to the Israeli NGO Ir Amim, by 2018 an estimated one hundred twenty thousand Palestinians were living behind the section of the separation barrier in and around Jerusalem that Israel built in the early 2000s during the second intifada. The route of the barrier follows the municipal borders in some spots and cuts into the West Bank in others to encompass the large Israeli settlement blocs surrounding the city. Cutting inside municipal boundaries at two points, the barrier isolates one-third of the city's Arab population on the other side. Even though they are officially residents of Jerusalem who pay municipal taxes, this leaves them with few municipal services and requires them to pass through checkpoints to enter the rest of the city.[5]

Land and population engineering are at the core of Israeli policies that have profoundly impacted all aspects of Palestinian life in Jerusalem for the last half century, limiting opportunities for development, mobility, and commerce. In 2017 the poverty rate for Arabs in Jerusalem was 78 percent compared with 25 percent for the Jewish population and 45 percent for the city overall.[6]

An analysis by Ir Amim of the Jerusalem 2013 municipal budget, comprising city and national government funds, found that only 10.1 percent was invested in east Jerusalem for its 37 percent of the population;[7] in 2017, the organization reported a shortage of 1,938 classrooms there.[8] The Association for Civil Rights in Israel reported in 2017 that the city operated four social-welfare services offices in east Jerusalem compared with nineteen serving the city's Jewish residents, with each social worker in east Jerusalem handling an average of 339 cases compared with an average of 194 cases for social workers in the rest of the city.[9]

From 1967 to 2017 the city's Arab population grew nearly fivefold—slightly more than double the rate of Jewish population growth.[10] However, according to data published in 2019 by Peace Now, since 1967 the Israeli government has initiated construction in east Jerusalem of 55,335 housing units in Jewish neighborhoods, 99 percent of the total, compared with 600 units, or 1 percent of the total, in Arab neighborhoods.[11] Arab Jerusalemites face great difficulty in obtaining building permits for a range of reasons: ownership of 90 percent of land in the eastern part of the city is not listed in the state land registry;[12] many neighborhoods lack master plans on which permit applications can be based; and right-wing members of the city council often raise political opposition.[13]

After a two-year campaign to obtain data from the municipality of Jerusalem, in September 2019 Peace Now published an analysis indicating that between 1991 and 2018, the municipality issued only 16.5 percent of all building permits to Palestinians in east Jerusalem, despite their constituting one-third or more of the city's population; 45.7 percent of permits issued during the period were for construction by Jewish Israelis in west Jerusalem; and the remaining 37.8 percent of permits were approved for Jewish Israelis to build in urban settlement areas in east Jerusalem.[14] The pattern was characterized by the Associated Press as "strong evidence of decades of systematic discrimination" and a "refusal to grant permits to Palestinian residents [that] has confined them to crowded, poorly served neighborhoods, with around half the population believed to be at risk of having their homes demolished."[15] The Peace Now data analysis also found "a dramatic increase" in the number of permits issued to enlarge areas of Israeli urban settlement in east Jerusalem during the first two years of the Trump administration: the city issued permits to build 1,861 such housing units in 2017–18, a 60 percent increase over the 1,162 such permits issued in 2015–16.[16]

As a result, Peace Now concluded, "in the absence of [municipal housing] planning and with virtually no chance of obtaining building permits, east Jerusalem Palestinian residents are forced to build without permits and live under the constant threat of demolition," with nearly 200 Palestinian-built residential and nonresidential structures in east Jerusalem demolished each year from 2016 to 2019 alone.[17] The Association for Civil Rights in Israel has estimated the number of Palestinian housing units under threat of demolition in east Jerusalem to be as high as 20,000;[18] the Israeli human-rights organization B'Tselem has indicated that between 2004 and October 2019, 964 Arab housing units were demolished in east Jerusalem—with at least 145 demolitions carried out by owners who were served demolition orders—leaving 3,118 Palestinians homeless, including 1,671 minors.[19]

Despite systemic and systematic policy inequities toward Arab Jerusalemites and ongoing international consensus on the legal status of east Jerusalem, in December 2017 President Donald Trump proclaimed U.S. recognition of Jerusalem as the capital of Israel, an act of geopolitical fiat upending nearly seventy years of U.S. policy. Signaling the relocation of the U.S. Embassy from Tel Aviv to Jerusalem, Trump declared, "Today we finally acknowledge the obvious."[20]

In September 2018, in a failed attempt to compel Palestinian negotiators to return to peace talks, the Trump administration halted $25 million in aid for the East Jerusalem Hospital Network,[21] part of an overall cut in bilateral aid to the Palestinian Authority exceeding $200 million.[22]

Obscured by policy and geopolitics, the presence of Jerusalem's Arabs, historical and current, is nonetheless obvious and vibrant— their lived experiences refracting a distinctive pattern in the Palestinian kaleidoscope.

Imad Khatib's family is but one that traces its lineage in Jerusalem through the centuries. "Khatib" means preacher in Arabic and is a common surname; Khatib himself is descended from the Tamimi branch. He was born in Jerusalem in 1960 and grew up with his parents and seven sisters in Wadi Joz, less than half a mile from Bab al-Zahra. He attended kindergarten through high school in the neighborhood, his childhood punctuated by the 1967 war.

Khatib went to Egypt to earn his bachelor's degree in mechanical engineering. After a brief teaching stint at the polytechnic in Hebron, on British and German government scholarships he earned his master's degree in renewable-energy engineering in Cardiff and his PhD in environmental technology engineering in Karlsruhe, focusing on mathematical modeling of airborne pollution.

After finishing his doctorate, in 1998 Khatib was working for the BASF chemical company in Germany and married with three young children. It was five years into the era of the Oslo peace accords, and his wife, Rania, also born in Jerusalem, suggested that the family return to their roots. "We heard about the peace and the chance of raising our children in Jerusalem without being afraid," he recalls. So they returned, and he went about establishing his academic career in Hebron.

In 1999 Khatib became the founding director of the university's renewable energy and environmental research unit, raising funds for five labs, one focusing on energy efficiency of commercial, industrial, and residential buildings and another on water-quality monitoring in marginalized Hebron communities. In 2000 he began an eighteen-year tenure as secretary general of the Palestine Academy for Science and Technology; from 2003 to 2010 he was principal investigator for a

German initiative focused on impacts of climate change on the hydrology cycle of the Jordan River catchment area, a major reservoir for the eastern aquifer of the West Bank. In 2014 Khatib became president of the Palestine Polytechnic University.

He recalls that the early years of his return were marked by a "honeymoon" period of sorts between Israel and the Palestine Liberation Organization, cosignatories to the Oslo Accords. "There was plenty of money coming into the region for so-called people-to-people activity, to bring people together for reconciliation, for understanding each other." Fathi Arafat, the brother of PLO leader Yasser Arafat and chairman of the Palestine Red Crescent Society, tapped Khatib to be a codirector of the Palestinian-Israeli Environmental Secretariat, known as PIES.

"I was very interested, because this would be my first exposure to the Israeli Left—to those who actually were very much willing to make peace with the Palestinians," he recalls. Prompted by Fathi Arafat's urging that the environment knows no political boundaries, Khatib accepted a part-time position working alongside a progressive Israeli activist. "I felt that this was an opportunity just to check—is it right? Are we going for reconciliation, are we going to make peace? Are the Israelis going to recognize the Palestinians?"

Khatib looks back on an amicable relationship with Paul, his Israeli codirector. "He came from South Africa. He was against apartheid. He was against all Israeli right-wing measures against Palestinians. He was a help for me; he was decent. That's why I thought there might be a way," Khatib remembers.

Despite their collegial harmony, external factors would prove increasingly disruptive. "By that time, several Israeli organizations wanted to be part of these people-to-people projects," Khatib says. "There were millions of dollars from the USA and Europe, especially Norway." An offer of financial support for PIES came from an Israeli organization tied to an agency with a history of expropriating Palestinian lands. In agreement with Paul, Khatib refused.

In another incident, an Israeli scientist specializing in migratory birds offered to host Palestinian students but did not disclose his identity as a settler, to which Paul alerted Khatib. He says Paul came under increasing pressure from elements on the Israeli Left, so much so that he resigned as codirector. With the eruption in 2000 of the second intifada, the PIES initiative faded away.

Khatib still remembers the sting of a conversation he had at the time with an Israeli architect of the Oslo Accords who was also a professor and peace activist. The two were talking about Yasser Arafat, and Khatib recalls that his interlocutor took a tough stance.

"I said, 'Why are you saying that?' He said: 'We made a choice to grant the Palestinians a homeland in Judea and Samaria'"—terms for the West Bank used by right-wing, expansionist proponents of a so-called Greater Israel. "I said: 'Aren't you a leftist? You are talking this way about these lands?' He said, 'Yes, these are Judea and Samaria.' I found myself facing someone who did not recognize Palestinians as legitimate people of this land.

"I told him: 'You accept those [Jews] who are coming from Ethiopia and those who are coming from Russia, accept them to come and settle on my land.' He said: 'This is not your land, Imad. Let us face it. This is not your land.'"

But Khatib sees evidence to the contrary all around him in Jerusalem. He sees it when he walks through the Old City, where Muslim Arabs account for three-quarters of its estimated thirty-eight thousand residents and Christian Arabs about 18 percent.[23] He sees it when he revisits his grammar and high schools in Wadi Joz. And when passing by the Jewish west Jerusalem neighborhoods of Baka and Ein Kerem, he sees it in the many still-extant dwellings that were built and inhabited, before 1948, by Palestinian Arabs.

"Our narrative is linked to the monuments, to the alleys, the buildings and arches that are part of our historical archaeology," Khatib says. "This is evidence for us that we belong to this country."

When it comes to belonging, citizenship is a prime marker. However, approximately 95 percent of Arab Jerusalemites—including those born in the city and whose families have lived here for generations—are not citizens of Israel.[24]

Rather than considering them natives, the state confers upon them permanent-resident status, with residency permits that are subject to revocation by the Ministry of the Interior. "They can take it and leave me without an identity. This is inhumane," says Khatib, who is a permanent resident of Jerusalem along with the rest of his family.

From 1967 to 2014, approximately 14,500 Palestinians lost their right to live in Jerusalem[25]—about two-thirds between 1997 and 2011, and most by virtue of having spent seven or more years abroad. (Jewish Israelis, including settlers, can live abroad for indefinite periods without losing their citizenship.) Since 2006 the ministry has also added lack of allegiance to the state as a basis for revoking residency permits of those deemed to be "terrorists" for reasons including throwing stones or belonging to Islamic political parties.[26]

Palestinian permanent residents of Jerusalem get medical and social-welfare benefits and can vote in local elections. But they cannot vote in national parliamentary elections or obtain Israeli passports. They may apply for citizenship: from 2003 to 2018, 10,305 did so, and 3,413, or one-third, were granted it in an application process that averages six to seven years.[27]

Khatib maintains that at the core of Arab daily life in Jerusalem, with all its inherent difficulties, lies the underlying notion that the large-scale displacement of Palestinians that resulted from the 1948 and 1967 Israeli-Arab wars can never be repeated. "We are not in a position to leave our country, whatever the Israelis are doing," he says. "There is no Palestinian who will accept becoming a refugee again.

"That's why there is a consciousness among all Palestinians living in Jerusalem that we have to adapt. You feel that you are intimidated every day with measures that you have to accept. This is our city, and we have to keep resisting peacefully."

That means Palestinians keeping on with the details of their everyday lives, he says—ensuring their children's education; enduring long waits and humiliating treatment by Israeli soldiers at city checkpoints; not reacting to the taunts of Israeli children whose families have settled in Arab neighborhoods of east Jerusalem, including in the Old City.

The landscape of conflict does not, however, extinguish the impetus to create. Khatib has coauthored a collection of profiles of ten prominent Palestinian Jerusalemites of the twentieth century, narratives that detail their contributions to "preserving the Arabness of Jerusalem."[28] Published in Arabic locally in 2018, the volume covers a range of personalities, from Elizabeth Hanna Nasir, a social worker who established a community center to assist Palestinian girls and young women separated from their families in the wake of the 1948 war, to Faisal Al-Husseini, a political figure who advocated for the Palestinian cause on the international stage and served many roles at home, including minister for Jerusalem affairs in the Palestinian Authority.

In daily lives both exceptional and quotidian, Palestinians in Jerusalem fortify and preserve a tightly knit social fabric with a sense of common purpose heightened by shared predicament. "Christians and Muslims live as neighbors," Khatib says. "We don't think twice: You are Christian, you are Muslim. No. We know that we are all under the same Israeli measures, we are all alike. We help each other." During two weeks of unrest at the Al-Aqsa compound in July 2017 sparked by the killing of two Israeli police officers, Israel installed and then removed metal detectors at entrance points to the shrine. When he went to pray at the site, Khatib found that many Christians, among them friends of his, had come to the barricades to protest. "They were there beside us, standing with us."

Such a fabric cannot be frayed, he insists. "This is the culture that we share, the narrative that we all have.

"The only thing you can do is to be steadfast," Imad Khatib says.

"The only thing you can do is to keep your life in Jerusalem."

Mahmoud Muna was in the audience on the third night of the Kalimat Palestinian literature festival, in the French-German Cultural Center on Peace Street in Ramallah.

A principal organizer of the festival, Muna had worked for nine months to plan the five-day event held the first week of November 2018. Ten Palestinian and four international writers of fiction, poetry, travel, journalism, memoir, and history appeared at five venues in as many days. They began in east Jerusalem—where Muna is proprietor of The Bookshop at the American Colony Hotel—then proceeded to Nablus, Ramallah, Bethlehem, and finally Haifa.

The theme on this third evening was writing the personal and the political. One of five speakers, Gavin Francis, the Scottish physician and acclaimed medical and travel writer, began: "I live in

Edinburgh, and that city is relatively peaceful. There's not a great deal of political agitation or complication that I have to deal with on a day-to-day basis.

"Medicine, the act of being a doctor, of engaging in a consultation—that is purely personal," he said. "It's about an empathetic engagement. It's about an encounter between me and another individual, trying to understand their suffering. And it's my attempt to ease that suffering through some kind of dialogue, entering into a kind of imaginative understanding of what it's like to be that person."

After reading passages about his medical stints and travels in the Indian Himalayas and in West Africa near Senegal, Francis concluded: "My job as a doctor is enormously rewarding. It's about engaging very much with the personal. I'm fortunate not to have to deal very much with the political where I live and practice, but I'm hoping that in this discussion, we can take it forward."[29]

The Palestinian-American writer Susan Abulhawa was also to have attended the festival but had been deported at Ben-Gurion Airport in Tel Aviv days earlier.[30] Joining the event in Ramallah by phone, she followed Francis with a counterpoint.

"We all exist within a political context, whatever that context might be. We create our art and our literature within this political context. I don't think there is, or there can be, a separation. It's a bit like separating water from a river or trying to tease out the woman from the mother," Abulhawa said.

"Even in situations where people who live in more stable political environments create art and they try to say that this is not political, it has no political connotations, even that is a political statement, because it says something politically to be able to be disengaged from what one perceives as political.

"As Palestinians, everything we do, even something seemingly disengaged from politics," she asserted, "is necessarily political because we are a people whose very existence is being denied. Everything that asserts our existence, everything that asserts our historic presence, is necessarily then political."[31]

Five weeks later, Muna is in his shop at the stately American Colony Hotel, a century-old oasis of calm amid the cacophony of east Jerusalem frequented by international travelers, diplomats, and journalists alike. An elegant composition of blond limestone, arched windows, and vaulted ceilings, it has an interior dressed in period furniture and Oriental carpets and a landscape adorned with gardens, courtyards, and palm trees. The bookstore sits opposite the hotel's main entrance, fronted by a terrace and arched doorway and window trimmed in Jerusalem stone, of a piece with the setting.

Surrounded by ceiling-high shelves packed with volumes about Palestine, the Israel-Palestine conflict, the Middle East, and Arab history, Muna says the Francis-Abulhawa exchange was, for him, a singular moment of Kalimat, which means "words" in Arabic. It was singular amid the challenges of moving the fourteen writers and their books from city to city and through military checkpoints; singular among the workshops that the writers held with students at Al-Quds, An-Najah, Birzeit, and Bethlehem universities.[32]

As Francis spoke, Muna says, "I could see what was going on inside the Palestinian heads. From his point of view, Francis was telling a personal story. From the Palestinian perspective, this is very political. He's telling them about the world, he's telling them about himself. But the way they perceive it is about the politics, *their* politics and their inability to travel and to cross the border. He can cross borders in two, five, twenty minutes and be in another country. For them, this is unimaginable."

But, Muna says, for him it was a moment of clarity.

"International writers have the privilege to actually avoid the political and write the personal. In the West, politics is somehow related to the news, or to the president, or to the parliament. Politics here is a big umbrella. Everything comes under it. Absolutely everything. Anything I write is political, because the umbrella of politics covers every aspect of my life."

An essayist himself, Muna has written that in Jerusalem, unlike in many parts of the world, culture is not a conduit for entertainment but "the vehicle for social and political change . . . an unshakable buttress to identity." For Palestinian cultural planners and managers, culture is synonymous with resilience and steadfastness.[33] And that, he says, imposes upon them a responsibility to find and plan events that have meaning for their society, "so you're not doing something that is repetitive or needless or pointless."

And so, Muna took up the challenge of staging Kalimat, which was cosponsored by the Educational Bookshop, also run by his family, and the Kenyon Institute, both in Jerusalem, with funding and support from international and local partners.[34] While literature festivals around the world are often sponsored by ministries of culture or by municipalities, Palestinians in Jerusalem have no such representation. "Your identity is Palestinian, but you are in an Israeli-controlled geographical area," Muna notes, musing that staging a Palestinian literature festival from a footing in Jerusalem is akin to picking a fight of sorts.

"You are choosing to do something, and you know it will introduce a lot of challenges and problems for you. But you try to do it. It gives you a sense that you are not just trying to survive the moment.

"You actually want to change the moment."

Born in Jerusalem in 1982, the youngest of six brothers and a sister, Mahmoud Muna frames the narrative of his childhood: "I grew up in a family that valued books and education."

He completed his first ten years of schooling in the Shuafat refugee camp in the northeast corner of the city, where his father, Ahmed, taught mathematics for thirty-nine years. The family lived in the middle-class neighborhood of Musrara, on the border between east and west Jerusalem; accompanying his father to the camp and studying there afforded Muna a different Palestinian perspective.

"I grew up in a refugee camp where I didn't belong. I wasn't a refugee, but I can tell you the full experience of the camp. My dad was deputy headmaster, so he had to start his day very early, and he would often stay after for meetings and visits in the camp—to this person whose house was flooded, with that student who had problems with his parents." When his father retired, Muna finished his last two years of high school, the *tawjihi* college prep, at the private St. George's School in east Jerusalem.

His ability to move from the poorest Arab school in the city to one of the most affluent stays with Muna to this day. "I have been privileged to be able to come into the camp and be able to leave the camp, because other kids couldn't leave. Many Palestinians from middle-class families wouldn't know what life is like in the camp," he says.

The second axis of Muna's childhood was his family's bookshop, which his father opened in 1984 to fill his afternoon time after teaching in the mornings in Shuafat. Ahmed Muna, who was born in Jerusalem in 1936 and earned a teaching certificate, took over part of a commercial space at 22 Salah-Eddin Street, in east Jerusalem's central business district, that was owned and run as a book and stationery shop before 1948 by the family of renowned Palestinian writer and intellectual Edward Said.

Over the years that Muna worked after school and weekends at the Educational Bookshop, his brothers returned from studying abroad and eventually took it over from their father. In 1999, Munthir Fahmi, a native Jerusalemite who would become known as "the bookseller of Jerusalem," opened a branch of the shop at the American Colony Hotel with stock from the Munas' store on Salah-Eddin Street. In summers throughout his own college years, Muna would return to Jerusalem from abroad to work as Fahmi's assistant.

Muna began his higher education at Al-Quds University in Jerusalem but went to the United Kingdom after the second intifada erupted in late 2000. Within two years, checkpoints and construction of the Israeli separation barrier lengthened his daily travel between home and campus from twenty-five minutes to ninety and from three kilometers to twenty-five; violence was hitting closer to home. "During those years a lot of things were happening around me, a lot of friends died," he recalls.

A member of the millennial generation "who wanted to change the world through the keyboard," Muna finished the last two years of his undergraduate degree in computer science in 2006 at the University of Sussex. He then changed course, earning a master's degree in media from Sussex in 2007 and a second master's in communication from King's College London in 2009.

Again, Muna refers to his sense of privilege, heightened in the UK as he considered the cost of one of his ten-week lecture courses compared with what his former classmates in the refugee camp paid for their schooling. Along with that, he says, was his ability to be abroad during a time of political turmoil and violence at home. "I was privileged to be in and out from the problems back home while other people could not do that," he says. "So I felt this was a time when I needed to be a messenger of those problems."

Sussex, he says, known for "its radical legacies and positions on struggles around the world," was a natural locus for his entry into student activism. The intifada generated much interest on campus about the conflict; Muna organized discussions, invited Palestinian music groups to perform in the UK, and led student delegations on trips to the Palestinian territories.[35]

Returning to Jerusalem after his studies, Muna joined the family business alongside his brothers Imad, Iyad, and Nihad, finding an easy segue from his campus activism to organizing cultural events at the bookshops. By 2014 he had assumed responsibility for daily operations at the American Colony location along with the "bookseller of Jerusalem" moniker. The shop carries 1,200 English-language titles and has a mainly international clientele reflecting that of the hotel. A half kilometer away, the Salah-Eddin Street shop houses a café and carries a similar number of Arabic- and English-language titles that cater to a mostly local audience.

In both locations, patrons find classics of Palestinian fiction and poetry by vanguard writers including Ghassan Kanafani, Emile Habibi, and Mahmoud Darwish as well as nonfiction works of criticism and social history by Edward Said, Rashid Khalidi, Salim Tamari, Raja Shehadeh, and Nur Masalha. Along with works by international authors, the shops also offer titles by noted Israeli writers including Amos Oz, David Grossman, Ilan Pappé, and Jeff Halper. For lighter fare, Muna says, Palestinian male readers under thirty enjoy motivational and self-help books; female readers gravitate to romance novels and other fiction.

His work as a literary curator extends beyond commerce to creating and mediating spaces—such as the Kalimat festival—that link writers and readers. "I often not only help the reader find the best book," he says, "but also help the writer find the best story—a character, an inspiration. Connecting people facilitates the whole landscape."

The Jerusalem landscape has been radically altered since 1967, not only in its geography and demography but also in its outlets for Arab culture—fortifying the nexus, for Palestinians, between the personal and the political.

Before 1948, Muna has written, "Jerusalem was a Mecca of culture. Writers, artists and singers, intellectuals and journalists from all across the Arab world would flock to the city," among them the legendary Egyptian singer Umm Kulthoum.[36] The Jerusalem-based Palestine Broadcasting Service—established in 1936 during the British mandate, with the main tower in Ramallah—produced cultural programming, including live music broadcasts, in Arabic, Hebrew, and English, transmitted along with interviews of regional celebrities, poets, and writers over the radio waves.[37]

Between 1948 and 1967, when east Jerusalem was under Jordanian control, Jordan administered elections for the Jerusalem Municipality, known as Amanat al-Quds, in 1951, 1955, 1959, and 1963. After its conquest of the eastern part of the city in 1967, Israel dissolved this Arab council, which continued to operate symbolically from Amman.[38] Conferred with permanent-resident status rather than citizenship since 1967, the majority of Palestinian east Jerusalemites have boycotted elections for the Israeli-controlled municipality of Jerusalem, with voting rates declining from 21–22 percent in 1969 to 5–8 percent in 1993 to 0.7–1.6 percent in 2013.[39]

The link between politics and culture is apparent in city budgets: in 2013 funding for cultural activity in east Jerusalem amounted to 3.4 percent of total culture department allocations for the whole city, despite 37 percent of the population being Arab.[40] This has impacted cultural infrastructure as well as programming in east Jerusalem, with cinemas, theaters, museums, libraries, and sport facilities either in short supply or in need of rehabilitation—or both.[41]

Eight cultural institutions are active in east Jerusalem, Muna says: a theater organization, a museum, a music school, two art galleries, a multidisciplinary cultural center, and his family's two bookshops. None receives funds from the Jerusalem municipality because they don't apply, a choice that is both political and pragmatic.

The former is a matter of national consciousness akin to the voting boycott—and aligns with international law and consensus, which do not recognize Israel's de facto annexation of east Jerusalem and deem it illegal. Palestinians view the municipality as an Israeli institution; dealing with it normalizes and legitimizes the occupation.

Practically speaking, Muna says, "any meaningful cultural activity I'm going to do in Jerusalem is going to challenge that. So there's no way of finding any shared platform or shared common interest. Our cultural activity is for reinforcing Palestinian identity in east Jerusalem," which is neither an objective nor a goal of the municipality, he notes. "That's exactly what they don't want to do.

"If I go to them and say I'm going to create a modern dance group, they probably would fund it. But I'm not going to do modern dance because that's not what my community wants. What my community wants is *debke*"—traditional Palestinian folk dance—"to relate to the land and to the struggle and to the Palestinian question, which the municipality is not willing to fund."

Further, the Palestinian Authority, based in Ramallah, is prohibited by the Paris Protocol of the Oslo Accords from funding cultural activity, and activity of any kind, in Jerusalem until such indefinite time when the final-status stage of the conflict is reached.

This leaves Palestinian cultural planners largely dependent on international donors—mostly foreign consulates and international NGOs—that have funding parameters and objectives of their own. The donor-driven culture, Muna has written, has marginalized many local artists, compelling them to seek opportunities abroad for exhibitions, performances, and other engagements as well as resulting in internal cultural immigration to other cities that has yielded a "salty-sweet competition" between Jerusalem and Ramallah.[42]

The conundrums that Palestinian Jerusalemites face are many. They reside in Israeli-controlled territory that according to broad international consensus stands to be negotiated as the future capital of an independent Palestinian state. They are subject to marginalizing policies of the municipality. Their cultural institutions cannot receive support from the Palestinian Authority. These circumstances collided when the Arab League named Jerusalem to the "Arab Capital of Culture" initiative for 2009 in conjunction with the UNESCO Cultural Capitals Program.

Since 1996 the Arab League has designated a different Arab capital for the distinction each year. In November 2006 culture ministers from the league's twenty-two member states issued a resolution declaring that they chose Jerusalem for 2009 to "foster cultural activity within and beyond Jerusalem to support its resolve, strengthen its Arab and cultural identity, and develop aspects of daily life in all cultural, social, media, and economic arenas, in addition to intensifying Arab participation in support of the city."[43]

Coordination between Palestinian government officials in Ramallah and Gaza to plan the events of 2009 proved elusive;[44] funding promised from Arab countries and the broader international community proved scant.[45] Given the political undertones of the celebration and involvement of the Palestinian Authority in its planning, Israeli interventions also posed direct challenges. In March 2008 the Israeli minister of public security shut down an event at the El-Hakawati Theatre in east Jerusalem staged to announce the winner of a logo contest for 2009, alleging that the gathering was an activity of the PA.[46]

On the opening day of the celebration in east Jerusalem on March 21, 2009, according to one of its planners, Varsen Aghabekian, "We had children in the streets with balloons, we had clowns and people doing traditional dances in the streets—and these people, unarmed, were chased by soldiers and policemen." Aghabekian, executive director of the 2009 Capital of Arab Culture project, told the *Guardian*: "The formal ceremony planned for the same evening didn't happen because it was shut down at the last minute. Luckily, we had prerecorded it the day before."[47]

The *Jerusalem Post* reported that Israeli police broke up a total of eight events in the eastern part of the city that day, including a soccer match, a women's conference, and a student rally in the Old City. At Al-Quds University, police detained two female employees for planning to distribute T-shirts advertising the events, and students were blocked from entering the campus.[48] In May, police twice shut down events at a six-day Palestinian literature festival attended by international writers in east Jerusalem, and authorities shuttered a media center set up there in advance of Pope Benedict's visit to the city.[49]

Even so, Aghabekian later reported, by mid-2009 more than 250 cultural activities had been staged by Palestinian governmental institutions and NGOs, with over 40 percent taking place in east Jerusalem. Palestinian governorates throughout the West Bank held Jerusalem culture weeks "with attention focused on Palestinians in Jerusalem and the denial of their rights under occupation."[50]

To narrate is power, Edward Said has written, and when the powerful attempt to block the formation and emergence of narratives of those whom they subjugate, the link between culture and power crystalizes. Narratives of emancipation and enlightenment, Said observed, have inspired and mobilized people the world over to fight for their freedoms.[51]

No less so in Jerusalem. Muna says there is a "cultural warrior" aspect to his work: being a curator of cultural activity requires fighting the system, social conventions, and stereotypes not only in artistic pursuits but also in daily life. "This defines an active member of society in Jerusalem more than any other city," he says, "if you can be on the edge but contain the anger, the frustration, and the stress."

The stresses of daily life for Arab Jerusalemites are many, Muna says, at once reserved about speaking on a personal level but acknowledging that his own perspectives enwrap the experiences of his community as a whole.

"The genius thing about this occupation, or the devilish side of it, is that it has reinvented itself, cloned itself differently to different Palestinians depending on their geographical location," he says. "So it's not enough to say, 'I'm a Palestinian' to reflect on my physical identity and challenges and aspirations. A Palestinian in Jerusalem is different from a Palestinian in the West Bank and a Palestinian in Gaza, unfortunately. One of the biggest challenges we will have after liberation, hopefully soon, is how to stitch back these identities and create one shared common identity again."

Palestinians in Jerusalem, Muna says, experience constant friction with what he calls the "soft occupation." For all of their distinctive burdens and challenges, Palestinians in the West Bank and Gaza Strip generally do not encounter Israeli soldiers and police on a daily basis. They do not participate directly in the Israeli economy, or use the Israeli public transport system, or have to speak two languages, Muna says—realities that Palestinians in Jerusalem face every day.

They may be subject to checkpoints near their homes; businesses in east Jerusalem suffer, he says, because the eastern part of the city is strangled. The traffic jams that occur throughout the day and the shortage of public parking due to a lack of municipal development in their neighborhoods causes many Palestinians to double-park.

In other parts of the world, even in west Jerusalem, Muna says, drivers who double-park while sitting in their cars are treated by the spirit of the law when police tell them to move. "Here, you get a ticket, and you know why you get a ticket. This," he says with an exasperated sigh, "is the example of *everything*."

A trip to the bank to receive a wire transfer turns into a failed exercise because the Israeli clerk will not accept a bank statement and ATM card from a Palestinian east Jerusalemite as proof that the account is his. Palestinians who apply for mortgages to build houses in Arab neighborhoods such as the Mount of Olives, Issawiyya, Silwan, Beit Hanina, and Shuafat are routinely rejected by Israeli banks, Muna says, which deem them high-risk areas.

"So what do you do," he asks rhetorically, "if you're a young person who has never thrown stones, who wants to live a life any Israeli would want? What do you want me to do? I'm trying to be a nice citizen, a human being.

"Here, it's by the book. But the book happens to be in Hebrew, and you don't know Hebrew very well. And the people in front of you have defined themselves and you in the language of enemies and others.

"You are always treated exactly by the text, a text that you don't have a better understanding of, a text that you don't have a relation to. You try to understand it, but there are always barriers.

"You are not," Muna says, "inside."

Yet it is from within his society that Muna seeks direction, sees hope— and in his estimation, Palestinian writers have a distinct role to play.

"In today's Palestine, we lack vision from the politicians for what's ahead. There must be someone else to take the responsibility of presenting a new vision. This is the role of writers," he says. "A writer who does not see his writing as part of this process for social and political change, for creating space for debates and for promoting a vision for the future, is not necessarily a writer in Palestine."

On the political level, he says, Palestinians have not always communicated their message to the world skillfully. "Even with a few exceptional individuals and a few exceptional years, the Palestinians have been quite unlucky about how to tell their story. We always had a gap between where the world is and our approach to it.

"In times when the world was internationalist, speaking about equal rights and liberties and human rights, we were stuck in a very nationalist paradigm. Now we have moved to the international language of equal rights and human rights, but the world is already in another zone, in a nationalist phase. We have been out of sync."

From the power of the written word, though, and his role in facilitating its transmission, Muna summons optimism. Fresh off the success of the Kalimat festival, in early 2019 the Educational Bookshop on Salah-Eddin Street presented in its Jerusalem Literary Salon Reja-e Busailah, author of *In the Land of My Birth: A Palestinian Boyhood*, a memoir of his coming of age as a blind youth in the years leading up to the 1948 war. Palestinian social historian Salim Tamari and noted Lebanese novelist Elias Khoury joined the event via Skype. The salon also hosted British academic Michael Dumper, author of *Jerusalem Unbound: Geography, History, and the Future of the Holy City*, which chronicles changes imposed by Israel in the city since 1967 and the resilience of its Arab population.

"The future will have to be better for the Palestinians," Muna says. "I don't think anything can happen that's going to be worse than what we have already seen."

And contested though their city is, when Palestinians speak about Jerusalem, "they mean their Jerusalem," he says. "They mean east Jerusalem. The Old City. And the part of west Jerusalem that is historical. When they say Jerusalem, they speak about the Jerusalem that they know. They know Jaffa Street—yes, that's the heart of west Jerusalem. And part of west Jerusalem is the Jerusalem that they know—Katamon, Baka, French Hill. They speak about Jerusalem as Talbiyyeh and Katamon, where the Arab houses used to be. They're not interested in the bigger part of Jerusalem beyond that, which is mostly residential, mostly newly built. It's not built in their way, it's not built on their city."

Muna's tone mellows when he considers the place in Jerusalem— beyond the bookshops and the home that he shares with his wife,

Mai, and their three young daughters in the Mount of Olives—that speaks to him most.

"I like the small alleyways of the Old City. When I walk in the Old City of Jerusalem, I start to speak to the stones. Or rather, I imagine that I'm having a conversation with them. I ask them questions and start to imagine what their responses are."

He says he often hears the stones laughing—at Palestinians, Israelis, tourists. Especially the tourists, he says, who come and see a city that's not really Jerusalem, a city of myths and legends. A city whose narrative has been created for their entertainment.

And he hears the stones laugh at Palestinians and Israelis too for not really understanding Jerusalem. "Not a single civilization has *not* tried to occupy, control, conquer Jerusalem. Not a single civilization has succeeded. You have two choices in Jerusalem as a civilization, as a government, as a people. You either end up in the history books as someone who built, or you end up in the history books as someone who destroyed.

"We're trying to do exactly what the previous ones before us have done. Trying to control the city and call it ours. No one controls Jerusalem."

Mahmoud Muna laughs softly. "If you really know the history of Jerusalem, then you know you're just a passing moment in it."

At the age of not quite four, Nadia Harhash asked her mother whether God is male or female.

I thought he had to be male, she would later write, *because everyone preferred males. I silently questioned the masculine dominance of this "fact," because the origins of life are from femininity. How could my mother, the creator of children, remain in the shadow of my father, who we rarely saw? How could the branch be stronger than the tree, and more dominating, while the tree, the origin, remained subordinate and obedient?*[52]

From an early age, Harhash was not only independent in spirit but also aware of the patriarchal society around her. Born in the Wadi Joz neighborhood of Jerusalem in 1971, she started to walk when she was very young—so much so that to keep her from wandering, her grandfather Mustapha would sometimes tie one end of a rope around her ankle and the other around a black iron rod planted deep in the ground.

"This girl is not a girl made for this life," he declared—and even as she felt his love and idolized him as she grew, the rope stayed with her. *I felt its effects for many years,* Harhash would write in *In the Shadows of Men*, her narrative of her life in Jerusalem. *Whatever I did, I remained tied to something that always held me back.*

Even so, as a kindergartner she found herself free to roam one day unshackled. Dropped off by her father, Issam, at her school across from the Damascus Gate of the Old City, she discovered that neither classmates nor teachers were there. So young Nadia navigated the nearby neighborhoods on her own, finding her father's workplace by trial and error.

Her family would recount the story with pride for years. *How could a four-year-old child travel from her school to her father's office on her own?* she mused in *Shadows*, recalling: *As I grew up, this memory helped me imagine myself as Supergirl. From that day on, I became the girl in charge, the one who could do everything.*

Growing up in A-Ram, northeast of the municipal boundary of Jerusalem, Harhash was the oldest of nine children—with seven more girls born before the first and only boy. The long wave of female children eddied turbulently through the family, washing over their mother, Ilham, most forcefully. *Girl after girl after girl was born, and the dreams of our mother broke around us, their shrapnel scattered and then reshaped into another dream far away from us—the dream of the male,* Harhash has written. *When a boy arrived, life began to flourish in our home. My mother's happiness flooded the earth and sky, and it overwhelmed us. Finally, we were bonded with this world. Finally, we had an existence. Finally, we had a brother.*

In their middle-class family to which she ascribes "ordinary behaviors and average education," Harhash and her sisters were nonetheless treated with compassion. Their mother insisted that they attend private schools, even though the family was not wealthy. Their father worked long hours in the family's car-sales and taxi businesses to support them; their grandfather also contributed to their education. From her father, Harhash says she learned modesty and self-sufficiency; from her mother, to face and overcome challenges.

Still, there was something else she had to remember. *Grow tired, strive, struggle, and resist, yet, of that one thing always remain aware: You are a woman. Your horizons are limited. Your actions come with great responsibility. Any misstep is a black mark that will later reflect on your sisters.*

Her mother told her: "Be careful. You are a girl. Be educated so that education can be your weapon. Work hard so you won't need anyone to support you."

This advice Harhash took to heart. The threads of her adulthood—in her roles as a wife, divorced woman, and single mother—are woven into a tapestry of lifelong learning, continual questioning, and a quest to be her own person.

She shares details of her life in Jerusalem on a sunny Saturday afternoon in the house that her father finished building for the family in 1989 in the genteel neighborhood of Beit Hanina; Harhash has just painted the front door teal blue. At ease, surrounded by the cocoon of family, she wears a black V-neck pullover and grey sweat pants, silver crescent-moon and hamsa necklaces, and her long dark hair plaited in a single braid.

Daughter Serena, sixteen, comes in with a friend, fresh from school exams; Issam passes through briefly with a cheery greeting. Grandmother Faiza, ninety, sits quietly smoking next to the kitchen windows, through which seep traffic noises from the old Jerusalem–Beit Hanina main road. Imm Omar, the housekeeper, goes about her chores in the high-ceilinged abode filled with crammed bookcases and children's artwork on the walls. Zoey, a yellow mini Labrador, scampers underfoot.

After finishing her primary and secondary schooling at Schmidt's Girls College, in the early 1990s Harhash enrolled at the Hebrew University of Jerusalem to study political science while simultaneously studying law through a distance-learning program of Beirut Arab University, traveling to Jordan in the summers to sit exams. During those years of the first intifada, she completed the law degree but left her Hebrew University studies unfinished.

"I loved political science," she says, recalling her aspirations for a career in diplomacy that were ultimately frustrated by circumstances of alienation. "But I felt that I was wasting my time, because we didn't have a government. We didn't have a state."

Her experience on the Mt. Scopus campus during those violent and politically turbulent years evokes the Palestinian outsider in Jerusalem among the Israeli majority. "Even though I was studying at the Hebrew University, I didn't see Israel," she says. "I didn't see Israelis. I always thought that the occupation would go away. As much as they"—Israelis—"came from nowhere in my head, they would disappear the way they came." Language was also a barrier. A resident of the city but not a citizen of the state, Harhash registered at the university as an international student, enabling her to submit her work in English and other languages for the first three years. "I couldn't face Hebrew," she remembers. "Something inside me was blocking it." But in the last year of her studies, there was no way around the requirement of completing the final seminar in Hebrew.

Having finished her law degree, Harhash was married and pregnant with her first child when she withdrew from the university. She wed at twenty-one, determined to fulfill her duty in a society that encourages women to marry young. But she was also determined to become the woman that her mother, who married at fifteen and gave birth to her at sixteen, could not have been—*the woman who demanded, and took more from life.* The die for conflict between social duty and individualism was cast: *I was an obedient wife, as my mother wanted me to be, and I was strong, as she wanted me to become.*

After two years in the United States, Harhash and her husband returned in 1995, settling down with their young daughter, Hiva, in the center of east Jerusalem between Sheikh Jarrah and Wadi Joz. Despite economic and educational disparities in their backgrounds, Harhash believed that she could build a life with her husband, coupling her drive with his strong work ethic. Without regret or fanfare, she traded the material ease of her childhood for a young married life of starting from scratch.

The couple opened a coffee-vending business with two machines bought with their savings, adding three more with a loan from her father and the sale of her wedding gold. Harhash worked full-time beside her husband: "All that he had in the business was something that we did together," she remembers.

The two machines grew to twenty, installed in major supermarkets in the city and near schools and universities in Jerusalem, Bethlehem, and Ramallah. The couple expanded the business into coffee supply. Harhash managed the office; her husband maintained the machines. "We were growing," she recalls. "Building our own career was very good. It was a very special time in my life on that level. But it was a horrific time on the marital level."

Even as she worked full-time, having three more children within five years—and attending to the school and health needs of the couple's three daughters and son, ferrying them to swimming, tennis, and music lessons as they grew—Harhash faced resentment from her husband that turned increasingly aggressive in their home life. *My husband was demanding, and he complained constantly. I lived with a man whose expectations could never be met.*

Embedded in those expectations was that Harhash not stray from a narrow path. The rope that her grandfather had tied around her ankle during childhood persisted, metaphorically, into married adulthood. Her husband expressed dissatisfaction with her appearance; he forbade her to visit libraries. In her mothering, she resisted: *I was secretly raising my children to pursue dreams hidden from them by the patriarchy. I wanted my children to hear a single message from me: Become who you want to become.*

Harhash endured her husband's increasing intolerance until a severe beating left her with a broken rib. To avert investigation, at the hospital she said she had fallen down stairs. But privately, she has written, *the chaos of my senses exploded inside me and erupted in all directions within me, and I was no longer capable of controlling it or even calming it down.*

In 2004, after thirteen years of marriage, Harhash took her children, left her husband, and began her life anew.

She did not decide to breach her status as a married woman of means easily or without angst: *How do you say no? How do you leave a life filled with glory and money? How do you rebel against a life that most women dream of? What do you want? Do you think you are the only woman who was ever insulted in her home?*

She was not. Despite her advanced education, successful career, and high income, her marital troubles mirrored those of other east Jerusalem women of varied levels of privilege. A 2017 study by the Palestinian NGO Juzoor for Health and Social Development found that 55 percent of participants had been exposed to domestic violence, and only 18 percent felt empowered to participate in family decisions and community life outside their homes.[53]

Low employment rates—only 5 percent held full-time jobs and 21 percent worked part-time—were attributed both to state violence and mobility restrictions imposed by the occupation[54] as well as gender stereotypes, "including a husband's perceived insecurity. Such factors, added together, make Palestinian Jerusalemite women almost completely dependent upon husbands and fathers for income," the study concluded, based on research conducted among 953 women from the Old City, Shuafat refugee camp, A-Ram, Issawiyya, and Jabel Mukaber.[55]

Inability to make independent household decisions was reported by 26 percent of study participants; 94 percent said discrimination against women participating in public life exists, with nearly half saying they were unable to join women's organizations or attend training courses. More than 98 percent indicated violence against women and children as a preeminent issue, with the study finding most incidents of domestic violence against adult women perpetrated by husbands or ex-husbands. Exposure to physical violence from a close relative was found to increase fivefold among separated, divorced, and widowed women.[56]

With no financial support from her family, Harhash summoned the strength to push forward with her divorce, making no claims on the couple's house or business and forgoing the monetary settlement due her according to her marriage contract. *I believed it was my right as a free Muslim woman. I was told I was free, and I decided to regain my freedom at that moment. I didn't realize, of course, that freedom for a woman in a patriarchal society is impossible. All I aspired to do was take a breath without a man watching over me. My heart was pleading for life.*

In December 2004 Harhash moved out; her divorce became official the following May. She moved with her children to a rented apartment in Beit Hanina, during their first months sleeping on mattresses on the floor and making do without refrigerator, stove, and washing machine. Trading material comfort for her independence, Harhash countered strife with certainty.

When I left my husband, I took with me a map that I drew carefully and modestly. The most important thing was that I would never again rely on a man. I had to remember that the greatest gain from the divorce was getting away, unlocking those chains and freeing myself from the requirements of a man and his constraints on me.

I resembled the olive tree in my country. You can uproot it, and yet it continues to grow. You leave it without water, and it is not bothered by thirst.

At the same time, Harhash embarked on a decade of court battles over custody and support issues. At the secular Israeli court in Givat Shaul, her ex-husband's lawyer demanded that she—deemed to be out of line with the role of a traditional Palestinian woman—justify how she could read a novel, *The Schopenhauer Cure*, while still having time to care for her children.

At home and in public she was repeatedly confronted by family members sent by her ex-husband to claim their children, scenes that culminated in various police stations at the Russian Compound, in Pisgat Ze'ev, and on Salah-Eddin Street. A court order affirming her fitness as a parent followed, and the children remained with her.

For ten years after she left her husband, Harhash plumbed the depths of volatility as a divorced woman in a society insistent on preserving male prerogative as a key to social order. A society in which, she asserts, men and women contribute evenly to sustaining the patriarchy—women by raising their sons to take their place in it; men by assuming those very roles. Hostility came from many directions, including family members and women friends to whom she had suddenly become a pariah.

In an instant, I became like a contagious disease. Everyone tried to stay far away from me. Divorce became a divorce from society, not just from the man. As if leaving the flock makes the sky smaller, no matter how spacious it seems. It remains a sky controlled by pre-set rules.

It was as if my divorce threatened to break apart all the marriages in society. Suddenly, I became a threat to every man and woman, and a threat to my own family—both my married and unmarried sisters. I brought disgrace when I asked for divorce. Women conspired against me, even my mother and my sisters. My husband was backed by an army of men dedicated to serving him and distorting me.

It was only from her father that Harhash received reassurance. He asked her what she wanted. She replied: "I want a man who carries piety towards the God in me."

Regrouping after divorce, Harhash went back to work away from the business she had built with her husband, only to be confronted by aftershocks of their split. *When I was desperately searching for a job, I would enter an office and find my ex-husband in front of the window, sometimes like a ghost and sometimes like a monster. No employer wanted to deal with an obsessed, annoying ex-husband constantly tracking the wife who'd left him. Everywhere I went, my problems preceded me.* A job at an institution run by a relative of her ex-husband was rescinded when his family applied pressure.

Harhash pushed forward, opening a daycare center in her parents' home in Beit Hanina and moving in with Hiva, son Abdel-Nour, and toddlers Yasmina and Serena. As she struggled to regain her equilibrium, she willed for them a life different from hers, just as she had projected for herself a life different from that of her mother before her. *How could I pretend to raise the next generation with better values when I could not be a good example myself? I wanted them to grow up with enough power that they could be the shapers of their own destinies. What I tried to do as a divorced mother was to give each child a brush and allow him to paint whatever he wanted into our life's portrait.*

It was with her children at swimming lessons at the YMCA in west Jerusalem that Harhash began to view Israelis differently. "It was one of the very few places, if not the only place in Jerusalem, that really makes you feel this strong sense of shared ownership of the place," she recalls. "Nobody questions why you are there. You can be a Palestinian and enjoy being there. And Israelis would also feel the same." From being among families from both communities, Harhash segued into becoming active in the Israeli-Palestinian women's peace movement. "Being an activist starts by recognizing the existence of the other and accepting them. You try to make the place where you are a place that can fit in everyone," she says.

Soon after her divorce, Harhash attended a conference on the Mount of Olives held by Women in Black, a peace and justice movement that started in Jerusalem in 1988 during the first intifada. From there she began to participate in activities of the Coalition of Women for Peace, the Tel Aviv–based hub for such groups around the country.

"I met remarkable women," Harhash recalls of her coactivists, in particular the Israeli women. "I learned a lot about what it means to be an intellectual—that you can disagree with someone on major issues, and yet, when you leave that room, you become friends again." It was a mode of discourse that was new to her.

"This is a major part of what makes Israelis more powerful than us," she says. "You can freely express what you think without feeling afraid that something bad will happen to you after you leave that room." The women would argue forcefully over issues, then share a meal together. "This is one of the most important lessons I've ever learned," Harhash says, "to be outspoken. Your voice becomes so important, even though you could be the youngest, the least important among them all."

Her activity in the coalition and an interfaith women's dialogue group in Jerusalem helped Harhash fill the social void created by her divorce. "It was a time when I needed to be involved. I needed to feel effective. I was exploring things, I was maturing on all levels: the women's level, the political level, the social level, the personal level."

The support she received from Israeli women—"women who barely knew me," she recalls—came from a wellspring of compassion, and it buoyed Harhash during her transition from a married woman respected within her society to a divorced woman castigated by it. "I was living inside a big fire. I needed to feel sane, to feel that whatever I was doing was not crazy, not outrageous," she says. One Israeli woman even offered to accompany her to a court hearing to face her ex-husband.

Of these friends and acquaintances, Harhash has written: *They pulled me towards a place of empowerment. They insisted I was far*

more capable, stronger and tougher than I believed. They also real-
ized how much I needed the support of others—the support that comes
with a word, a look, even a simple sigh of understanding.

I needed to be reminded that I existed, that I had value. After a
long period of collapse after collapse, with destruction raining down on
top of me, I needed to be reminded of my worth.

Like many who recover from emotional trauma, Harhash healed gradually, reclaiming her self-worth through study, work, and developing her writer's voice. She earned two master's degrees: one in Islamic philosophy online from the Freie Universität Berlin in 2015, the other in Jerusalem studies from Al-Quds University in Jerusalem in 2016—delving into women's issues for both theses.[57] She began to publish essays and commentaries in local and international media outlets.

From 2008 to 2016, she held administrative positions at Al-Quds, coordinating its various research institutes and centers and updating its bylaws and regulations. She also worked to advance accreditation of its various degree programs offered in Jerusalem, outside the main campus, which is located in Abu Dis.

Working at the university also heightened Harhash's political sense of place. In the face of Israel's overwhelming dominance in Jerusalem, she says, "the only thing we are left with is us—people and institutions. Every single person who can make a difference can have an effect on the future of Jerusalem. Every single building or institution that is educational, that is still characterized by being Palestinian, is important and is needed in our political fight. You cannot *not* mix the political and the social in Jerusalem. Everything you do is an act of politics here."

Her later years at Al-Quds coincided with recurring waves of violence that seized the city and its environs following the breakdown of peace negotiations in April 2014 and the seven-week war in Gaza that summer and continued through 2015 into 2016. From her office in the finance building on the Abu Dis campus, about three kilometers east of the Old City but partitioned from Jerusalem by the Israeli separation barrier, Harhash found herself on what she described in an October 2015 Huffington Post essay as a shooting line, the campus having fallen into a state of anxiety and become a place of confrontation.[58]

"The moment you enter the campus at 7:30 and see an army vehicle there, you know there will be trouble that day," she recalls. "You cannot but see them in this invasive way. At some point it becomes uncontrollable. All it takes is just one person to throw a stone."

Harhash chronicled her encounters with the occupation in *Shadows*: She waited at a checkpoint in Shuafat for two hours, her vehicle second in an ever-growing line as the young soldier in charge leisurely ate a cracker. She shouted at him; he demanded her identity card and pointed his gun at her head.

She submitted at Ben-Gurion Airport to targeted screening with an ultraviolet X-ray machine that revealed the minutest details of her body, down to stretch marks on her abdomen from her pregnancies. She told the security agent: "There used to be Palestinian children in there."

She has asserted in resolute and forceful prose that Palestinian women suffer two forms of tyranny: not only the patriarchy of their society but also the indignities of the occupation.

Living under years of occupation has diminished the value of life among the Palestinian people. Life feels so miserable and worthless that death seems merely to be a change, not a loss. Young men are eager to go and fight, knowing they will likely be killed, because this would not be a loss to them.

Israel has successfully convinced us that our lives and our deaths are equivalent. Living in that state of humiliation, oppression, and suppression changes the nature of our souls and robs us of our joy for life. Life needs a space for hope to thrive, and such spaces have been shut and locked for young Palestinians.

During periods of heightened tension, Harhash feared that her own children might be moved to acts of self-sacrifice. *Horror knocked at my heart each time my youngest daughter sat in front of the TV and asked, "What would you do if I became a martyr? Why do we live? Look at all this injustice. What did these children do to deserve this? Why do we live such a life in the first place?"*

So she began to take Yasmina and Serena, then young adolescents, on trips to the Old City. "I would walk with them, bring food, and we would sit and eat on the stairs at the Damascus Gate," she recalls.

"This was our act of resistance, me and my daughters, just to prove that we own this place."

Harhash's independent voice resonates in her media writing published at home and abroad. She contributes political analyses regularly to Rai al-Youm, a digital news and opinion site published in Arabic from London. She has blogged occasionally for *Al Jazeera* Arabic. She has also been a frequent contributor to the Palestinian news agency Wattan, based in Ramallah, and she considers the pieces she has published there to have had a strong imprint. "Wattan allows me to reflect directly. It's like having the pulse of the place. It tests my integrity," she says.

Her frequent columns have commanded the attention of Palestinian leaders, and Harhash has pulled no punches when writing about politics and security issues as well as Palestinian civil society. Her words have not been censored, but on occasions when her editors have deemed particular topics she has written about to be too sensitive, they have opted not to publish her. She also maintains a blog,[59] where she posts without restriction. "This," she says, "is the power of being a free writer."

In December 2018 Harhash published a column in Wattan about Suha Jbara, age thirty-one, who had been arrested by Palestinian security agents in her home in the West Bank village of Turmus'ayya a month earlier, assaulted while being interrogated, and then imprisoned in Jericho on charges withheld from her attorneys.[60]

Amnesty International intervened in the case—referring to Jbara as a social activist involved with Islamic charities who had denied under interrogation that she had collected and distributed funds illegally. The human-rights organization reported that Jbara had been beaten, slammed against a wall, and threatened with sexual violence by interrogators. She had not been allowed to read her testimony before signing it and had been subjected to continual pressure to end her hunger strike.[61]

Public response from Palestinian quarters on Jbara's case was mute, however, spurring Harhash to call it out in Wattan. "We Palestinians describe the brutality of Israeli detention policies," she says, "and then we allow such a crime to take place. There is something wrong in how we deal with this as a society. I wrote: Where is the women's movement in Palestine in this case? She is a political prisoner, and she's being violated.

"If you don't act on such an issue," Harhash demands, "then when do you act?"

As the sun begins its descent in the late-afternoon hour and fills her house in Beit Hanina with soft light, Nadia Harhash is at home in Jerusalem, the nuances of her identity and sense of place of a piece. Ever prolific, in 2019 she published a novel that follows the paths of four women in Jerusalem named Maryam, their journeys linked to the past, bound up in the present, and weaving themes of sacrifice, suffering, and liberation.[62]

The need for freedom, she has written, is the first human instinct. But in her quest for personal liberation, Harhash declines to think of herself as a feminist, preferring instead the term *womanist*.

"The source of power in being a woman is genuine," she says. "It puts me on an equal level of creation," she asserts, adding that being a woman is a natural state, just like being a man. "I don't need to become a feminist in order to ask for what I deserve to have."

Like her personal struggles, the fight for her homeland is just, Harhash has written in *Shadows*.

It is about rights. Rights cannot be lost as long as there are people who demand them, and the demands will remain as long as there is a living, breathing Palestinian.

But change must also come from within, she believes.

There is something in our heritage that undoubtedly shapes our identity. I cannot say I don't want it, or that I try to rid myself of it. But everything that taints and distorts this heritage should be thrown out if the human inside us wants to find his humanity.

As for her city, she says, "I see Jerusalem as Jerusalem, as one unit. I don't see west Jerusalem as *not* being part of what represents me as a Jerusalemite." She doesn't want to see the city cut into two pieces, with chunks of east Jerusalem carved out to form the capital of a Palestinian state.

"It's like a diamond ring. Jerusalem is a ring, and the diamond of it is that sphere of Al-Aqsa and the Dome of the Rock, all of the Old City. There is this diamond, but the ring is all of Jerusalem.

"I don't want it to be taken away from me."

CHAPTER 5

In Gaza,
They Are Not Numbers

Areej Al-Madhoun sat at the long table in the competition hall, gesturing with her hands as she imagined counting beads on a Chinese abacus. She had eight minutes to solve 255 arithmetic problems: addition, subtraction, multiplication, and division, no electronic calculators or pencil-and-paper calculations allowed.

She was fourteen years old, a ninth-grader far from her home in Jabalia, the largest Palestinian refugee camp in the Gaza Strip. On this, her first trip abroad, she had traveled nearly eight thousand kilometers to compete in the biennial Intelligent Mental-Arithmetic (IMA) Competition held on December 16, 2012, in Malaysia. She was competing as an individual, but Areej knew that she represented Palestine; she represented Gaza; and she represented Jabalia, a pupil from *Banat Jabalia al-'idādiyya Ba* (B), a girls' preparatory school in the camp.

As Areej labored at her task, she also knew that her competitors—twenty-five hundred other youths from countries spanning Egypt to the Philippines—had dreamed, as she had, of being the best, of winning the first prize. "My plan was to win the competition, not just to participate," she recounts six years later. "Preparing for the competition, I had a story in my mind, a voice that said: 'The winner in this international competition is Areej Al-Madhoun from Palestine.'"[1]

She had trained for the competition as an extracurricular activity outside of her regular schoolwork, attending sessions at the IMA center in Gaza City. But her training focused on math problems her father had prepared for her to practice at home using a timer he bought for her to test her speed.

"The core idea is the abacus," she says. When she started to train, she used one of the beaded devices but soon set it aside. "When our hands are working, we are solving the problems imagining the abacus." But the real objective, she says, is not solving math problems but strengthening mental capacity. "You use both halves of your brain by using both of your hands. Solving the questions quickly improves many things: self-confidence, memory, focus. When your brain works well, then you can do anything by practicing."

In Jabalia Areej had worked up to solving 242 of 255 problems without error. But in Malaysia she had come down with a fever and the flu from her travels, and the peak of her preparation at home had coincided with the eight-day war in Gaza between Israel and Hamas just weeks before.[2] Fatigued and ill at the competition, she managed to solve just 182 problems, all correctly.

But that was the top score, and she won first prize.

Mathematics comes easily to Areej, who was born in Jabalia in 1998. "There is a sense between my brain and numbers," she says. Developing her strength in math fuels her power of imagination, enabling her to command abstract thinking that she uses not only to solve math problems but also to envision her future.

She began training at the IMA center in Gaza City in 2011 and won first prize in an all-Palestine competition that year. In December 2012, with no external funding, she and twenty-one other Palestinian pupils from Gaza and the West Bank traveled to compete in Malaysia. The ten West Bankers crossed into Jordan and flew via Amman; the twelve Gazans rode a bus through the Sinai to Cairo, flew to Saudi Arabia, and after a fourteen-hour layover continued on to Kuala Lumpur. "The traveling was so expensive for us," Areej says. "It was hard for our families. You have to spend time, you have to spend money—and then you may return without winning."

But out of the thousands of contestants, the Palestinians captured five of the top ten places, with four of the five winners from Gaza. Areej won first place; a pupil from Hebron in the West Bank second place; two from Khan Yunis the fourth and fifth places; and a pupil from Rafah the sixth. "After that," she says, "we left it for the world.

"For me it was a success. But for my country it was a great victory after the war. We did our best to tell the world that we are not just numbers, we Palestinians," she says, and she quotes the Palestinian poet Rafeef Ziadah: "*We Palestinians wake up every morning to teach the rest of the world life, sir.*"[3]

The moment of victory was bittersweet, Areej recalls. "When they announced that I got the first prize, I remembered many things. It was a mix of happiness and bad feelings after the war. I lost many friends, many memories." Her best friend had been killed by the Israeli military, one of eighty-seven Palestinian noncombatants to die, thirty-two of them minors.[4] Areej had continued to train for the competition through her tears.

"This is the life in Gaza," she says. "But for me there's no one . . ."— she takes a long pause—". . . no one who can take my dreams from me.

"If you ask me, 'How old are you, Areej?' I'll tell you three wars. And it may be four wars," she says on the day before her twenty-first birthday.

"This is the life in Gaza. You do your best not to be just a number in this world. And to be always full of hope."

Following her victory in the international competition, Areej finished preparatory and high school in Jabalia and in 2016 enrolled at the Islamic University of Gaza—one of twenty-eight universities and colleges in the Strip with a total enrollment exceeding eighty thousand students[5]—to study for a bachelor's degree in computer and electrical engineering. Halfway through her five-year program, her courses had included data structure and algorithms, digital electronics, sequential digital design, contralinear control systems, embedded systems, and software engineering.

"The power of mathematics comes from its application," she says. "The aim of these subjects is how to be a problem solver, how to think out of the box. This is the core effect of computer engineering: how to see things around you."

At the same time, Areej also imagines knowledge pathways for future graduate study in other scientific fields such as bioinformatics, which combines biology, mathematics, computer science, and artificial intelligence—among other sciences—in genomics to analyze the genetic basis of disease. Her interest in biology was sparked when she achieved a perfect score on a high school exam, and she has continued to explore the field on her own—connecting with the global scientific community by reading research papers online and watching related YouTube videos. She has explored CRISPR-Cas9—in her words, "the genetic-editing revolution that scientists are thinking about these days around the world"—a family of DNA sequences that play a key role in antiviral defense.

Advanced scientific fields such as bioinformatics and artificial intelligence are not taught at universities in the Gaza Strip, however, so she would have to study abroad to pursue them. But due to the prevailing restrictions on and uncertainties of life in Gaza, opportunities may be hard to come by. "I don't have a complete idea or decision about how to help people here," she says. "But I can have ideas, I can have plans."

She considers contributing in some way to advancing the state of medicine in Gaza, spurred by visits to hospitals in the aftermath of the wars there in 2012 and 2014. "It was horrible," she says. "I saw how people died. Doctors could do nothing—not because they aren't good doctors. They are intelligent, amazing, and under the conditions of war they did incredible things, unexpected things." Human capacity is abundant, but opportunities to obtain advanced training and to import sophisticated medical equipment and supplies from outside of Gaza are limited.

These conditions, however, do not hinder Areej's capacity to absorb new ideas and envision how she might apply them. She watched a YouTube interview with the Italian astronaut Paolo Nespoli, a European Space Agency engineer who logged 313 days in space on three missions. "He said the Earth is like a ship flying in the universe. We can see the borders between the countries from space, but we don't understand that we live on the same ship, and the people who are sitting in the front need to understand what the people in the back are doing."

Areej says that when people in Gaza ask her whether she would return if she is able to travel abroad to pursue advanced degrees, "my answer has been and will always be that I will *not* be outside Gaza all the time. I just want to have a chance to make my dreams come true, and then come back to Gaza to make it better. Palestinians live in the back of the ship, and the strong countries sit in the front. This is the equation.

"I don't want to go and help the strong countries. The world is not waiting for Areej to make that difference. It's all about my country. There's no dream in my mind, no idea that doesn't have Palestine at the beginning.

"Gaza is full of intelligent people, and we all have dreams. I have lived my whole life in Gaza, but I'm not from Gaza. I'm a refugee. I'm from Ashkelon," she says, calling the town of her ancestors by the name that is used in English today. "But Gaza is my land. Gaza is the place that teaches me the meaning of life, teaches me the meaning of patience, the meaning of doing your best.

"If I travel outside Gaza, I can do it. I want to do something for the growth of humanity. We are on the same ship."

As she prepares for the next levels of her education, Areej charts two parallel courses: the track on which she won't be able to travel outside Gaza and the track on which she will. In the meantime, she moves forward amid a perpetual state of uncertainty and war, her optimism imbued with a strong dose of realism.

"You get a call that tells you your best friend has died. Your school is not there anymore. Your family are not well. When I leave my home, I don't know what the situation around us will be," she says.

"But I still bring my books, my laptop. I study, I work hard, because I have a dream. If you are under war, do you focus on your dreams? Or think about if there is any chance for having a better life?

"And each time I feel what an unfair world this is, I say that there's no problem, keep doing well, you can do it.

"And I just might tell myself that I am Palestinian."

The Al-Madhoun family's roots are in the Arab town of Asqalan, also called al-Majdal,[6] on the Mediterranean coast thirteen kilometers north of the Gaza Strip and eighteen kilometers north of Jabalia. On the eve of the war in May 1948, the Palestinian inhabitants of Asqalan, which was known for its weaving industry, numbered approximately ten thousand; in October–November of that year, almost all became refugees.[7]

By October 1950 no Arabs remained in Asqalan, the result of wartime engagement between Israeli and Egyptian military forces in the south of the country and Israel's expulsion of the town's indigenous Palestinian civilians. Asqalan had been renamed Ashkelon and was being repopulated with a growing number of Jewish Israelis.[8] It was a single episode of a methodical policy of forced population transfer that prestate Jewish paramilitary forces and then the Israeli army carried out in Palestinian towns and villages throughout the country, from the prewar spring of 1948 through the 1949 armistice with the surrounding Arab countries well into 1950.

Ramadan Al-Madhoun, Areej's paternal grandfather, was twelve years old in 1948 when the Palestinian exodus from Asqalan—where his family had owned a factory that produced rugs and traditional Palestinian clothing—propelled them into the Gaza Strip and compelled them to restart their lives as refugees, first in the al-Shati, or Beach, camp and then in the Jabalia camp.[9]

Mahmoud Al-Madhoun, Areej's father, was born in al-Shati in 1971, and his family moved to Jabalia when he was five years old. Immediately following the 1948 war, 35,000 refugees had settled in the camp, which is located north of Gaza City near a village of the same name. By 2020 the number of registered refugees living in Jabalia, which covers a mere 1.4 square kilometers, had more than tripled to approximately 113,990, the largest of the eight refugee camps in the Gaza Strip.[10] Jabalia's population accounts for approximately one-fifth of the nearly 600,000 refugees living in the eight camps and 8 percent of Gaza's approximately 1.4 million refugees, who in turn make up 73 percent of its total population of 1.9 million.[11]

One of ten children, Mahmoud attended elementary through high school in Jabalia. He earned a two-year diploma in Arabic from Al-Azhar University and a bachelor's degree in English literature from the Islamic University of Gaza, both in Gaza City, and teaches eighth- and ninth-grade English at an UNRWA preparatory school in the camp.[12] His wife, Rania, holds a diploma in multimedia science from Palestine Technical College in Deir al-Balah. All of their children, Areej and her three brothers, were born in Jabalia; the oldest, Ahmed, was studying political science and international relations in Malaysia when Areej was studying computer and electrical engineering in Gaza.

The importance of education is a salient thread woven into the tapestry of Palestinian lives, whether they are lived in cities or towns, rural villages or refugee camps. Like many Palestinian parents, Mahmoud Al-Madhoun considers himself duty-bound to provide for his children's education, and he has recited a credo to Areej and her siblings that she remembers readily and manifests in her determination to excel. *Al-istithmār al-haqīqi lil-'āba' yakūn fi abnā'ihim*: The real investment of parents is in their children.

"Our children are everything, the most precious gift that God has given us," Mahmoud says. "They are your heart that is moving outside your body. Our greatest test is how to treat and educate them. Our secret of happiness is to see them successful and creative. To let them achieve that, it is our duty to give all that we can.

"It is my promise to them to work hard to make them happy, strong, and powerful. Energetic and full of hope, courageous. To make them unbreakable and well educated. Being educated and skillful means that you have the key to a better life. It is an indispensable necessity. Palestinian society looks with respect at educated people."

Mahmoud's striving to support his daughter's education has not been limited to encouraging her success in classrooms from elementary school to university. Often, she recalls, he would take her for walks through Jabalia when she was sixteen and seventeen, sometimes alone and sometimes with her brothers, for an hour in the early evenings. "Daddy gave us a very good life, but he always wanted us to be aware of and feel people around us," she says. They walked through a moving, breathing canvas of poverty and suffering, manifestations of the extremely high population density pervading the camp, whose more than one hundred thousand residents live in a space just over one-half of a square mile, many in substandard conditions.[13]

"We would walk around and talk, a father with his daughter," Areej remembers. "Sometimes we walked between houses of families that live in very hard situations. The houses are very narrow, and the streets are very narrow. You can hear people when they are talking: people who can't earn their living easily. The father who can't bring his family any food. I heard that with my own ears, a father who was talking with his wife and told her, 'I don't have money. I have been out of the house since 6 a.m., and I don't have one shekel.' And the sound of his young baby crying. It was really hard to hear that. I wrote that in my diary.

"This is a common problem in Gaza," she says. "Tens of thousands of people, especially youth, don't have work. This is the reality for many people here." By 2018 the average unemployment rate in the Gaza Strip had exceeded 50 percent—among the highest in the world—and the number of refugees relying on UNRWA for food assistance had increased to nearly 1 million out of a total 1.4 million.[14]

Her father also meant the walks to be object lessons for Areej to develop self-sufficiency. "We would walk in different areas to know the streets and the area around us. This is one of the life lessons. You have to know the situations around you," Areej says. "You have to know how to do everything by yourself. Don't wait for direct help from your father or your mother. For me as a girl, I go to the university by myself without any help, I go everyplace by myself. And Daddy supports that. He always says: 'You have to feel very confident and you have to try to do everything by yourself. As a father, I will be an adviser for you.'"

The undergirding of parental support and the warmth of extended family life embrace Areej, easing the displacement of refugeeism that has transcended generations and fortifying her laser-like sense of purpose. "To live with a big family is a very special and good thing," she says. Since moving in February 2019 from Jabalia to the seaside neighborhood of al-Karameh in Gaza City, about four kilometers west, Areej's family returns to the camp to be with their kin on Fridays. There are uncles, aunts, and cousins for her to see, but "the very special person who I really miss and wait every weekend to visit is my grandma," she says of her father's mother, Yusra, who was born in Asqalan in 1946.

"Each time she tells me: 'You are the very special girl in the whole family.' Each time she says, 'Areej, you remind me of little Yusra, because I always wanted to study, to have education, but the situation wasn't good.' I can sit and talk with her for many hours. She tells me everything about Palestine, about Asqalan, about the stories of her life.

"She listens to me talk for an hour about my plans, my education, my problems, about the future. She smiles and then she tells me, 'Oh, Areej, I can't understand anything of that. But I support you and I believe in you.' I can't forget the words my grandma told me before I traveled to the international math competition: 'I will pray for you to get the first prize. But you have to remember that I believe in you, my little Areej.'"

The support of family is a clear stream bubbling through Areej's reflections on the predicament of refugee life in Gaza and her own place in it, ordinary details of everyday lives lived under extraordinary circumstances.

"Forcing Palestinians to leave their cities and villages did not happen yesterday," she says, musing that in the present day, Palestinian refugee camps are not groups of tents, as outsiders might imagine. In Jabalia, she says, "some parts of camp are very poor, and the roads are very narrow, and people don't earn their livings easily. But for me, thank God, my circumstances don't compare with the situation that many others are living."

She measures her comfort, in part, by the fact that in al-Karameh as in Jabalia, she has her own room "in a wide and beautiful house. I have my own laptop. I can study and do many things." She measures her family's good fortune, in part, by their ability to have a generator to bolster the meager and unreliable supply of electricity that Gazans without generators must endure—sometimes four hours a day, six hours on a good day, she says, and on bad days none at all. In Jabalia the Al-Madhouns bought a generator to power their home; in al-Karameh they pay to share a generator with neighbors that powers electricity and water to multiple households. Privately generated electricity is about seven to nine times more expensive per kilowatt hour than that from the public power grid.[15]

Her grandfather Ramadan built the house in which she grew up in Jabalia with no assistance, Areej says. "He was not a rich man, and he was not an employee"—but rather the proprietor of a small grocery store when her father was young and eventually the owner of what is considered a supermarket by local standards. By 1989 Ramadan had saved enough to start building a five-story structure of 210 square meters per floor in which to live with Yusra, their sons, and their sons' families.

Twenty years and a generation later, the extended Al-Madhoun family living in the house that Ramadan built numbered thirty-four before Areej's family moved to al-Karameh: grandmother Yusra on one floor; one uncle's family of twelve on a second floor; Areej's family of six on a third floor; two uncles' families totaling ten people on a subdivided fourth floor; and another uncle's family of five on the fifth floor.

Ramadan died when Areej was eight, but her memories of him remain vivid. "He wasn't an educated man, but he did his best in this life to build this building. He was a very special person. I still remember how much he supported us when we came back from school with certificates at the end of the year. In the second grade, just before he died, I went to him and said, 'Oh, Grandfather, I'm the first in my class. I got 100 percent, and my teacher told me that not everyone can get 100 percent.' He said: 'I believe and I trust that Mahmoud's family will be different. And especially Areej.'"

In the mornings from his supermarket, she remembers, "each time he saw me before I went to school, he waved and said, 'Goodbye, my little scientist.' He was not educated, but he could write and read. He was cultured—*muthaqqaf*,"she says, translating the adjective into Arabic. "He always believed in me. And before he died, he told me that one day, I will be something very big in this world."

Her family moved to al-Karameh on the parallel determination of her father, Mahmoud, son of Ramadan. "Because of the hard situations that Palestinian youth are living these days, my father feels it is one of his duties to prepare a better life for every one of his children. The second house that I'm living in now is going to be a gift from my father to one of us. He told me he plans to buy a house for every one of us, *insha'Allah*. This is not easy. This is very expensive. This is very hard, and not everyone in Gaza can do it.

"But Daddy struggles to offer that to us."

Areej wakes up every day at 4 a.m. and prepares to pray the dawn *al-fajr* prayer, the first of her five daily devotions. Many mornings she walks five minutes from her home in al-Karameh to the Mediterranean coast, where she refreshes herself for the day ahead by taking in the vast beauty of the sea. Back home, she eats the breakfast that her mother sets out for her: milk every day and a rotation of cake, eggs, cheese, or bread with butter and strawberry jam. Areej writes in her diary and texts her friends.

Saturdays through Wednesdays, she heads to the Islamic University of Gaza, hailing a shared taxi for the ride with three other passengers. For thirty to forty-five minutes, depending on the traffic, she dons earbuds and listens to music, Qur'an recitations, or audio books on her phone. Sometimes she reviews material for her classes, which begin at 8 a.m. Often her days on campus end at 3 p.m., other times an hour or two later. Computer and electrical engineering lectures last one to three hours, and she also attends two-to-three-hour weekly lab sessions and discussion sections for basic courses.

Most days she returns home around 5 p.m. The family eats together and shares the details of their days—hers at the university, those of her father and two younger brothers, Mohammed and Abdallah, at school in Jabalia, and her mother's in and around the house. "Sometimes we watch a movie or tell jokes," Areej says. "This is a special time for family."

After the sunset *al-maghrib* prayer (she has prayed the afternoon *al-'asr* and *al-dhuhur* prayers at the university), she devotes the remaining hours of her day to study: reading, working on assignments and projects, preparing for presentations, often for three hours or so. She prays the nighttime *al-'ishā'* prayer, the last of the day, and sometimes continues with her work as late as 1 a.m. Bedtime is usually around 10, though, but no matter the hour of repose, her new day will start at 4 a.m.

On Thursday and Friday weekend days there is time for painting and drawing, for visiting with relatives and friends. Sometimes Areej does embroidery with her mother, sometimes she goes for walks with her father and brothers. Every day she writes in her diary. There are occasional outings with friends, she says, including parties. "We have fun in this life. But because we are all at the university, we don't have much time to spend with each other. So, most of the time we talk on social media." On her twentieth birthday friends surprised her at the university that day with a chocolate cake iced with the greeting *Sana sa'ida, Newtonna al-qādim*: Happy birthday, our next Newton.

Sometimes local groups invite her to talk about her life and successes. "They ask me: Do you spend all of your time studying and preparing for these achievements, or are you a normal girl? This is a very common question.

"Each time I say: I'm just like any normal girl. I like drawing. I like joking. I like going to parties. I like nail polish. I like everything that normal girls do. I have a specific daily routine. I know what is important and what is more important. And I control my life according to that, according to my dreams. I don't allow any situation or problem, any complex things around me, to affect my goals."

Living in the conflict zone of Gaza, Areej pushes forward resolutely, despite not knowing what will happen or what to expect on any given day. In early May 2019, on the first day of a three-day escalation of hostilities between Israel and Hamas, she was in the university library. "I was writing before the bombs started falling and kept writing after that," she recalls. Addressing the bombs directly, she wrote: *"Hey, are you kidding? I'm in the library. I'm here just to feel comfortable and quiet, reading a book, writing my memories. What's wrong with you? Did they send you to break my moment? Well, it's a very silly idea—and I'll stay here!"*

But as the Israeli bombardment intensified, she could hear that it was near the campus. Sirens sounded, and lectures were canceled. In the shared-taxi ride home, she heard explosions around her and remembers thinking: "Oh, car, please go quickly. I just want to be with my family. No matter if we are all safe or not, but just to be together."

On most days her street in al-Karameh is quiet, and she hears the voices of children on weekends when they come outside to play soccer in the street. But this night she was awake at 3 a.m., listening to the cries of her neighbors' children and babies as she sat low on the floor of her room rather than higher up on her bed, listening to the radio for news about the bombs still falling outside.

The exterior chaos did not disrupt the sanctum and order of her room, its centerpiece a white wooden desk with three drawers and two small cabinets. On one corner of the desk among other small knickknacks sits a cup of paintbrushes; on the other an iPad and a red rose. Immediately above are hung eleven small white cards in a neat semicircle, clipped with small colored clothespins to a string and inscribed with lines of poetry, inspirational sayings, and a math formula, all penned neatly in Areej's hand. Above the cards is displayed an array of postcard-sized photos and illustrations, many depicting scientists and science themes.

Next to the whiteboard on the wall is a small wooden shelving unit filled with her careful arrangements of tempera, acrylic, and oil paints, school notebooks, and chemistry and physics textbooks. One side nook holds a jar of seashells, another nook a bowl of potpourri, and another small packages of fruit-flavored marshmallow candies and chocolate wafers for snacking when Areej studies or paints or entertains friends.

And that night she wrote:

Well, the bombs are not kidding. These may be my last words, so please, if my iPad is not destroyed, open the notes. I'm a girl who cares about details and privacy, so you can't read them without the password: **********.

I don't know who is the one I'm talking with, or who is the reader of these words. I just want you to tell the world that I was the happiest baby, child, and young girl in this world. I'm happiest because of my family, because of the supportive people, because of Palestine.

Yes, I said it, because of Palestine! The Palestinian flag on my desk, the Holy Qur'an, the red rose, the gifts and awards that I got, the success in my life. Tell the whole world that I was full of life and full of love. That I didn't hate anyone in this life. And that I had many dreams.

From a great distance, voice-to-voice over the internet rather than face-to-face in person,[16] Areej muses: "I don't want to say that wars are normal situations. But as a Palestinian living in Gaza, I'm used to living in such a situation. If I stopped dreaming [during] each war, then I couldn't have been the first in the international competition, since it was after the war of 2012. I lost many friends, many relatives, many close people around me. But I had a dream. And that dream was to win the first prize.

"We are not in normal circumstances. But this does not mean that we will give up our dreams. I can't imagine my life without dreaming and making progress."

She makes a distinction between the sides of herself that she calls "Areej" and "the Palestinian Areej."

As Areej, she says, "I have this family, this house, my father is working. I have my own room, my laptop, I study at a good university. I have a good situation, I am happy. I'm so lucky to have this family and the fighters in my life—my mom and dad who work hard to give us a comfortable home and good education."

As the Palestinian Areej, she says, "I have lived through wars, lost chances to travel. I expect that in the future, I may lose more chances. I have different plans—Plan A if I can travel, Plan B if I can't travel.

"It's all about how to do it in the right way. When you have a different situation, you have to be more responsible. If a student in any other country has to work for two hours, I have to work for twelve hours."

On one of the notecards hanging above her desk she has written in English a declaration of encouragement to herself: *Remember, No one [else] is Areej, and that is my POWER!* And then a quotation of a favorite saying: *"Work while they sleep / Learn while they party / Save while they spend / Then live like they dream."*

"I just want to be able to do something for Palestinians, for Gaza, for everything in this world," Areej Al-Madhoun says.

"As Daddy always tells us, if there is anyone who can do that, then you can do that and more."

Every personal narrative of life in the Gaza Strip, like that of Areej Al-Madhoun, is unique. Yet each narrative also echoes common realities of harsh conditions and pervasive uncertainty. The context for personal narratives is part of a larger historical arc, the starting point of which and points of emphasis along the way are a matter of subjective interpretation. Historical arcs, however, are anchored by objective fixed points.

Following the Six-Day War of 1967, Israel occupied the West Bank, Gaza Strip, Sinai Peninsula, east Jerusalem, and Golan Heights and immediately began settling Israeli civilians in contravention of the

Fourth Geneva Convention. Israeli settlement in the West Bank, east Jerusalem, and the Golan Heights continues to the present day, despite continual and consistent international iterations, in the form of multiple United Nations Security Council resolutions, of its illegality according to international law.

In the first two decades of Israeli occupation after 1967, the secular nationalist Palestine Liberation Organization and its ruling Fatah faction were based first in Jordan, then in Lebanon, and finally in Tunisia. Operating from outside Palestinian territory, the PLO could not, either through political or military means, stem the growth and proliferation of Israeli settlement and its damaging impacts on the Palestinian population, from land confiscation to restrictions on mobility to deadly confrontations with Israeli soldiers and settlers. In response, and on the crest of the wave of political Islam that swept the region following the Iranian revolution of 1979, in 1987 the Islamic resistance movement Hamas was established on the ground amid the Palestinian population in Gaza and the West Bank, with social-service and armed wings.

Since the establishment of the Fatah-controlled Palestinian Authority in the West Bank in 1994 following the 1993 Oslo peace accords between Israel and the PLO, the United States has channeled aid to PA security forces in order to thwart Hamas and other Islamic factions in the West Bank, which have struck Israeli soldiers and settlers in the occupied territories as well as civilians in Israel.

Israel unilaterally withdrew its settlers and military forces from the Gaza Strip in 2005 following the second intifada. At the same time, in more than a decade following Oslo, Israeli settlement in the West Bank and east Jerusalem had continued apace, and the Fatah-led PLO had made little headway in bilateral negotiations with Israel. In January 2006 elections were held for the second Palestinian Legislative Council of the Palestinian Authority in the West Bank and Gaza Strip; under international observation, they were deemed to have been free and fair.

Hamas, the main component of the "Change and Reform" list, won 74 of the 132 seats, its electoral strength derived from the deeply rooted grassroots base it had cultivated and served for nearly two decades through its social-welfare programs. Fatah, its leadership widely perceived by Palestinian voters as corrupt and the Palestinian Authority it led seen as working collaboratively with Israel—according to the tenets of Oslo and with limited benefit to the Palestinian population—garnered forty-five seats.

In March 2006 Hamas leader Ismail Haniyeh formed a new government. Following the capture of an Israeli soldier in Gaza in June 2006, Israel invaded the West Bank and Gaza Strip, destroying civilian infrastructure and arresting dozens of Hamas supporters and elected members of the legislative council, including cabinet ministers, and preventing other Hamas leaders, including elected officials, from traveling from Gaza to the West Bank. In February 2007 Fatah and Hamas formed a national unity government, but the power struggle between the factions continued.

In June 2007 Hamas fighters prevailed in the Gaza Strip, ousting Fatah officials there, and the unity government based in the West Bank fell. Since then the two territories have been governed for the most part separately, the PA in control of the West Bank and receiving international recognition and economic aid, and Hamas in control of the Gaza Strip, shunned by the United States and European governments. Attempts at reconciliation between Fatah and Hamas have been sporadic and results superficial.

As of 2020 Hamas maintained exclusive political and military control on the ground in the Gaza Strip. However, Israel retained control of the airspace over Gaza, the majority of its territorial waters, and the northern border crossing at the Erez checkpoint. Egypt, which has a peace treaty with Israel and receives significant U.S. military aid, maintained control of the Gaza's southern border crossing at Rafah.

Citing the context of "50 years of occupation, 10 years of Hamas rule and [Israeli- and Egyptian-imposed] blockade and internal Palestinian division," OCHA, the United Nations Office for the Coordination of Humanitarian Affairs, Occupied Palestinian Territory, concluded in 2017 that

1. . . . recurrent rounds of conflict have compounded an already precarious humanitarian situation in Gaza, generating significant displacement and undermining the quality of health,

education, water and sanitation services. The destruction of productive assets has also contributed to high unemployment, food insecurity and aid dependency. Children have been particularly impacted by the conflict, leaving them with a deep sense of insecurity, fear and hopelessness.

2. Major escalations have resulted in large-scale loss of life and injury. . . .

3. Restrictions on the import of construction materials, and funding gaps, have delayed the reconstruction and repair of destroyed and damaged homes, prolonging displacement. . . .

4. The conduct of the hostilities by both sides has involved serious violations of international humanitarian law, including of the principles of distinction, proportionality and precaution in attack.[17]

The Israel-Hamas dynamic in the Gaza Strip since 2007 has been characterized in a RAND Corporation assessment as "how an advanced military fought a weaker, yet highly adaptive, irregular force." This has compelled Israel to adopt a strategy of deterrence based on the idiomatic concept of "mowing the grass," "accepting its inability to permanently solve the problem and instead repeatedly targeting leadership of Palestinian militant organizations to keep violence manageable. It needs to exert enough force to deter Hamas from attacking but not so much that it topples the regime. As one Israeli defense analyst put it, 'We want to break their bones without putting them in the hospital.'"[18]

The international humanitarian community has documented and, in some cases, challenged the impacts of that strategy, in particular on the majority civilian, noncombatant Palestinian population of the Gaza Strip. The reports also cite as contributing factors restrictions by Egypt on movement through Rafah, the activity of armed Palestinian factions, and intra-Palestinian political discord.

Human Rights Watch (HRW) reported that in 2019, "Israel's twelve-year closure of Gaza, exacerbated by Egyptian restrictions on its border with Gaza, limits access to educational, economic and other opportunities, medical care, clean water and electricity." While the average daily electricity supply nearly doubled to twelve hours from

2018 due to "additional fuel purchased by Qatar through Israeli vendors, the continuing shortfall compromises Gaza's water supply and sewage treatment." Israeli restrictions on delivery of construction materials, ostensibly to prevent their use for military purposes such as building tunnels, coupled with a lack of funding continued to slow efforts to rebuild housing units destroyed by Israel in the 2014 Gaza war, with over twelve thousand Gazans remaining displaced more than five years later. Israeli forces have continued to shoot live ammunition at Palestinian demonstrators inside Gaza "who posed no imminent threat to life, pursuant to open-fire orders from senior officials that contravene international human rights standards," HRW reported.[19]

OCHA reported that Gaza's population of nearly two million—which inhabits 365 square kilometers (141 square miles), with a population density of approximately 5,203 persons per square kilometer (13,475 per square mile)—is "'locked in,' denied free access to the remainder of the occupied Palestinian territory and the outside world. Movement restrictions imposed by Israel since the early 1990s and intensified in June 2007, following the takeover of Gaza by Hamas, have severely undermined the living conditions. The isolation of Gaza has been exacerbated by restrictions imposed by the Egyptian authorities on its single passengers crossing (Rafah), as well as by the internal Palestinian divide."[20]

In July 2013 OCHA documented the extent of Israel's imposition of Access Restricted Areas (ARA) in the Gaza Strip and called for a balance between respect for international law and Israel's security concerns. "Since September 2000, Israel has tightened restrictions on Palestinian access to the sea and to land located near the fence with Israel, citing security concerns," OCHA reported, "undermin[ing] the security and livelihoods of Palestinians. Access to schools for children living in the ARA on land can be dangerous and classes are often disrupted." The agency also stated that "additional risks to civilian life and property have stemmed from activities of Palestinian armed groups operating in the access-restricted areas on land." However, it concluded: "Restrictions imposed [by Israel] on access to land and sea and the methods used to enforce them raise serious concerns under international law. These restrictions should be removed to the fullest extent possible; measures imposed to address Israel's security concerns must not result in disproportionate harm to the lives and livelihoods of Palestinian civilians. The use of force must be in conformity with Israel's obligations under international law."[21]

In August 2013 the secretary-general of the United Nations concluded in a report to the UN Human Rights Commission that Israel's imposition of the ARA in particular and the blockade overall "target and impose hardship on the civilian population," amounting to collective punishment and "effectively penalizing them for acts they have not committed."[22]

> The ARA undermines the livelihoods of tens of thousands of Gazans, violating their human rights, including rights to work, to freely dispose of their natural wealth and resources, to an adequate standard of living and to food, which includes the possibility of feeding oneself directly from productive land or natural resources. Israel's methods of enforcement often violate Palestinians' civil rights, including the rights to life, liberty and security.
>
> While parties to an armed conflict may take security measures, such measures must comply with international law and should be necessary and proportional. Numerous statements made by Israeli officials in their professional capacities have made clear that the blockade is being imposed to apply pressure to the de facto authorities, and in response to acts committed by various groups in Gaza, including Palestinian armed groups, towards or in relation to Israel. However, the blockade and related restrictions target and impose hardship on the civilian population, effectively penalizing them for acts they have not committed. As such, these measures contravene article 33 of the Geneva Convention relative to the Protection of Civilian Persons in Time of War (Convention IV) prohibiting collective penalties.[23]

The report also stated that Palestinian "accountability for violations of international law committed by the de facto authorities or armed groups in Gaza, including the killing of civilians, must be ensured."[24]

The most severe manifestations of the ongoing cycle of instability, conflict, and destruction to play out in the Gaza Strip resulted from the seven-week war fought by Israel and Hamas (along with the

Islamic Jihad faction) from July 8 to August 26, 2014. Given Israel's vast military superiority, the magnitude of human casualties was stunning and disproportionate, as was the extent of physical destruction. Israel carried out more than 6,000 airstrikes in Gaza (with 15 hits on residential buildings killing 115 children and 50 women); Palestinian armed groups fired 4,881 rockets and 1,753 mortars toward and into Israel.[25] Numbers do not tell the whole story of the impacts of the war and the human stories behind them, but they are an important contextualizing factor all the same.

According to the United Nations, 2,251 Palestinians, including 1,462 civilians, were killed, among them 551 children and 299 women; 73 Israelis were killed, 67 of them combat soldiers and 6 civilians in Israel.[26] A total of 11,231 Palestinians were injured, including 3,436 children and 3,540 women, with 10 percent suffering permanent physical disability; and up to 1,600 Israelis were injured, including 270 children. More than 1,500 Palestinian children were orphaned, and 142 Palestinian families had three or more members killed in the same incident.[27] At the height of the hostilities, 500,000 Palestinians, accounting for 28 percent of the Gaza population, were displaced, with 18,000 housing units destroyed in whole or part.[28]

The economic impacts of the war were also disproportionate. Direct damages to the Israeli economy were estimated at $25 million, with "a contraction of output in the tourism and manufacturing sectors" estimated at $903 million.[29] By contrast, the Palestinian Authority estimated the cost of rebuilding destroyed and damaged housing (including whole neighborhoods), schools, hospitals, the electrical grid, and other infrastructure in the Gaza Strip at $7.8 billion.[30] Of the $5.4 billion pledged by nations attending the Cairo Conference of October 2014, donors had disbursed only 51 percent by the end of 2016.[31]

Life in Gaza was very different a generation ago, before the closures, before the blockade, before the cycle of warfare between Israel and Hamas. Najwa Sheikh-Ahmad describes a sea change—"a huge deterioration in all aspects of life"—over the course of the more than two decades she has worked for UNRWA since 1996.

"In 1996 the Palestinian Authority had just come to Gaza. People were hoping to have their independent state, a solution to their plight.

Jobs were available, international organizations were in Gaza in huge numbers, and many people were working for them," she says, speaking as acting public information officer in UNRWA's Gaza field office in mid-2019.[32] "People were working in Israel and the Gulf countries and traveling to the West Bank with no restriction. This made people feel free somehow.

"The economy was growing—Gaza was very alive," she says, noting as examples that with no restriction on movement, furniture factories exported their products to Israel, the West Bank, and Europe; and sewing factories did business with Israeli companies that sent fabrics to be stitched into garments in Gaza due to the quality and price of the work.

Even as they waited for political progress that would enable Palestinian self-determination, "people at that time were living a good life. The situation was very promising," Sheikh-Ahmad says.

But beginning with the outbreak of the second intifada in 2000, conditions began to deteriorate with the closing of the borders and increased restrictions on movement, followed in 2007 by imposition of the blockade that has continually stymied the economy. In 1995 there were approximately seven hundred thousand refugees in Gaza, about 14 percent of whom were receiving food assistance from UNRWA; by 2019 the refugee population had doubled to 1.4 million, and the rate of those receiving food assistance had increased fivefold.[33] "All of these circumstances changed life in Gaza," Sheikh-Ahmad says. "This impacts the way the people deal with each other, the way they think about their future, the way they plan for their future."

As life in Gaza goes for its 1.9 million inhabitants, so it goes for the 1.4 million refugees who account for nearly three-quarters of the total population, approximately six hundred thousand or over 40 percent of whom were living in eight refugee camps throughout the Strip as of 2020. In its 2019 emergency appeal, UNRWA reported that 68 percent of all Gaza households were experiencing food insecurity; the overall unemployment rate had reached 54.9 percent; the GDP per capita had dropped to $410, down 9 percent from 2017; and poverty among individuals throughout Gaza had increased from 38.8 percent in 2011 to 53 percent in 2017.[34]

Among the 1.4 million refugees, approximately 1 million, or 72 percent, were dependent on emergency food assistance—a tenfold increase over the 100,000 Gaza refugees who required such support in 2000.[35] Of those depending on food assistance in 2018, nearly two-thirds, or 620,310, were classified as abject poor (living on less than $1.74 per person per day); and more than one-third, or 389,680, were classified as absolute poor (living on between $1.74 per person per day and $3.87 per person per day).[36] For the Gaza population overall, the public electric grid could supply an average of only five hours of electricity a day; and the flow of wastewater directly into the Mediterranean averaged four times that of international standards, diminishing access to clean water and increasing health risks.[37]

In January 2019 the commissioner-general of UNRWA called for $1.2 billion to fund the agency's programs for the year to support 5.4 million Palestinian refugees across the region in Gaza, the West Bank (including east Jerusalem), Jordan, Syria, and Lebanon. The total included $750 million for core services encompassing education, health, and relief and social services and a targeted emergency appeal of $138 million for humanitarian aid for refugees in Gaza and the West Bank.[38] The emergency appeal designated $127.5 million for Gaza (including approximately $94.5 million in emergency food assistance, $3.5 million in mental health and psychosocial support, and $2.6 million for emergency health services)[39] and $10.5 million for the West Bank.[40]

In July 2018 the agency had reported a shortfall of $217 million, referencing the Trump administration's decision to cut nearly $300 million in support from the fiscal 2017 level and to end future funding.[41] A statement issued by the U.S. Department of State on August 31, 2018, declared that "the United States was no longer willing to shoulder the very disproportionate share of the burden of UNRWA's costs that we had assumed for many years," characterizing the agency as an "irredeemably flawed operation" and the Palestinian refugees it serves as "UNRWA's endlessly and exponentially expanding community of beneficiaries." Prior to that point, the U.S. had been UNRWA's largest single donor since the agency began operations in 1950.[42]

As the number and needs of refugees in Gaza continued to increase, international funding for the agency had been on the wane before the Trump cut, however. As recently as the mid-2000s, UNRWA operated with little or no budget deficit each year and few emergency appeals, according to Sheikh-Ahmad, but other events in the region—including humanitarian crises resulting from the civil wars in Syria and Yemen—have diverted the attention of donor countries. "UNRWA is no longer the main concern for the international community," which in focusing on more recent conflicts may also be internalizing the longevity of the plight of Palestinian refugees, a salient factor in the stagnant, seven-decade Israel-Palestine conflict, she says.

"The donor countries have been giving money over and over again every year to support the refugee population, hoping that a just solution will be found. Logically, some donors argue that they have been giving money for over 70 years, but nothing has changed."

The aggregation of hardship in Gaza has led to desperation among the general population and particularly among youth, casting a pall of gloom over daily life, Sheikh-Ahmad says. Rates of drug use and divorce are on the rise. "There are some issues that have started to surface that we were not aware of in previous years," she notes, citing increasing numbers of suicides and suicide attempts among youth.

"They don't have any kind of hope, they don't have any kind of future. They don't have faith in our almighty that things will change," she says. "They start to cross the red lines and react to the pressure they are living under. There is no work, no money, no stable life. Parents can't offer their children pocket money for school. The number of people seeking mental-health support is increasing."[43]

The social fabric in Gaza is "*mumazzaq*—torn to shreds," says Sheikh-Ahmad, herself a refugee who was born in the Khan Younis camp in 1972 and earned a bachelor's degree in education from Al-Azhar University in Gaza City. Her family's pre-1948 roots are in al-Majdal; those of her husband, Taher, who was born in the Nuseirat refugee camp in Gaza, are in nearby Julis. Together they have five children.

"As a mother, I cannot plan for my children's future," she says. "I'm not sure if there will be another war and they will be killed." Her two older sons are studying abroad: "I'm not sure when I will be able to see them or when they will return from an open world where they have opportunities to build their futures outside."

In Gaza, Najwa Sheikh-Ahmad says, "we are living the daily life because we don't have any other solution. It's not a matter of resilience. Because we have no other solution, we can *only* live our daily lives."

Ahmed Alnaouq remembered how his older brother Ayman would give him a soft punch on the shoulder with every greeting, and Ahmed would tease him back, saying, "Your ducks are hungry. Feed them or they're going to die of starvation." But that seemed unlikely, as what began as a flock of ten soon increased to fifty under Ayman's care.[44]

Growing up, Ahmed and Ayman, four years apart, would swap stories of their school days in Deir al-Balah, the central Gaza Strip city named for its profusion of palm trees. Ayman would describe funny skits he had acted in; Ahmed would relate difficult math problems he had solved. Ahmed remembered the humorous side of Ayman, who would balance a stick on his nose and walk without it falling, and compose songs on the spot, to the delight of their siblings. Ahmed remembered his brother's compassionate side—how Ayman brought the family ice cream with chocolate to numb the pain of their older sister's divorce—and his serious side, how he recited the lines of his favorite poems and his own tales of the life he envisioned in heaven.[45]

Ayman always won the school competition for reciting passages from the Holy Koran from memory, Ahmed would write of his brother a year after he was killed in the Gaza war of 2014. *He would come home afterward, proud and happy, and share pieces of a chocolate bar he had won as a prize.*[46]

At the same time that Ahmed remembered his chess contests with Ayman and their spirited computer gaming—Age of Empires was a favorite—he also remembered imploring his brother to take him to observe, from a distance, the Israeli tanks and soldiers on the military base that separated Deir al-Balah from the nearby Israeli settlement of Kfar Darom before Israel withdrew from the Gaza Strip in 2005.

He didn't want to take me, Ahmed wrote, *but he finally relented. When we got close and saw a tank approaching, I ran away, horrified, and hid behind a big tree. "Are you happy now?" Ayman demanded furiously. "I told you many times they can kill you so easily. They do not differentiate between kids and fighters!"*[47]

In 2013, when he was twenty-two, Ayman became a fighter, joining the Al-Qassam brigades, the armed wing of Hamas. Ayman was killed by an F-16 missile on his way to face Israeli forces on July 19, 2014, eleven days into the seven-week war.

Ahmed remembered that just a month before, the family had been happily preparing for Ayman's wedding the following year, painting the walls of the small apartment he would share with his bride-to-be. Having earned a postsecondary certificate in financial management, Ayman was working as an accountant at the time of his death while studying at Al-Quds Open University in Gaza City for his bachelor's degree in commerce. *He planned to be the most accomplished accountant and establish his own business that would finance an orphan-care organization*, Ahmed wrote.[48]

And Ahmed also remembered: *He always believed in me and had faith that I would make a difference in this unfair world. I really believed in him and supported his decision to join the military brigades, but I won't follow his exact steps. I will fight on in my own way: I will fight with words. . . .*

I will show the world the life, the hope and the beauty of the Gazan people who will never give up their pride, independence and bravery.[49]

Born in 1994, Ahmed grew up in Deir al-Balah. The family roots of his father, Nasri, were planted in Jaffa and Gaza City before 1948—and the family of his mother, Basima, originated in the city of Beersheba in the Negev desert. As refugees in Deir al-Balah, Nasri and Basima raised nine children born within twelve years—five daughters and four sons, with Ahmed the eighth in line, Ayman the sixth. The family did not live in a refugee camp, but the children attended UNRWA primary schools.[50]

After finishing high school in Deir al-Balah, Nasri went to work to support his mother and siblings after his father died. To support his own growing family, he worked for years as a construction laborer in Israel. In the year 2000, during the second Palestinian uprising, Israel closed the borders of Gaza and the West Bank due to escalating violence, throwing tens of thousands of Palestinians out of work. Nasri bought a ramshackle taxi and worked as a driver in Deir al-Balah for fourteen years, but his economic fortunes declined, the family of eleven living in a 120-square-meter apartment.

"We were raised very poor," says Ahmed as a young man of twenty-five and university graduate. "We were all close in age, and all nine of us were in school at the same time. My parents would always tell me that education was very important, but they didn't have the time to teach me or to follow up with my lessons. They were working all the time just to provide us with the necessities." Even so, he recalls excelling in school, "and that's what made my life a bit better."

But in 2000, as soon as he began first grade, the second intifada broke out. Every two or three days, he remembers, Israeli forces would enter Deir al-Balah. Demonstrations would erupt, and he and his classmates would take to the streets. "Many from my school would go near the Israeli forces and throw stones. It was a very big part of my life. It was difficult to see that Israel invaded our city with their tanks. It was horrifying. But that was the routine of our life."

The sounds of Israeli helicopters, F-16 jets, and drones also became routine; the cacophony of ordnance explosions, bombs, and tanks in the ongoing war of occupation, resistance, and retaliation became the grisly music of Gaza. "I was very accustomed to the kinds of weapons the Israelis were using against us," Ahmed recalls. "And that was not OK, because I was young. I should have been accustomed to playing with toys, not hearing the sounds of bullets and bombs and shelling. But that was an integral part of our life."

He would write, *Apaches hovering over the sky in Gaza became a routine sight as I walked to school*,[51] noting that during the second intifada, Israel carried out most assassinations of Palestinian resistance leaders using U.S.-supplied Apache helicopters. He became aware of Israeli drones in 2008, and years later would write one an epistolary message: *I didn't want to write you this letter, but I was provoked— you could say I was driven to it by your incessant nagging, keeping us up all night long. I remember when I saw you for the first time. You were terrifying—tiny, but terrifying nonetheless. When I heard your low, persistent whine, I had no idea what you were. Your sound alone caused chills to go up and down my spine. Then, seeing your sleek, silvery shape in the sky filled me with wonder and fear.*[52]

By the time Ahmed reached the age of twenty, the year his brother was killed, his short life had been punctuated by the three Gaza wars of 2008–9, 2012, and 2014. The third war was particularly cataclysmic, the sheer magnitude of its human casualties and material destruction indelibly scarring psyches and landscapes.

"After the war when I lost my brother and many of my friends, it was devastating," he says. "I went to the borders and I saw that all the homes, all the houses close to the border were damaged. It was a massacre, actually. Thousands of people had been killed, many of my friends had been killed, hundreds of thousands of people had been displaced from their homes. I felt so hopeless.

"Someone in this state of mind could only think of one thing, which was to follow in the steps of my lost brother, to honor his memory. I wanted to be like him, I wanted to fight for his cause."

Ahmed kept Ayman's picture in place of his own on his Facebook page for a year. Some months after the war ended, he received a message from an American journalist he had met at a friend's birthday party in 2012 who had heard that Ayman had been killed. Ahmed told her that he was thinking of joining the armed resistance. She urged him to find another way to advocate for his people and suggested that he write about Ayman.

"At that time I didn't believe in the value of writing, in the value of defending human rights, because I thought that no one would care about us," Ahmed recalls. "But she said: 'Please write your story, write about your brother.'"

In December 2014 an essay he wrote in tribute to Ayman was among the first postings on a website that the journalist had launched, We Are Not Numbers, with the tagline: "Palestinian youth tell the human stories behind the numbers in the news."[53] Reaction to his essay—much of it from Western readers outside of Gaza—was immediate and supportive. It became a turning point, challenging and displacing his thoughts of following his brother's path.

"After I wrote about my brother and I saw how many people reacted, something changed in my psychology," he says. "Seeing that the world does care about the Palestinians, and that the world might stand up with the Palestinians against occupation and injustice taught me that the peaceful approach is the most significant one, the most deserving one."

In late 2014 Ahmed—who was majoring in English literature at Al-Azhar University in Gaza City with the aim of working for an NGO or international media outlet—began to volunteer with the fledgling We Are Not Numbers. By early 2015 he was employed as the assistant project manager; in mid-2016 he became project manager.

The blockade of Gaza—Palestinians and international solidarity activists often refer to it as "the siege"—isolates its inhabitants from the outside world to a remarkable degree. But the seal is not hermetic.

Mentoring two brothers in Deir al-Balah on their applications for U.S. university scholarships in 2012, Pam Bailey was invited to their home for a birthday party. There she met their friends, among them Ahmed Alnaouq. He and several of the others then connected with her on Facebook.

Bailey, an American journalist and public relations professional, had left her corporate job in the United States at age fifty-one in search of work with social purpose. After trips to Israel and the West Bank in 2007 and 2008, she segued into Palestinian solidarity activism, returning to spend most of 2009–12 in Gaza, teaching English and social media skills on a volunteer basis and reporting periodically for the Inter Press Service news agency. Back in the U.S. in 2014, after the war she became consumed with worry about the friends she had made in Gaza and resumed contact with Ahmed.[54]

"He was depressed and lost," she recalls. "He could not envision a future for himself, other than perhaps following his brother into the resistance forces. Gaza seemed like a prison with no door and becoming smaller all the time."

Ahmed, she knew, was not unique: Many young people in Gaza have lost relatives or close friends to violence; up to 70 percent of youths are unemployed and cannot help support their families. "Many don't see any point to their lives," she says. "They make up more than half of Gaza's population. What does this mean for the future of Palestine and the region?"

Bailey encouraged Ahmed to channel his grief and hopelessness into writing about Ayman and worked with him for three months on his essay. Soon after it was published, she says, "I saw him start to emerge from a very black place and discover a sense of purpose, a feeling of self-worth. And with that comes hope and a whole host of positive ripple effects." She found the relationship to be mutually beneficial, gaining an adopted son of sorts and a deeper knowledge of the region and the human condition.

Bailey was also inspired to undertake a new endeavor, establishing We Are Not Numbers to bring stories, written in English, of young Palestinians like Ahmed to international attention while helping them break through their isolation by forging connections beyond Gaza.

Bailey matches writers aged fifteen to twenty-nine with volunteer international mentors, all professional writers and editors in journalism, literature, and public relations. Some mentors provide only technical writing assistance; others also engage in relationship building via real-time social media contact. Mentors read submissions for a sense of story, coaching writers to take a show-don't-tell approach using details and quotes, and make technical corrections for grammar, brevity, and transitions. Writers review the edits, which they can question and challenge. Bailey does a final read of all pieces before publishing them on the website.

By late 2020 We Are Not Numbers had published 806 journalism, personal essay, and literary pieces by 246 young Palestinian writers coached by 144 international mentors. The site accepts submissions from young Palestinians no matter where they live; most writers published on the site are from Gaza with other contributors from the West Bank, Lebanon, Turkey, Chile, Belgium, and the United States. Writers are not paid for publishing on We Are Not Numbers (WANN), but some are compensated when Bailey places their reporting pieces with external media outlets.[55]

The meticulous work of recruiting writers, pairing them with mentors, and bringing their work to publication is bookended by the continuous challenge of fundraising. Bailey reached out to her international civil society contacts early on, securing support from the Euro-Mediterranean Human Rights Monitor[56] for the part-time salary of the first project manager of WANN, creating its website, and securing office space in Gaza City.

Since mid-2017 We Are Not Numbers has operated independently, relying on crowdfunding appeals for approximately 85 percent of its $30,000 annual budget.[57] It has also partnered with U.S.-based Rebuilding Alliance.[58] Until the project is registered as a nongovernmental organization, U.S.-based Nonviolence International serves as its fiscal sponsor, channeling tax-deductible donations to WANN.[59]

Sundays through Thursdays, Ahmed commuted to work from Deir al-Balah in a shared taxi, known in the region as a *service*. The eighteen-kilometer trip each way to and from the capital of Gaza City takes thirty to forty minutes and costs about five shekels, or $1.50. As project manager for We Are Not Numbers, along with colleagues working as a team, he focused on organizing workshops for writers, making connections with local and international NGOs, and giving media interviews.

In October 2017 Ahmed directed the Palestinian Youth News Agency, a journalism academy supported by the U.S. Department of State. WANN selected twenty-five university graduates to age twenty-nine from throughout the Gaza Strip for an intensive weeklong training course followed by a year of weekly workshops. Taught by local Palestinian media professionals, instruction focused on news and feature reporting, in English, for international media outlets.[60] Graduates of the academy continue to write for WANN, some placing their pieces with international outlets and getting paid for their work. In Gaza, Ahmed says, "we have so many people who can write in English, who can use their English to generate income."

He views the practice of journalism not only as a livelihood but also as a means to a higher end. "When you are living in a conflict zone and you can write and you can be heard, it is your moral obligation to tell the truth about what's going on," he says. "You can't have a pen and see people who are dying and suffering and you don't write about it.

"In Gaza we need journalists who can be the voice for the voiceless in Palestine. We need writers who write for international media outlets because Palestinian voices are not heard in the West. The Israeli point of view is *ultra*-heard. We need a generation of Palestinians who can defend their human rights in the English language to the international audience. This is very important."

At the same time, there is a two-way factor in play when WANN writers are exposed to nationalities, religions, and beliefs that are absent in Gaza. The shackles of physical isolation experienced by Gazans looking to communicate the details of their lives and points of view to the world from the inside out are loosened by connections with sympathetic mentors and readers looking to learn about Gaza from the outside in.

In a personal essay published in 2019, Ali Abusheikh, partnerships coordinator for We Are Not Numbers, wrote that as a university exchange student in Chicago he met many American Jews sympathetic to the Palestinian cause, "or at least willing to listen and learn. But most Gazans have very little contact with Jewish people since they are not allowed to travel, and the only Israelis to whom we are exposed are in tanks, warplanes or checkpoints. So, it's not surprising that many Palestinians regard them with distrust."[61]

We Are Not Numbers helps bridge that gap, he wrote. An American Jewish woman named Ruth from West Hartford, Connecticut, reached out to Abusheikh and other WANN writers—all of whom have profile pages on the site that link to their social media accounts.

"Ruth is the first Jewish person I've been able to talk with openly about Zionism, Judaism, anti-Semitism," Abusheikh wrote. "We truly listen to each other. Ruth cares and is very humble about the limits of what she knows. I can voice any point of view without fear of hurting or angering her and thus losing her friendship. Ruth is the first to check on me and the other writers when she hears Israel is attacking Gaza. It's become personal for her."

Such give-and-take fuels Ahmed's passion for his work, which he expresses in idiomatic English with a flowing cadence. "It is so important for the English-speaking audience to know the reality of what's going on on the ground in Palestine, for the world to stop being ignorant about the Palestinian issue, the Palestinian-Israeli conflict," he says. "Having others look at us as humans—not as terrorists and not as numbers—is so important for us Palestinians.

"It's so important for us to be seen as fully human. It's so important for human rights, for humanity, for dignity. It's so important for the West to know the truth, because maybe, if the peoples of Western societies know the truth, they can pressure their governments to stop being biased in favor of Israel, to be neutral, to support human rights."

For Ahmed, We Are Not Numbers is an arrow sailing toward that target, parallel to the trajectory of his own self-discovery. "It changed my life, literally turned it upside down. It gave me a voice. It taught me how to write, and it taught me the importance of writing, for myself and for my people."

In addition to personal essays, Ahmed has also published journalism pieces on the WANN site. He reported on a kite-flying campaign carried out in the spring of 2018 during six weeks of protest by Gazans along the Israeli border leading up to the seventieth anniversary of the Palestinian *nakba*, or catastrophe, of 1948, when Israel gained its independence. He has detailed the crisis faced by Palestinian NGOs in the Gaza Strip due to cutbacks in international funding, restrictions imposed by Israel, and internal Palestinian political divisions. He has profiled Syrian refugees hoping to rebuild their lives by resettling in the Gaza Strip.[62]

"Before I worked for We Are Not Numbers, I didn't know the value of myself to the world," Ahmed says. "I did not know that I can make a difference. But I discovered myself. I discovered how much I can be valuable to humanity, how much I can be valuable to Palestine.

"How much I can be valuable for participating in ending the Palestinian-Israeli conflict."

At age twenty-four, Ahmed had never left the Gaza Strip. When he would watch movies depicting life in the outside world, he would feel torn. When he would sleep and dream of traveling to pray at the Al-Aqsa mosque in Jerusalem, he awoke happy, only to have that pleasure overshadowed by the reality of his immobility. "Gaza was like a prison for me before I traveled," he says. "That mood dominated my life. All I thought about was how to escape. Not forever, but to try something new, to meet new people."

His first trip out of Gaza was sparked by that hunger for freedom. But during his seven-month odyssey in Egypt, he was confronted with confinement of a different stripe, tainted by effects of the conflict spilling over the border.

In June 2018 he decided, on the spur of the moment, to take advantage of the open border with Egypt during the holy month of Ramadan. At the Rafah crossing in the southern tip of the Gaza Strip, Ahmed was asked to pay a hefty "coordination fee" of $1,200, in reality a routine bribe paid by Palestinian travelers in order to exit. He borrowed the funds, but the steep price seemed worth it. He continued on to the bustling capital. "It was very new for me, the life in Cairo," he recalls. "I loved it." He remained there with friends for six months, renewing his Egyptian residency permit before leaving the city briefly in November to represent We Are Not Numbers at the World Youth Forum in the Red Sea resort city of Sharm el-Sheikh.

When he returned to Cairo, Ahmed went to the Thai embassy to apply for a visa to attend the model United Nations conference in Bangkok but was told he lacked the correct type of Egyptian permit. When he returned to the visa department, Egyptian officials told him the renewed permit he held was a fake.

An interrogation led to a court appearance at which a judge ordered Ahmed to be released, but he was not freed. Instead, he says, he was jailed and interrogated on a broad range of topics for the next two weeks, including his nonexistent political affiliations in Gaza. He was held in solitary confinement in a cold, dirty cell with no blankets, meager food, and no way to contact friends, family, or a lawyer. A deportation order followed, but over two more weeks he was moved through a series of prisons. In each, he says, he was verbally abused by his captors, who made repeated references to Palestinians as "dirty" and "terrorists."

"The officer who imprisoned me told me: Just because you are a Palestinian, I will not let you go. Other officers told me: Just because you are a Palestinian, we are treating you this way.

"They have been under systematic brainwashing," Ahmed says. "The media in Egypt depicts the Palestinians as terrorists and very bad people. I was told by every single Egyptian I met that we, the Palestinians, sold our lands to the Israelis seventy years ago, and that's why we are living under occupation today. They are told this by their leaders, by their media, and they believe with all their hearts that we are guilty. They don't know about the massacres committed against the Palestinian people, about the refugees and how we fled our lands."

After being imprisoned for a month, he was deported back to Gaza in January 2019, but the Egyptian authorities would not return his passport. Replacement passports are issued by the Palestinian Authority in Ramallah—and Ahmed, like the vast majority of Gazans, could not obtain a permit to travel to the West Bank. He returned to his work at We Are Not Numbers with invitations to attend international conferences in London and Tunis, to which he could not travel without a passport.

He was back home, a captive of sorts still and again.

That the pen is mightier than the sword is a maxim also known in Arabic. Translated literally as *al-qalam 'aqwā min as-sayf*, it resonates for Ahmed.

"Regarding our cause, our conflict with Israel, they are way mightier than us," he says. "If we are going to fight them with our arms and weapons, we don't have a chance to beat them. And in fact, I don't want to beat them. I don't want to kill them. I just want them to respect us and to live with us peacefully.

"So, in the case of Palestine, the pen is mightier than the sword. Because with the pen we can write about our suffering, we can write about their aggression, we can write about their human-rights violations, and we can write about our right to this land, our right to live freely. And our right to have our human rights.

"We have a choice; we have a chance. If we show the world the reality on the ground, people will be convinced we are on the right track. If we write, maybe the world will stand by us, and if the world stands by us, they can pressure Israel to stop its violation of our human rights."

With these ideas in mind, Ahmed won a prestigious Chevening scholarship, sponsored by the British government, to study for a master's degree in international journalism beginning in the fall of 2019. He applied to and was accepted by universities in Leeds, Durham, and Sussex. At one of those institutions, he envisioned, he would face rigorous standards of writing, reading, and analysis, propelling him to stretch his intellect and hone his skills. He would be able to break free from the isolation of Gaza by meeting people of different nationalities, cultures, and beliefs outside the zone of occupation. He would step outside his own comfort zone and, in so doing, advance his people's cause.

But still lacking his passport in mid-September 2019, when the ten other Chevening recipients from Gaza traveled to the UK, he wrote on Facebook of his dismay at being left behind. Advised by a commenter to post a last-ditch appeal via the social media network to Palestinian president Mahmoud Abbas, Ahmed resisted—having months before been told by the prime minister's office that his passport would not be reissued. But then he relented, and immediately hundreds on Facebook began to share his appeal. Within twelve hours, he says, the Palestinian intelligence services contacted him; two days later his new passport was issued; four weeks later he received a visa in Amman, Jordan, and flew to the UK. By mid-October Ahmed was in residence as a master's student at the University of Leeds, his determination intact. In September 2020 he completed his degree, with distinction.

"I believe that we can best advocate for our human rights through journalism," he says, aware of the fine line between reporting and advocacy but approaching that line according to the context of his lived experience as a Palestinian from Gaza. "If a journalist is neutral, if a journalist is a human being, if a journalist believes in the value and importance of human rights, he would tell the real story as it is."

The completeness and complexity of that real story, in Ahmed's view, does not often find expression in Western news media, and by name he calls out reporting of the conflict by outlets including CNN, the BBC, and the *New York Times*. "They never advocate for human rights," he opines. "But if a true journalist wants to write about the conflict, he or she would write from a human-rights perspective." This, he believes, would advance the process of conflict resolution. "The two," he says, "correlate perfectly."

Inspired by the work of Saudi journalist Jamal Khashoggi, widely believed to have been murdered in 2018 at the hands of his own government, Ahmed paid tribute to him in an essay published by We Are Not Numbers, writing, in part:

You were not Palestinian, but I claim you as one of my leaders. Your death is my inspiration to follow in your footsteps, speaking truth to power.

It is ironic that you were murdered for your words, yet they went viral when you were killed. This was not a win for despots like Saudi Crown Prince Mohammed bin Salman. It was a flame that ignited waiting matches like me. . . .

What I learned gave me hope for the strength of the human spirit. . . .

Many shed tears over your murder. But I believe your death is a rallying cry for all human rights defenders and those who previously silenced themselves in the presence of tyrants.

Instead of squelching your voice, bin Salman and other oppressors have given new life to your words, which now are slogans for people longing to be free. . . .

In your writings, you protected no one. You criticized the Saudi regime and its opponents indiscriminately. . . . This taught me to be a seeker of truth, no matter where it leads me. . . .

You taught me that words are indeed mightier than bullets.

Mr. Khashoggi, I know you are not be [sic] able to read this, but I hope your soul knows that your sacrifice has changed the life of a young writer from Gaza.

May you rest in power.[63]

Ahmed moves forward with his vision of reaching out to the world as a journalist and effecting change. If Ayman were still alive, Ahmed believes, his brother would understand and respect his choices, just as he says he respects those who make the choices that his brother did. Five years after his brother's death, Ahmed says: "Ayman lived the same circumstances I did in my life. He'd been through wars, he'd been through the occupation, he'd been through the siege, he lost many friends, and he lost many loved ones. He had his reasons for choosing the armed resistance."

In the first of two essays about Ayman for We Are Not Numbers, Ahmed wrote that his brother did not take up arms immediately, but first became active in Hamas's social-service wing. *Ayman had become a member of Hamas because it gave him a way to be active in standing up for his family and his people. He focused on aid for needy people, making him beloved in the neighborhood. However, in 2012,*

Israel again invaded our land for eight terrible days. When this war was over, Ayman was not the same. Now he wanted to join Hamas' armed-resistance force. He vowed he would protect his people; he swore he would defend his homeland. It was not so easy though; he had to try many times before he was accepted.[64]

At the time Ayman was killed on his way to confront Israeli forces in July 2014, Ahmed says, his brother had never committed an act of violence.

Ahmed believes that Westerners misconstrue the nature of those who choose to resist by force of arms. "I think if Ayman were here, he would love to have me study journalism and advocate for the Palestinians' rights. Ayman was educated, he was understanding, he was supportive. He would respect whatever I choose for my future."

That future of choices, though, is bound up with great uncertainty. "Being a Gazan affects every aspect of your life," Ahmed says. "Everything I think about is finding an end for this conflict. If I were not a Palestinian, I would have other dreams. I love physics, I love mathematics. I adore calligraphy. But I can't pursue these things because there are other more important things that dominate my mind."

In an online exchange with an Indian writer in 2016, Ahmed asked what she knew about Gaza without having been there. He was struck by her response, and it has stuck with him. "Gaza is a place where children are not innocent anymore," she wrote in their Facebook chat.

Recollecting the anecdote, Ahmed sighs. "When I walk in the streets of Gaza and see the faces of children four, five, six years old, they look older than they are. All the suffering makes us grow old before our time. This burdens us, makes us more mature about injustice and justice at the same time.

"It will make me grow older faster, make me die younger, make me more focused on what's going on in the world, more so than people in other parts of the world.

"We the Palestinian people have suffered a lot," Ahmed says. "It's enough. Enough fighting, enough struggling, enough living under all these circumstances. I did not choose to live here. I did not choose to be at war with Israel. I was born in this country, and I am forced to endure its consequences. I am a peaceful person."

Ahmed Alnaouq does not relinquish optimism to weariness. "I believe that oppression will end one day," he says. "I don't believe oppression can last forever. I'm not sure when this will happen. I'm not sure when we will get our rights.

"Maybe it will take a lifetime to end the Israeli occupation. Maybe less, maybe more. I don't know. But eventually, things will be better," he says.

"Better."

CHAPTER 6

Imperatives of Narrative

To be entrusted with someone's narrative is a privilege. A source agrees to open the door to her life and share details of her daily routine, a chronology of her work and accomplishments as a student or teacher or doctor or businessperson. A source agrees to open his personal space to share the details of his family background and perspectives and opinions on matters of import. To grant such access to a researcher or a scholar or a journalist is an act of faith. To be on the receiving end of such an act of faith is a privilege.

It is incumbent upon the receiver—the writer who constructs the narrative—to render the source's words accurately and to represent her ideas not only in the context that they were spoken in but also within the broader context of the issues at hand, so that the intent and meaning of the source's words and ideas can be clearly understood. It is also incumbent upon the writer to find the best possible balance of presenting the source's words directly, and at length—so that he is speaking for himself—within the framework of the story that the writer herself constructs to support and convey a theme of her own creation. In weaving the source's words and ideas into a story that conveys the writer's vision lies the challenge of not assuming the source's voice, of not speaking *for* him.

This is especially so when the space briefly shared by the source and the writer is a contested space, one that the writer can enter and exit at will—another aspect of her privilege—but one that the source may not be able to, a "marginal space that is not a site of domination but a place of resistance," in the words of American scholar and activist bell hooks,[1] who suggests that the writer may consider the source as subordinate: "No need to hear your voice when I can talk about you better than you can speak about yourself. No need to hear your voice. Only tell me about your pain. I want to know your story. And then I will tell it back to you in a new way. Tell it back to you in such a way that it has become mine, my own. Re-writing you I write myself anew. I am still author, authority."[2]

And even when the writer does not consciously assume a power-dynamic position, the issue of her privilege still hovers, even when her intent is to shed light on how and against what the source may be resisting. "The banality of evil," the American writer and photographer Teju Cole has written, "transmutes into the banality of sentimentality. The world is nothing but a problem to be solved by enthusiasm"—that is, the enthusiasm of the writer, presumably for telling the story, which in the telling may belie a savior complex "that is not about justice," Cole asserts. "It is about having a big emotional experience that validates privilege."[3]

The task of constructing narrative is challenged further still. Even before the process of composing and posing questions—and exercising the privilege of constructing that framework—before the writer begins to observe the source's surroundings and interact with him, the writer's subjectivity can filter or otherwise affect the very nature of that interaction: how she perceives the matter at hand, beyond the material aspects of the source's physical space, beyond what he has to say. "Seeing comes before words," the English critic, writer, and artist John Berger has written. "It is seeing which establishes our place in the surrounding world; we explain that world with words, but words can never undo the fact that we are surrounded by it. The relation between what we see and what we know is never settled. . . . The way we see things is affected by what we know or what we believe."[4]

The challenges in compiling the collection of narratives that is *Stories from Palestine* are not merely intellectual, moral, and philosophical. There is also the challenge of access. Not access to the sources themselves, per se, for they and those who have served as bridges to them have been overwhelmingly cooperative and ready to assist. Physically, most of the locales referenced herein—with the exception of the Gaza Strip, where barriers to entry by outsiders are substantial but nonetheless pale in comparison to barriers to egress by the Palestinians who live there—have also been accessible. This physical accessibility has allowed for face-to-face contact with most of the sources and for firsthand observation of their surroundings. In cases where this was not possible, including Gaza, digital communication technology has enabled real-time, direct voice contact with other sources over great distances, across many time zones, and at no expense.

The issue of access arises in the obscuring of Palestinian society itself by the imposed conditions of occupation under which Palestinians live—and in effect, this obscuring impacts the audience as well as having consequences for the sources themselves and for those who would attempt to interact with them. This obscuration serves to discourage if not prevent entirely some outsiders from interacting with Palestinians directly, interactions that can yield broader knowledge about their everyday lived existence and understanding of their humanity. This obscuring lessens the type and quality if not the quantity of information that is publicly accessible, and it renders the audience's task of assessing what is accessible—of making sense of it and judging its credibility—more challenging.

For reasons attributed to security, Israeli citizens not in military service are prohibited from entering Gaza. Throughout the West Bank, red warning signs posted near Palestinian cities, towns, and villages declare in Hebrew, Arabic, and English:

> This Road leads To Area "A"
> Under The Palestinian Authority
> The Entrance For Israeli
> Citizens Is Forbidden,
> Dangerous To Your Lives
> And Is Against The Israeli Law

and

This Road Leads To
Palestinian Village
The Entrance For
Israeli Citizens
Is Dangerous

In addition to segregating Israelis from Palestinians and their environments in the West Bank and Gaza Strip, the occupation imposes a distancing of some official representatives of the international community who seek to document qualitative human rights issues, while at the same time allowing for the collection of quantitative metrics of Palestinian life that measure and map demographics, territory, and resources.[5] United Nations designees known as "Special Rapporteur on the situation of human rights in the Palestinian territories occupied since 1967" have routinely and systematically been denied direct physical access to Palestinian individuals and institutions in the West Bank and Gaza Strip for the purpose of compiling assessments. The report of Special Rapporteur Richard Falk, presented to the Human Rights Council of the UN General Assembly in January 2014, emphasized

> the importance of this mandate as providing an independent witness to the evolving effects of the continuing occupation of Palestine by Israel. This exposure is centered upon the presentation of information received on the persistence of severe violations of international humanitarian law and international human rights law. . . . It was unfortunate that Israel refused even minimal cooperation with this mandate to the extent of allowing the Special Rapporteur to have access to occupied Palestine during the past six years or of responding to several urgent appeals addressing specific situations of immediate concern that fell within the purview of the mandate.[6]

The 2017 report of Special Rapporteur Michael Lynk stated: "The Special Rapporteur would like to draw attention once again to the fact that he has not been granted access to the Occupied Palestinian Territory, nor have his requests to meet with the Permanent Representative of Israel to the United Nations been accepted"; and Lynk consequently based his report "primarily on written submissions as well as consultations with civil society representatives, victims, witnesses, and United Nations representatives."[7] The 2018 and 2019 Special Rapporteur reports were submitted under the same circumstances, with the preamble in both reports noting in identical language: "The Special Rapporteur re-emphasizes that an open dialogue with all parties is an essential element of his work in support of the protection and promotion of human rights. He further notes that access to the Occupied Palestinian Territory is a key element in the development of a comprehensive understanding of the human rights situation on the ground."[8]

Such restrictions on access, coupled with the imperatives of geopolitics that often limit and code the public statements of diplomatic representatives, make it all the more imperative that other observers fortunate enough to have physical access to engage and interact relatively freely with Palestinians—including academics, journalists, and activists from a range of civil societies, including Israel—do so in venues that are not limited to arenas of protest and violent confrontation. Seeing Palestinians' creative and productive endeavors and listening to them speak about their work and everyday lives—absent the notion of "news" or "trends"—is the space from which it is possible for narratives of Palestinian humanity to emerge.

From his lab on the campus of the Arab American University, physics professor Atef Qasrawi conducts cutting-edge research that advances information technology. His work in solid-state physics and electronics can be applied to increase computer speeds and data-storage capacities; the bulky and nano-thick microwave tunneling devices and pyrochlore ceramics he designs are used in sensing, data transfer, and transferring signals in mobile phones and other devices; his work on visible light communications renders them more effective than microwave transmissions to enable faster video streaming.[9]

Born in 1968 in the village of Mesliyah, near Jenin in the northern West Bank, Qasrawi was the fourth among seven brothers and five sisters; their father supported the family as a stone mason. After earning his bachelor's through PhD degrees in physics from the Middle East Technical University in Turkey, he taught for seven years at Atilim University, in Ankara, then returned to the West Bank to teach and establish his research career. Palestinian scientists face limitations imposed by Israel on the types of scientific machines and instruments that can be imported; Palestinian universities emphasize teaching over research because they rely on student tuitions for revenue due to limited funding from the Palestinian Authority.

These factors stunt the growth of the Palestinian scientific community, Qasrawi says, but he has published more than 190 research articles in international science citation-indexed journals; won research grants from Saudi Arabia and Turkey and in Palestine, and been ranked among the top 2.5 percent of scientists among more than 15 million users worldwide of the ResearchGate social network. While maintaining a long-standing research partnership with other physicists from three Turkish and three Saudi universities, he chooses to remain in Palestine. "The reason is simple," he says. "I must find my work here to build my country." He has served as a trustee for the Palestinian Higher Council for Innovation and Excellence since 2013.

His optimism is fueled by his students on the bachelor's, master's, and PhD levels at the Arab American University, where he has taught since 2008 and supervised more than thirty graduate students. "Every student, whatever is happening, is here for education. The way of thinking among youth has changed," he says, noting that the Israeli military routinely shut down Palestinian campuses over student protests during the uprisings of 1987–93 and 2000–2004. He notes that female students are particularly motivated, overcoming social limitations on activity outside the home by excelling in their studies.

"Palestinians must work three times more than people in other societies because of the conditions of the occupation," Atef Qasrawi says. "In ten years, if we continue this way, we will be able to catch up with the world. We must fight with science, not stones."

At the Palestinian Circus School (PCS), based in Birzeit—established in 2006 as part of the international social circus movement, which emphasizes development of social skills, building self-esteem, and expressing creativity rather than training professional circus performers—Mohammad Abu Taleb found a career as an artist and teacher.[10]

Born in 1991, Abu Taleb grew up in Jenin in the middle of a family of eight brothers and sisters. He did not excel in school but was active in sports, playing basketball and handball, earning a black belt, and winning championships in tae kwon do. When his father, a high school English teacher, died in 2008, his mother insisted that he continue his studies after finishing high school, but he did not pass the *tawjihi* matriculation exams and began to work as an auto mechanic. When representatives of the Palestinian Circus School visited Jenin and demonstrated some techniques that year, Abu Taleb, his twin brother, Ahmad, and two cousins recognized the opportunity for something new and signed on, participating in local workshops. In 2009 they began commuting to Ramallah once a week to hone skills including acrobatics, juggling, and rope climbing. They found that circus training offered variety over routine: "Every day is something new, with trust-building games, team-building, ice-breaking," Abu Taleb says—techniques the circus school also uses in workshops it conducts for children across the West Bank.

In 2011 Abu Taleb moved from Jenin to Ramallah to take up the circus full-time, and his world continued to open up. "I had always felt shy," he says. "I got angry easily, it was hard to trust people. But with circus, my personality started to change by talking with people, meeting new people, from here and outside." He improved his English by listening to circus artists visiting Palestine from Belgium, France, and Germany; he learned to interact with females his age who were troupe colleagues.

Abu Taleb has performed throughout Western Europe with the Palestinian Circus School, touring the United Kingdom, Denmark, Germany, and Belgium in 2018 with *Sarab*, whose title is Arabic for "mirage." The show, which depicts scenes of Arab refugees struggling to find sanctuary, is based on interviews that troupe members conducted while in Turkey, Jordan, and Germany to teach circus workshops from 2014 to 2017 at the height of the Syrian civil war. PCS productions often convey social themes, with original stage works referencing life under occupation. "One of the goals is to let audiences know about the Palestinian issue," Abu Taleb says, "to show our stories, our life. We are present in the world. We are alive; we fight the occupation in our way."

At home in the West Bank, Abu Taleb finds another type of fulfillment by teaching and performing for Palestinian children and youths living in a conflict-ridden environment. "When I look in the eyes of children and see them happy for an hour or thirty minutes, taking them out of their lives keeps me going," he says.

And to older skeptics who question the need for a Palestinian circus, Mohammad Abu Taleb draws on the confidence he has developed within it to reply: "Circus makes people alive. What are you doing for Palestine?"

Inside the one-room Palestine Museum of Natural History, in Bethlehem, a chukar partridge strikes a confident pose, the distinctive stripe banding its eyes and looping down to its upper chest answered by the vertical stripes on its flanks. The bird appears in a photo, next to which its genus name, *Alectoris chukar*, is posted in English over its Arabic appellation, *al-hajal*. Next to it is depicted a rock dove, *Columba livia*, in Arabic *hamam jbaili*, with spotted white beak and black double-band stripes adorning its gray body above the tail. Then there is the ostrich *Struthio camelus*, or *na'āma* in Arabic, its black-feathered body supported on long white legs and from which sprouts an even longer white neck topped by an intent gaze on the face of the bird.

Yes, there are birds in Palestine. And small mammals and insects, a variety of which are also on display in dried live form in the museum. Just outside is an elaborate, twelve-dunam botanic garden that includes a tortoise, small olive grove, pond ecosystem, greenhouse, recycling hut, vertical garden, and peacock among some 270 plant species. In the museum and garden, local and international visitors can begin to fathom the natural diversity of Palestine, a collection of flora and fauna existing in harmony with their environment despite so often being overshadowed by the manifestations of human conflict. In a corner of the museum, posted inconspicuously in a plastic sleeve hanging next to the Palestinian flag, the motto of the museum proclaims in English: *Respect; respect ourselves (empowerment, self-liberation); respect other human beings (regardless of background); respect earth and all living beings.*

The museum and garden are part of the Palestine Institute for Biodiversity and Sustainability, founded by Mazin Qumsiyeh and his wife, Jessie, and opened to the public in 2017 on a satellite campus of Bethlehem University. In 2018 the institute hosted 5,300 Palestinian adults and school children as well as international visitors from more than thirty countries, providing tours, workshops, and field trips on topics includ-ing biodiversity, climate change, recycling, and ecotourism. The insti-tute is also active in conservation projects and conducts and publishes research, with funders having included the British Council, National Geographic Society, Rotary International, Royal Belgian Institute of Natural Sciences, and United Nations Development Programme.[11]

In 2019 the institute opened a Palestine Ethnography exhibit, at-tracting over three thousand visitors and featuring agricultural ob-jects, a garden with herbal and medicinal plants, and a small cultural-heritage library. The institute reaches out beyond Bethlehem, in 2019 taking its programs on the road to 125 Palestinian cities, villages, and refugee camps and actively engaging sixty-five thousand social media users. In its short history, it has had 345 volunteers—92 in 2019 alone—from 35 countries.[12]

Qumsiyeh, who earned both his PhD in zoology and genetics and master's degree in zoology and systematic and evolutionary biology in the United States, was born in Beit Sahour in 1957 to parents who were teachers and later school principals. As a child Qumsiyeh would ac-company his uncle Sana Atallah, known as the first Palestinian zoolo-gist, on field-research trips in the surrounding valleys. "He had a keen eye and would say: 'Look, there is a chameleon here, a lizard there.' I learned to observe nature," Qumsiyeh recalls. When Atallah died in 1970, Qumsiyeh's grandfather Issa Atallah consoled him: "This is the way life works, you have to look at the positive side. I challenge you to become as successful as or more successful than your uncle." As Qumsiyeh came of age during the early years of the Israeli occupation after 1967, his grandfather told him that the starting point for dealing with the situation was in his mind. A half century later, Qumsiyeh quotes the maxim of South African antiapartheid activist Stephen Biko that "the greatest weapon in the hand of the oppressor is the mind of the oppressed"; and Qumsiyeh adds that he makes a conscious effort to ward off what he calls "mental colonization."[13]

"That's what freedom is," he says. "It's mental freedom. It's the choice of who you want to lead your life and what you want to do with your life." Finding optimism, he says, has to do with being a scientist and looking at data. "Palestine has twelve thousand years of history from the time of hunter-gatherers. In those twelve thousand years we had a relatively peaceful society except for a few periods of conflict," among which, he notes, were two centuries of the Crusades in the Middle Ages and the modern-day Israel-Palestine conflict with roots in the late nineteenth century. "We have to look at the big picture and say '*C'est la vie*, that's humanity.'" Societies based on a single religion or race ultimately fail, he asserts. "Diversity is the source of strength."

The biodiversity institute and natural history museum reflect that worldview, which Mazin Qumsiyeh maintains parallel to a spirit of defiance toward the occupation that envelops Palestinians' natural landscape. "I don't underestimate the challenges we face," he says. "We may fail. But if our chances of success are 60 percent, or 20 percent—or even zero percent—this would not change my behavior.

"I will still resist."

A through line of the narratives in *Stories from Palestine* is resistance. It is present, explicitly and implicitly, in the words spoken and ideas expressed by virtually all of the two dozen Palestinian sources interviewed. It is present in their accountings of activities of their individual daily lives and in their musings on the collective Palestinian predicament. The theme of resistance recurs across a broad range of productive and creative endeavors and occupations; it resonates across generations, among men and women, from professionals and entrepreneurs, artists and students, intellectuals and farmers. It is heard in villages, towns, cities, and refugee camps from the West Bank to east Jerusalem to the Gaza Strip.

As a group, the educational level of these sources skews high; most were interviewed in English. Thus, it is fair to note that in certain demographic respects they may not necessarily be *representative* of the 5 million Palestinians living in the West Bank, Jerusalem, and Gaza, the locales that they and many others around the world still envision as the basis for a future independent Palestinian state. At the same time, it is also important to acknowledge that whatever their individual trend lines, these sources live under conditions of Israeli occupation that affect Palestinians in all of these locales. Therefore, their narratives are not only *evocative* of the experience of the collective community but are also genuine and significant iterations of Palestinian *sumūd*, or steadfastness.

The narratives presented herein demonstrate human capacity and determination to carry on with ordinary functions of life under extraordinary circumstances. In the face of continually diminishing land resources and critical limitations on water supply methodically imposed by the Israeli occupation, Palestinian farmers persist in cultivating their land, as a means not only to livelihood but also to maintaining their physical presence on that land as a primary marker of cultural identity and historical continuity.

The high value and respect that Palestinian society accords education have been seen among other marginalized peoples and minority groups in the modern age. Unique to Palestinian society are the circumstances that continually hinder and intrude on the process of education, most notably the danger children face in traveling to their schools as well as the emotional and psychological burdens they carry into their classrooms. On occupied territory, Palestinians have built a higher education system that produces internationally recognized scientific research, despite limited financial and technical resources to support it, and that graduates tens of thousands of students each year despite the lack of adequate market capacity to absorb them. Overall, Palestinian society regards education as a singularly viable path forward, not only for the sake of individual status and achievement but also for the integrity of Palestinian society as a whole. Among themselves, Palestinians continue to negotiate intersectional issues of education, gender, and class, including opportunities for girls and young women and social acceptance of vocational and technical education to answer the need for skilled trade workers.

Palestinian cultural endeavors often carry a deliberate text or subtle subtext of resistance and freedom. Like people throughout the world, Palestinians want to enjoy life, be entertained, and consume. However, the *Stories* narratives that touch on theater, dance, literature, writing, circus, and beer making indicate a drive to mold cultural expression to reflect collective Palestinian determination to confront the occupation—and to show the world that Palestinians are present in it, creative and producing. Traditional mores in Palestinian society at times militate against cultural initiatives such as ballet and circus schools, but initial resistance often gives way to acceptance.

As a sizable minority in Jerusalem, Palestinians are confronted by Israeli policies that shrink their landscape, discriminate against them in allocation of public resources and services, and generally segregate if not alienate them from the city's Jewish majority. Such challenges imbue the modalities of Palestinian daily life in Jerusalem in realms spanning education, commerce, media, and the dynamics of family life. On an informal basis, many Palestinians equate Jerusalem with the neighborhoods they inhabit in east Jerusalem. Not surprisingly, Palestinians have deep affinity for the Old City, with its Arab residential quarters, markets, and holy sites of the Al-Aqsa and Dome of the Rock mosques, not only for their cultural and religious significance but also as testament to the enduring historical—and continuing— Arab and Palestinian presence in the city.

Nearly two million Palestinians live in the Gaza Strip, which since 2007 has been under virtual lockdown after Hamas came to power and has been the locus of three short wars between Islamic factions and Israel, the third of which, in 2014, imposed a particularly devastating degree of loss of life and damage to infrastructure that has yet to be fully restored. Nearly three-quarters of Gazans are refugees, and the population as a whole faces day-to-day uncertainty compounded by the physical isolation of Gaza from the rest of Palestine and the world. It is difficult if not inadvisable to suggest overarching or even general characterizations of worldview based on those expressed by two young Gazans in narratives constructed on the basis of a series of extensive voice interviews with each but without the benefit of in-person contact and observation. Nevertheless, it stands to reason—based on these sources' articulation, in English, of sheer will and determination to persist and to excel while at the same time confronting the harsh realities known to most if not all Gazans—that if it is possible to locate, listen to, and learn from two such young Palestinians in Gaza from thousands of miles away, then surely there is an inestimable number of others like them to be known and understood.

What, then, do we do with these glittering narratives? Are they merely stories? Is it enough to be entertained and/or informed by them? Should they spur some kind of activism? Who, in the telling and constructing and consideration of these narratives, has agency—which can be understood to encompass not only the ability to act independently and to make choices freely but also to be held accountable for those actions and choices?

It is within the source's agency to agree to speak on the record, to share his story, and to trust his interlocutor to convey his narrative—even if the source aims to leverage others' understanding in a way that may bring him and his community advantage. In the present context, many sources for this work—and Palestinians in general—express the belief that many Westerners either do not understand their predicament correctly, or their understanding is woefully incomplete, or some combination of the two.

It is within the writer's agency to take what is already compelling and not aim to attempt to make it more so, but to use her privilege of access to the ideas and conditions of sources in order to make that information more broadly known. In the present context, the objective behind presenting the narratives in *Stories from Palestine* is to suggest ways of seeing Palestinian society from angles that do not often appear in many mainstream media and scholarly representations.

The audience also has agency that comes with choosing to engage with the narrative. There is a further choice to be made, and that is for the reader to make a connection between the narrative and the sources and society it reflects, on the one hand, and himself or herself and the society to which he or she belongs, on the other. In the present context, this agency is the willingness to understand that the trajectory of the Israel-Palestine conflict neither now is nor has ever been solely the domain of Israelis and Palestinians. Although there have been significant but relatively limited impacts from the larger Arab and Muslim worlds, the course of the conflict has for over a century arguably been impacted in greater measure by the hegemonic interests—and, to a lesser extent, the cultural affinities—of Western societies, in particular those of Britain in the colonial era and then the United States from the mid-twentieth century until today.

Therefore, agency in engaging with Palestinian narratives also yields imperatives: the willingness to concede a connection between, on the one hand, the role that a free and democratic society plays, through its official policies, in influencing the course of an international conflict and, on the other, the obligations of membership in such a society. The Palestinian context epitomizes both the challenge and importance of understanding how one's own society contributes to a lack of parity between other societies in conflict. If Palestinians' struggle with Israel for freedom and independence is erroneously understood as a conflict between equals, then, it has been noted, the audience and the public at large "will have less desire and less impetus to act on behalf of justice."[14]

Ultimately, the narratives in Stories from Palestine do not yield a quaint painting of a distant landscape. Rather, they are a mirror reflecting not only what can be empirically experienced but also what can be critically known. As referenced above, in the context of another time, Edward Said observed that "Orientalism is—and does not simply represent—a considerable dimension of modern political-intellectual culture, and as such has less to do with the Orient than it does with 'our' world."[15] In the context of another place, Teju Cole asserted: "If Americans want to care about Africa, maybe they should consider evaluating American foreign policy, which they already play a direct role in through elections, before they impose themselves on Africa itself. The fact of the matter is that Nigeria is one of the top five oil suppliers to the U.S. and American policy is interested first and foremost in the flow of that oil. . . . If we are going to interfere in the lives of others, a little due diligence is a minimum requirement."[16]

Resolution of the Israel-Palestine conflict—elusive for over seventy years—is based on finding the equation of territory, security, and human rights that will satisfy Palestinian and Israeli needs for justice and add up to peace. But it is not up to Israelis and Palestinians alone to solve the equation. Other players will have to pitch in; outside formulas will have to be adjusted. During the long wait for peace, though, media and scholarly discourses have tended to pay less attention to Palestinians' human dignity and creative capacity, relying instead on frames emphasizing loss, suffering, and violence. Diplomatic and policy language, often echoed in the mainstream media with little analysis or question, tends to impose a false equivalence between Israelis and Palestinians, whose rights to security and dignity are equal but whose power to achieve them are not.

It is an open question whether or to what extent such unbalanced representations impact public opinion and in turn the formation of policy. It is difficult to fathom what tools can be used to measure and assess whether and how peacemaking may be hindered if one party to a conflict is routinely and overwhelmingly seen as being *in opposition*— consistently (although not *always*) represented, over time and through various modes of discourse, principally as fighting, struggling, clashing, and rejecting—with little parallel attendant focus on their producing and creating and determined efforts to maintain and sustain their place in the landscape while contributing to its betterment.

A 2019 Pew Research Center poll indicated that while 64 percent of Americans said they have a favorable opinion of the Israeli people and 41 percent have a favorable view of the Israeli government, 46 percent viewed the Palestinian people favorably but just 19 percent have a favorable opinion of the Palestinian government.[17] A 2018 Pew survey indicated that 46 percent of Americans said they sympathize more with Israelis in the Israel-Palestine conflict, 16 percent said they sympathize more with the Palestinians, and 38 percent expressed no preference—an overall balance of opinion reported to have shifted only slightly over the preceding four decades.[18]

It is a certainty, though, that policies leading to resolution of the Israel-Palestine conflict have failed to materialize for the better part of a century and that this failure has exacted incalculably high costs. The narratives in *Stories from Palestine* suggest a nexus between representation and outcome. Change often begins with the way we think; how we think is informed by our ways of seeing.

In the center of Birzeit, the Palestinian town north of Ramallah, a large graffito depicts a Palestinian fighter, his neck draped in a red-checkered *keffiyeh* scarf, a rifle poised upright over his left shoulder. The Arabic inscription translates: *We die standing as trees of Palestine.*[19] It is dated February 27, 2015; a rendering of the iconic key symbolizing the Palestinian right of return appears below. Minutes away, on a quiet street next door to a church, the Palestinian Circus School is housed in the old chemistry and physics building of Birzeit University, donated by the university's former president and nuclear physicist Hanna Nasir. A training room on the second floor is outfitted with a small trapeze and hanging rope used for aerial acrobatics; decals depicting juggling and tumbling decorate the windows. Behind the building is a giant blue big-top circus tent in which PCS troupe members give performances and teach children's workshops.

These two vignettes in Birzeit do not render the local landscape as necessarily binary: resistance or circus—but as organically integrated: resistance and circus.

There are many narratives to seek out and understand about Palestine—those that come directly from Palestinians themselves in their own memoirs, poetry, fiction, nonfiction, and film and those that are mediated by others, including scholars and journalists. *Stories from Palestine*, then, ends on a note from the latter realm. From his home in the Beit Hanina neighborhood of Jerusalem, Nazmi Jubeh, a history professor at Birzeit University, imparts the profound material and psychological impacts on Palestinian life in the city from 1967 until today—at once a literal rendering of local conditions as well as a metaphor, perhaps, for understanding a broader Palestinian context.[20]

"The Palestinians in east Jerusalem became poorer under Israeli occupation," says Jubeh, who was born in Jerusalem in 1955 and grew up in the Old City. "The majority before 1967 were middle class. Now the absolute majority, 78 percent, are living below the poverty line." Today, as a result of Israel's de facto annexation of east Jerusalem in 1967 and continual confiscation of land to build and enlarge settlements exclusively for Jewish Israelis, nearly 350,000 Palestinians live on less than 10 square kilometers in east Jerusalem, approximately 13 percent of the city's total land area, Jubeh estimates—despite their constituting 38 percent of the city's population. This has rendered many of their neighborhoods akin to slums, affecting every Palestinian in the city "regardless to which social class he or she belongs. Living in such slums is psychological, social terror," Jubeh asserts, replete with high levels of drug use and violence, including domestic violence. The shortage of parking spaces results in fights that have escalated to killings.

Issued permanent residency rather than citizenship, Palestinians in Jerusalem "have no political address in the city, no institutional address to mediate among us, to solve our problems," Jubeh says. "So people came back to methodology that was used a century ago, which is outside the rule of law, to retreat to the family as a social power.

You seek shelter in your family in order to secure yourself because the law is not there to help us. The law is the law of the occupier."

Palestinians experience segregation that is not only geographical but also social. "We are living with Israelis but absolutely separated," Jubeh says. "There are some services that we use together like hospitals, transportation to the airport. But we are trying our best, both sides, to ignore the existence of the other, as if they are not there, as if we are not there." In Jewish west Jerusalem, Palestinians "walk on Jaffa Street insecure," Jubeh says. "You do not belong to that society, but you are obliged to go there for one reason or another. Of course, there are exceptions. Some of us have good relations with Israelis, but this is not the rule."

Jubeh first encountered Israelis at age twelve in the Mughrabi Quarter of the Old City in June 1967, in the immediate aftermath of the Six-Day War. His family lived on the edge of the quarter, whose alleyways he navigated to reach school and his father's spice shop. He recalls seeing soldiers and ultra-Orthodox men dancing on ruins of the quarter in celebration of Israel's capture of the Old City and, with it, access to sacred Jewish sites. "This had a deep influence on my psychology and my relationship with Israelis," he says.

The physical logistics of life under occupation also have enduring impacts. For twenty-five years, five days a week, Jubeh has traveled fifty kilometers to and from Birzeit University via the obligatory congested and sometimes chaotic Qalandia checkpoint. "I don't know how long it will take to cross the checkpoint in any direction," he says. "I cannot plan my schedule. Sometimes it takes a few minutes, sometimes it takes two hours or more." He estimates that he spends a quarter of his daily workweek—"my work time, my production time"—waiting to cross the checkpoint, much more so in the years immediately following Oslo, less so more recently. Between 1993 and 2000, he says, "I managed to read one hundred books at the checkpoint. My car was a library."

The ramifications of such complications of daily life are common to societies in conflict zones around the world. "In general, every conflict produces a lot of violence," Jubeh says. "Societies are becoming more violent. They are becoming more aggressive in every aspect of life, which can be understood. Not everybody can get rid of the violence inside them in a positive way. Some do not manage. Some manage. I found my way of getting rid of anger at the checkpoint by reading."

At the same time, the longevity of the Israel-Palestine conflict sets Palestinian life apart from life in other modern conflict zones. "The difference between us and others is that we are living in this conflict for a century, and for more than five decades under direct control of the Israelis," Jubeh says. "They decide which books are allowed to come to the West Bank; they decide which kind of goods we can import. I cannot build without their permission, and I cannot travel without their permission."

It would be easier, Jubeh says, for him and his family to live in Birzeit, where an apartment of 100–120 square meters would cost approximately $100,000, compared with $500,000 for an apartment of the same size in Jerusalem. He would save further on car maintenance and gasoline and estimates that he would save at least two hours a day not having to pass through Qalandia.

But Nazmi Jubeh will stay in Jerusalem. "This is my city," he says. "Nothing will move me out of my city. We were driven from our homes in 1948.

"We will not repeat it."

N O T E S

INTRODUCTION. The Story behind the Stories

1. Interview with Madees Khoury, Taybeh, West Bank, June 5, 2018. Khoury's narrative continues in chapter 3.

2. While several Palestinian sources quoted in this work were interviewed in Arabic, the majority were interviewed in English. All but Khoury were born in Palestine.

3. The breadth and complexity of contemporary Palestinian life also includes the more than 1.5 million Palestinians who live in and are citizens of Israel (excluding east Jerusalem); approximately 3.2 million Palestinians living in refugee camps in Lebanon (475,075), Syria (552,000), and Jordan (2,206,736), according to UNRWA (United Nations Relief and Works Agency for Palestine Refugees in the Near East) figures as of October 2020 (https://www .unrwa.org/where-we-work); and Palestinians living elsewhere in the region and throughout the global diaspora. These distinct and diverse communities collectively account for over half the total Palestinian population worldwide, which taken together with the five million Palestinians living in the West Bank, east Jerusalem, and Gaza Strip is estimated by various sources to total between eleven million and twelve million.

4. This quotation originates with a peer reviewer who read and critiqued the *Stories from Palestine* manuscript but whose identity is not known to the author.

5. Anthony Bourdain, "Parts Unknown—Jerusalem," CNN, Sept. 15, 2013, http://edition.cnn.com/TRANSCRIPTS/1309/15/abpu.02.html. A narrative of Abdelfattah Abusrour appears in chapter 3.

6. "Girl from Gaza Takes First Prize in International Maths Competition," United Nations Relief and Works Agency for Palestine Refugees in the Near East (UNRWA), Jan. 14, 2013, https://www.unrwa.org/newsroom

/features/girl-gaza-takes-first-prize-international-maths-competition. A narrative of Areej Al-Madhoun appears in chapter 5.

7. *Sāmid* is the masculine singular form, *sāmida* is the feminine singular form, and *samidīn* is the plural form.

8. Raja Shehadeh, *Samed* [*sic*]: *Journal of a West Bank Palestinian* (New York: Adama Books, 1984), vii. (Originally published under the title *The Third Way* by Adam Publishers, Jerusalem.) As a national byword for Palestinians, *sumūd* has been used in various other contexts since the 1960s, including by the Palestine Liberation Organization in refugee camps in Jordan and Lebanon, particularly during the Lebanese civil war in the 1970s and '80s; in cultural expressions of Palestinians living inside Israel, prominent among them the poet Tawfiq Zayyad and novelist Emile Habibi; and by grassroots committees in the West Bank and Gaza Strip focused on self-sufficiency and decreased dependency on the Israeli economy during the first intifada in the late 1980s and early 1990s. (See Alexandra Rijke and Toine van Teeffelen, "To Exist Is to Resist: Sumud, Heroism, and the Everyday," *Jerusalem Quarterly* 59 [2014]: 86–99.) *Sumūd* has also been incorporated as an element of Islamic praxis, including resistance, among Palestinians by Hamas and Islamic Jihad. (See Anna Johansson and Stellan Vinthagen, "Dimensions of Everyday Resistance: The Palestinian Sumūd," *Journal of Political Power* 8, no. 1 [2015]: 121–22.)

9. Rijke and van Teeffelen, "To Exist Is to Resist," 94–95.

10. Ibid., 93.

11. Ibid., 90.

12. Johansson and Vinthagen, "Dimensions of Everyday Resistance," 110.

13. Lori Allen, "Getting by the Occupation: How Violence Became Normal during the Second Palestinian Intifada," *Cultural Anthropology* 23, no. 3 (August 2008): 456–57.

14. James C. Scott, *Weapons of the Weak: Everyday Forms of Peasant Resistance* (New Haven: Yale University Press, 1985), xvii, 302, cited in Jocelyn A. Hollander and Rachel L. Einwohner, "Conceptualizing Resistance," *Sociological Forum* 19, no. 4 (December 2004): 539.

15. Johansson and Vinthagen, "Dimensions of Everyday Resistance," 109.

16. Ibid., 111–13.

17. Shehadeh, *Samed*, 38–39.

18. Ibid., viii.

19. Raja Shehadeh and Jonathan Kuttab, *The West Bank and the Rule of Law* (Geneva: International Commission of Jurists and Law in the Service of Man, 1980). According to Al-Haq, the report analyzes the legal situation in the Israeli-occupied West Bank with regard to "the legislation and adminis-

tration of land rights, water rights, trading and commerce, town planning, trade unions, education, literature, and information. The report establishes that Israel has altered the existing laws and administration in such a way as to make the economy of the West Bank subordinate to the interests of Israel, and to facilitate the encroachment on the territory of Jewish settlements, which are universally condemned as a violation of international law." *The West Bank and the Rule of Law*, Al-Haq, July 19, 2011, http://www.alhaq .org/publications/publications-index/item/the-west-bank-and-the-rule -of-law.

20. Shehadeh, *Samed*, 67–70.

21. White House, *Peace to Prosperity: A Vision to Improve the Lives of the Palestinian and Israeli People* [*sic*], (Washington, DC: White House, 2020), https://www.whitehouse.gov/wp-content/uploads/2020/01/Peace-to -Prosperity-0120.pdf.

22. Aron Heller and Matthew Lee, "Trump Peace Plan Delights Israelis, Enrages Palestinians," Associated Press, Jan. 28, 2020, https://apnews.com /f7d36b9023309ce4b1e423b02abf52c6.

23. Joseph Krauss, "Key Points in Trump's Mideast Peace Plan," Associated Press, Jan. 28, 2020, https://apnews.com/5eb9a836e16ceec87ca7732985 aa551e.

24. Nathan Thrall, "Trump's Middle East Peace Plan Exposes the Ugly Truth," opinion, *New York Times*, Jan. 29, 2020, https://www.nytimes.com /2020/01/29/opinion/trump-peace-plan.html.

25. Krauss, "Key Points."

26. Heller and Lee, "Trump Peace Plan."

27. Steve Hendrix, Ruth Eglash, and Anne Gearan, "Jared Kushner Put a Knife 'in Netanyahu's Back' over Annexation Delay, Says Israeli Settler Leader," *Washington Post*, Feb. 4, 2020, https://www.washingtonpost.com /world/middle_east/reports-jared-kushner-angers-netanyahu-camp-by -slowing-annexation-moves/2020/02/04/82376ac6-4719-11ea-91ab-ce439aa 5c7c1_story.html.

28. Mehul Srivastava, "Trump's Middle East Peace Plan Falls Flat for Netanyahu Ahead of Israel Election," *Financial Times*, Feb. 11, 2020, https:// www.ft.com/content/2bcff144-4be7-11ea-95a0-43d18ec715f5.

29. "Three Short of Majority, Netanyahu Says He Won Election, Is 'Not Going Anywhere,'" *Times of Israel*, March 7, 2020, https://www.timesof israel.com/three-short-of-majority-netanyahu-says-he-won-election-not -going-anywhere/.

30. Colum Lynch and Robbie Gramer, "Trump Pressures Palestinians and Allies over Peace Plan," *Foreign Affairs*, Feb. 11, 2020, https://foreign

policy.com/2020/02/11/trump-pressures-palestinians-over-middle-east-peace
-plan-israel-netanyahu-abbas-olmert-united-nations-diplomacy/.

31. Eric Cortellessa and Raphael Ahren, "US Celebrates Withdrawal of UN Security Council Resolution against Peace Plan," *Times of Israel*, Feb. 11, 2020, https://www.timesofisrael.com/us-celebrates-withdrawal-of-un-security -council-resolution-against-peace-plan/.

32. Matthew Lee and Bradley Klapper, "Trump Declares Jerusalem Is-raeli Capital, Smashing US Policy," Associated Press, Dec. 6, 2017, https:// apnews.com/1d4e1824283f41eaa8422227fa8e6ea7/Trump-flouts-warnings ,-declares-Jerusalem-Israel's-capital.

33. Max Fisher, "The Jerusalem Issue, Explained," *New York Times*, Dec. 9, 2017, https://www.nytimes.com/2017/12/09/world/middleeast /jerusalem-trump-capital.html.

34. Mark Landler, "Trump Recognizes Jerusalem as Israel's Capital and Orders U.S. Embassy to Move," *New York Times*, Dec. 6, 2017, https:// www.nytimes.com/2017/12/06/world/middleeast/trump-jerusalem-israel -capital.html.

35. Fisher, "Jerusalem Issue, Explained."

36. Rick Noack, "Trump's Embassy Move Has Triggered Deadly Pro-tests. These Maps Explain Why," *Washington Post*, May 14, 2018, https:// www.washingtonpost.com/news/world/wp/2018/05/14/trumps-embassy -move-to-jerusalem-is-controversial-these-3-maps-explain-why/.

37. Jim Zanotti, "U.S. Foreign Aid to the Palestinians," Congressional Research Service, May 18, 2018, 3, https://fas.org/sgp/crs/mideast/RS22967 .pdf. The CRS reported: "President Trump has hinted that continued aid to the Palestinians might depend on Palestinian willingness to participate in U.S.-mediated peace initiatives with Israel."

38. Ibid.

39. See Noack, "Trump's Embassy Move."

40. Matthew Lee, "U.S. Cuts Aid to Palestinians by More than $200 Million," Associated Press, Aug. 24, 2018, https://www.apnews.com/3149b034 ef4a4b92a6dbb9c4aa1f5ca7. The report stated that the aid cut "comes as President Donald Trump and his Middle East point men, Jared Kushner and Jason Greenblatt, staff up their office to prepare for the rollout of a much-vaunted but as yet unclear peace plan for Israel and the Palestinians." See also Noack, "Trump's Embassy Move."

41. Lee, "U.S. Cuts Aid."

42. Edward Wong, "U.S. to End Funding to U. N. Agency That Helps Palestinian Refugees," *New York Times*, Aug. 31, 2018, https://www.nytimes .com/2018/08/31/us/politics/trump-unrwa-palestinians.html. The report

stated: "The move was pushed hardest by Jared Kushner, President Trump's son-in-law and top adviser on the Middle East, as part of a plan to compel Palestinian politicians to drop demands for many of those refugees to return to what they call their homeland, said the former official, R. David Harden, who worked at the United States Agency for International Development until April"; and: "Since 2010, the average annual contribution from the United States to the United Nations agency has been more than $350 million, a quarter of the agency's budget. In 2017, the United States contributed about $360 million."

43. Reuters, "Trump Cuts $25 Million in Aid for Palestinians in East Jerusalem Hospitals," Sept. 8, 2018, https://www.reuters.com/article/us-usa -palestinians-hospitals/trump-cuts-25-million-in-aid-for-palestinians-in -east-jerusalem-hospitals-idUSKCN1LO0O0.

44. Laurie Kellman, "Trump Closing Palestinian Mission in Pro-Israel Move," Associated Press, Sept. 10, 2018, https://apnews.com/22ab439a41004 2169cf96b0612fb8e5a.

45. Yara Bayoumy, "U.S. State Department Revokes PLO Ambassador Family Visas: Envoy," Reuters, Sept. 16, 2018, https://www.reuters.com/article /us-usa-palestinians/u-s-state-department-revokes-plo-ambassador-family -visas-envoy-idUSKCN1LW0RE.

46. Josh Lederman and Saphora Smith, "Trump Administration Cuts $25 Million in Aid for Palestinians in East Jerusalem Hospitals," NBC News, Sept. 9, 2018, https://www.nbcnews.com/news/world/trump-administration -cuts-25-million-aid-palestinians-east-jerusalem-hospitals-n907876.

47. Reuters, "Trump Signs Decree Recognizing Israeli Sovereignty over Golan Heights," March 25, 2019, https://www.reuters.com/article/us-usa -israel-golan/trump-signs-decree-recognizing-israeli-sovereignty-over-golan -heights-idUSKCN1R61XK.

48. Associated Press, "EU Rejects US Recognition of Israeli Control over Golan," March 27, 2019, https://apnews.com/68926b677f1b4bb3a663 5947d902cf73.

49. The Geneva Convention relative to the Protection of Civilian Persons in Time of War (known as the Fourth Geneva Convention and adopted in August 1949), article 49, paragraph 6, states: "The Occupying Power shall not deport or transfer parts of its own civilian population into the territory it occupies." UN Security Council Resolutions 446, 452 (1979), and 465 (1980) affirmed the applicability of the Fourth Geneva Convention "to the Arab territories occupied by Israel in 1967, including Jerusalem," and declared the settlements built by Israel on those territories to have "no legal validity."

In 1978, the State Department published in its "Digest of United States Practice in International Law" a three-page opinion by legal adviser Herbert Hansell concluding that "while Israel may undertake, in the occupied territories, actions necessary to meet its military needs and to provide for orderly government during the occupation . . . the establishment of the civilian settlements in those territories is inconsistent with international law"; in 1981 President Ronald Reagan, speaking to reporters, said he believed the settlements were "not illegal" but building new ones was "unnecessarily provocative." Bernard Gwertzman, "State Department; About the West Bank and the Emperor's Clothes," *New York Times*, Aug. 25, 1983, https://www.nytimes.com /1983/08/25/us/state-department-about-the-west-bank-and-the-emperor-s -clothes.html.

Prior to the Pompeo announcement in November 2019, all successive U.S. administrations since Reagan had skirted the issue of legality of Israeli settlements but consistently described them as impediments to peace. In December 2016 President Barack Obama, whose administration had referred to the settlements as "illegitimate," became the first U.S. president to withhold the U.S. veto in the UN Security Council on the matter, instead abstaining on a resolution calling the settlements "a flagrant violation under international law" and thus allowing it to pass. Karen De Young, Steve Hendrix, and John Hudson, "Trump Administration Says Israel's West Bank Settlements Do Not Violate International Law," *Washington Post*, Nov. 18, 2019, https:// www.washingtonpost.com/national-security/trump-administration-says -israels-west-bank-settlements-do-not-violate-international-law/2019/11/18 /38cdbb96-0a39-11ea-bd9d-c628fd48b3a0_story.html.

50. Matthew Lee, "US Angers Palestinians with Reversal on Israeli Settlements," Associated Press, Nov. 19, 2019, https://apnews.com/3da4fb36710 04679a91a7d4ae9ab4e57.

51. Lara Jakes and David M. Halbfinger, "In Shift, U.S. Says Israeli Settlements in West Bank Do Not Violate International Law," *New York Times*, Nov. 18, 2019, https://www.nytimes.com/2019/11/18/world/middleeast /trump-israel-west-bank-settlements.html.

52. Thrall, "Trump's Middle East Peace Plan."

53. Ibid.

54. "UN Security Council Working Methods: The Veto," Security Council Report, Sept. 30, 2019, https://www.securitycouncilreport.org /un-security-council-working-methods/the-veto.php, with link to table of all Security Council vetoes cast by all members, 1946–2019.

55. Thrall, "Trump's Middle East Peace Plan."

56. Jeremy M. Sharp, "U.S. Foreign Aid to Israel," Congressional Research Service, Aug. 7, 2019, unnumbered "Summary" page, https://fas.org/sgp/crs/mideast/RL33222.pdf.

57. [Author's name redacted], "U.S. Foreign Aid to Israel," Congressional Research Service, Dec. 22, 2016, 36, https://www.everycrsreport.com/files/20161222_RL33222_38d8a59f2caabdc9af8a6cdabfabb963ae8b63ae.pdf. The report charts year-by-year U.S. aid to Israel; aid from 1949 to 1967 equals $1.22 billion (out of a cumulative total through fiscal 2017 of $134.7 billion).

58. Sharp, "U.S. Foreign Aid to Israel," 27–30. Economic aid has included migration and refugee assistance for resettlement of Jewish immigrants in Israel as well as loan guarantees. From 1973 to 1991, U.S. aid to Israel for immigrant resettlement totaled $460 million; from 2000 to 2012 it totaled $519.3 million; and it has averaged approximately $10 million a year since through fiscal 2020. From fiscal years 2003 to 2019, the U.S. has extended approximately $57 billion to Israel in loan guarantees, enabling it to borrow from commercial banks at lower rates, from which Israel borrowed approximately $4.1 billion by issuing U.S.-backed bonds.

59. Ibid., 5.

60. Ibid., 1.

61. Ibid., 2.

62. Ibid., 3.

63. Ibid., 4.

64. Ibid., 2.

65. Ibid., n. 8. The CRS report attributes data on Israel's no. 8 ranking worldwide among arms exporters—accounting for 3.1 percent of world deliveries—to the Stockholm International Peace Research Institute.

66. Ibid., 8.

67. Ibid., 9.

68. Heller and Lee, "Trump Peace Plan."

69. Sharp, "U.S. Foreign Aid to Israel," 30. In fiscal 2003, the U.S. extended $1.1 billion in loan guarantees to Israel; $289.5 million was deducted for settlement activity, and Israel borrowed $1.6 billion, surpassing its allocation. In fiscal 2005, the U.S. extended $1.45 billion in guarantees; $795.8 million was deducted for settlement activity, and Israel borrowed $750 million.

70. Zanotti, "U.S. Foreign Aid to the Palestinians," unnumbered "Summary" page.

71. Ibid., 1n2.

72. Ibid., 11.

73. Ibid., 1.

74. Elior Levy, "The Many Layers of the Palestinian Security Forces," Ynetnews (Israel), April 26, 2016, https://www.ynetnews.com/articles/0,73 40,L-4795909,00.html. The report stated: "This security coordination between the PA and Israel removes Hamas from the picture, as this coordination is one of the central reasons that Hamas's military infrastructure is so shaky in the West Bank. Many of its military operatives are captured in their initial stages thanks to security coordination." (Ynetnews is the English-language, online version of *Yediot Aharonot*, the largest paid-circulation, Hebrew-language daily newspaper in Israel.)

75. U.S. Department of State, "Foreign Terrorist Organizations," https://www.state.gov/foreign-terrorist-organizations/.

76. Nicholas P. Roberts, "Reconsidering Terror and Terrorism: The Case for Hamas," Middle East Monitor memo, May 10, 2014, https://www.middleeastmonitor.com/20140510-reconsidering-terror-and-terrorism-the-case-for-hamas/; PDF of memo at https://www.middleeastmonitor.com/wp-content/uploads/downloads/briefing-paper/20140421_ReconsideringTerror andTerrorism.pdf. Roberts asserts: "Hamas remains a permanent actor on the stage of Palestinian politics, and, as the democratically elected government of the Hamas-Gaza state, it is a profoundly different organization than when it was founded in the late 1980s. . . . It is no longer accurate to judge the conflict through the framework of an Israeli police-security action against a local, marginal organization because Hamas is no longer that: it is a state-based political unit that negotiates with Israel and surrounding states daily."

77. Zanotti, "U.S. Foreign Aid to the Palestinians," 1–2.

78. Ibid., 4.

79. Ibid. The CRS report notes: "Indeed, Palestinians may be jailed by Israel as security threats for acts that some—or many—Americans might consider civil disobedience."

80. "Israel's Population Up to 9.25 Million, Though Growth Rate, Immigration Down," *Times of Israel*, September 16, 2020, https://www.timesofisrael.com/israels-population-up-to-9-25-million-but-growth-rate-immigration-down/.

81. Khaled Abu Toameh, "Palestinian Census: 4.7 Million in West Bank and Gaza Strip," *Times of Israel*, March 28, 2018, https://www.timesofisrael.com/palestinian-census-4-7-million-in-west-bank-and-gaza-strip/.

82. Aron Heller, "Israeli Demographer: Arabs Nearly Equal Jews in Holy Land," Associated Press, March 27, 2018, https://www.apnews.com/0bb2a5e1db634bc3b3ec961f2c70db34.

83. Michael Bachner, "Ahead of Jewish New Year, Israel's Population at 8.9 Million, Largely Content," *Times of Israel*, Sept. 4, 2018, https://www.timesofisrael.com/ahead-of-jewish-new-year-israels-population-at-8-9-million-largely-content/.

84. Abu Toameh, "Palestinian Census."

85. Ilan Ben Zion, "Israeli Parliament Passes Contentious Jewish Nation Bill," Associated Press, July 19, 2018, https://www.apnews.com/a9804a4476fb4123859aa7e3dd1ab871/Israeli-parliament-passes-contentious-Jewish-nation-bill.

86. White House, *Peace to Prosperity*, 13 (section 4, "Borders"; PDF p. 17). In the envisioned population transfer to the State of Palestine, the plan names ten Arab towns and villages in the central "Triangle" region of Israel—Kafr Qara, Ar'ara, Baha [*sic*; the correct spelling is "Baqa"] al-Gharbiyye, Umm al-Fahm, Qalansawe, Tayibe, Kafr Qasim, Tira, Kafr Bara, and Jaljulia—and states that in such an agreement, "the civil rights of the residents of the triangle communities would be subject to the applicable laws and judicial rulings of the relevant authorities."

According to the Israel Central Bureau of Statistics, the combined population of these towns and villages in 2018 numbered 257,094 ("Population and Density Per Sq. Km. in Localities with 5,000 Residents and More on 31.12.2018," https://www.cbs.gov.il/he/publications/doclib/2019/2.shnaton population/st02_24.pdf). See also Steve Hendrix and Sufian Taha, "Buried in Trump's Peace Plan, a Proposal That Could Strip Thousands of Israeli Arabs of Their Citizenship," *Washington Post*, Feb. 8, 2020, https://www.washingtonpost.com/world/middle_east/buried-in-trumps-peace-plan-a-proposal-that-could-strip-thousands-of-israeli-arabs-of-their-citizenship/2020/02/07/0b43ff0c-4696-11ea-91ab-ce439aa5c7c1_story.html.

87. Robert Entman's "cascade" model of communication theory posits that topics can flow from the general reader to civil society via the media and then appear on the radar screens of policy makers. Robert Entman, *Projections of Power: Framing News, Public Opinion, and U.S. Foreign Policy* (Chicago: University of Chicago Press, 2004).

88. Ben Ehrenreich, "The Resisters" (print-edition headline)/"Is This Where the Third Intifada Will Start?" (online version headline), *New York Times Magazine*, March 17, 2013, http://www.nytimes.com/2013/03/17/magazine/is-this-where-the-third-intifada-will-start.html.

89. Jodi Rudoren, "My Hobby Is Throwing Stones" (print-edition headline)/"In a West Bank Culture of Conflict, Boys Wield the Weapon at Hand," (online version headline), *New York Times*, Aug. 4, 2013, https://

www.nytimes.com/2013/08/05/world/middleeast/rocks-in-hand-a-boy
-fights-for-his-west-bank-village.html?_r=3&.

90. On March 12, 2015, the *Times* published "Netanyahu and the Settlements," by Jodi Rudoren and Jeremy Ashkenas, https://www.nytimes.com
/interactive/2015/03/12/world/middleeast/netanyahu-west-bank-settle
ments-israel-election.html?_r=0. The detailed and graphically rich report,
which appeared days before the election that Israeli prime minister Benjamin
Netanyahu would win, was replete with references to how settlement expansion has threatened prospects for a two-state resolution of the conflict. Describing decades of Israeli settlement building in the West Bank and the rapid
rate of expansion under Netanyahu, the report included maps as well as still
and interactive aerial photos of settlements in various stages of growth. However, the piece did not quote Palestinians directly, nor did it depict the physical obstacles and barriers to Palestinian movement and territorial contiguity
imposed by the settlements.

91. See Marda Dunsky, *Pens and Swords: How the American Mainstream Media Report the Israeli-Palestinian Conflict* (New York: Columbia
University Press, 2008).

92. See https://electronicintifada.net/; https://mondoweiss.net/; and
https://www.aljazeera.com/, et al.

93. Matti Hyvärinen, "Analyzing Narratives and Story-Telling," in *The
Sage Handbook of Social Research Methods*, ed. Pertti Alasuutari, Julia
Brannen, and Leonard Bickman (Thousand Oaks, CA: Sage, 2008), 450.

94. Ibid., 449–50.

95. Margarete Sandelowski, "Telling Stories: Narrative Approaches
in Qualitative Research," *IMAGE: Journal of Nursing Scholarship* 23, no. 3
(Fall 1991): 161.

96. Baruch Kimmerling and Joel S. Migdal, *Palestinians: The Making
of a People* (Harvard University Press, 1993); Rashid Khalidi, *Palestinian
Identity: The Construction of Modern National Consciousness* (Columbia
University Press, 1997); Rashid Khalidi, *The Iron Cage: The Story of the
Palestinian Struggle for Statehood* (Beacon Press, 2006); Ilan Pappé, *The
Ethnic Cleansing of Palestine* (Oneworld, 2006); Neve Gordon, *Israel's Oc-
cupation* (University of California Press, 2008); William A. Cook, *The
Plight of the Palestinians: A Long History of Destruction* (Palgrave Macmil-
lan, 2010); Ali Abunimah, *The Battle for Justice in Palestine* (Haymarket
Books, 2014); Marwan Darweish and Andrew Rigby, *Popular Protest in Pal-
estine: The Uncertain Future of Unarmed Resistance* (Pluto Press, 2015);
Ghada Ageel, *Apartheid in Palestine: Hard Laws and Harder Experiences*
(University of Alberta Press, 2016); Steven Salaita, *Inter/nationalism: De-

colonizing Native America and Palestine (University of Minnesota Press, 2016); and Mazen Masri, *The Dynamics of Exclusionary Constitutionalism: Israel as a Jewish and Democratic State* (Hart Publishing, 2017). These narrative emphases can also be seen in works on the Palestinian Arab minority in Israel, including Shira Robinson, *Citizen Strangers: Palestinians and the Birth of Israel's Liberal Settler State* (Stanford University Press, 2013), and Ilan Pappé, *The Forgotten Palestinians: A History of the Palestinians in Israel* (Yale University Press, 2011).

97. Mateo Hoke and Cate Malek, eds., *Palestine Speaks: Narratives of Life under Occupation* (McSweeney's, 2014). Other examples of this genre include Staughton Lynd, Sam Bahour, and Alice Lynd, eds., *Homeland: Oral Histories of Palestine and Palestinians* (Olive Branch Press, 1994); Laetitia Bucaille, *Growing Up Palestinian: Israeli Occupation and the Intifada Generation* (Princeton University Press, 2004); and Hatim Kanaaneh, *A Doctor in Galilee: The Life and Struggle of a Palestinian in Israel* (Pluto Press, 2008).

98. See Dunsky, *Pens and Swords*, 5–22.

99. Herbert J. Gans, *Deciding What's News* (New York: Pantheon, 1979), 39.

100. Ibid., 39–40.

101. Todd Gitlin, *The Whole World Is Watching: Mass Media in the Making and Unmaking of the New Left* (Berkeley: University of California Press, 1980), 263.

102. Spheres of consensus and deviance are discussed by Daniel C. Hallin in *The "Uncensored War": The Media and Vietnam* (New York: Oxford University Press, 1986), 135–36.

103. These three realms of discourse are addressed by Karim H. Karim in *Islamic Peril: Media and Global Violence* (Montreal: Black Rose Books, 2000), 5.

104. Ibid., 5, 23.

105. Gitlin, *Whole World Is Watching*, 257–58, 269.

106. Ibid., 6.

107. Ibid., 1–2.

108. Edward S. Herman and Noam Chomsky, *Manufacturing Consent: The Political Economy of the Mass Media* (New York: Pantheon, 2002), 40.

109. Its footage shot almost entirely by Emad Burnat, the 2011 documentary *5 Broken Cameras* was codirected by Guy Davidi. In addition to being nominated for an Oscar, the film also won the World Cinema Directing Award at the 2012 Sundance Film Festival as well as honors at festivals held in the Netherlands and Armenia.

110. Edward Said, *Orientalism* (New York: Vintage Books, 1979), 12.

111. The Palestinian Authority is the protogovernment in the West Bank, administering ministries and security forces but lacking territorial sovereignty. President Mahmoud Abbas, who is also chairman of the Palestine Liberation Organization (which represents the Palestinians in peace negotiations) and head of the Fatah party, was elected in January 2005 for a term that expired in 2009, with no further elections held as of 2020. The Gaza Strip has been controlled by the Islamic Resistance Movement, known in Arabic as Hamas, which won a plurality of votes in the January 2006 election and took full control of Gaza in June 2007 after protracted violent clashes with Fatah. Hamas has ruled Gaza according to conservative Islamic sensibilities and with no subsequent elections held as of 2020. In October 2017 the PA and Hamas reached a reconciliation agreement, the stability and feasibility of which remain fluid.

112. Birzeit University (Birzeit, est. 1924); Hebron University (Hebron, 1971); Bethlehem University (Bethlehem, 1973); An-Najah University (Nablus, 1977); Palestine Polytechnic University (Hebron, 1978); Islamic University of Gaza (Gaza City, 1978); Al-Quds University (Jerusalem, 1984); University College of Applied Sciences (Gaza City, 1998); Arab American University (Jenin, 2000); and Al-Aqsa University (Gaza City, 2000; formerly a teachers institute and college of education).

113. See the Palestinian Non-Governmental Organizations Network, http://www.pngo.net/our-members/. (Website was under maintenance in June 2020.)

114. World Bank data for 2018 indicate Israel's GDP at $370.5 billion and the combined West Bank and Gaza GDP at $14.6 billion. Between 1993 and 2011, GDP per capita in Israel rose from $16,029 to $32,123. By contrast, GDP per capita in the West Bank and Gaza Strip rose from $1,320 to $2,489; in Gaza the per capita GDP increased by less than $300 in two decades, reaching $1,534 in 2011. Thus, the per capita GDP disparity between Israelis and Palestinians more than doubled in the two decades after the Oslo process began in 1993 from $14,709 to $29,634. Neve Gordon, "The Oslo Accords' Calamities," *Al Jazeera*, Sept. 12, 2013, https://www.aljazeera.com/indepth/opinion/2013/09/201391295343390833.html.

CHAPTER 1. Made in Palestine

An earlier version of this chapter was published as "Made in Palestine" in *The Cairo Review of Global Affairs* 26 (Summer 2017): 60–71. Republished here with permission. See also https://www.thecairoreview.com/essays/made-in-palestine/.

1. Interview with Adnan Massad, Faqqu'a, West Bank, May 13, 2018.

2. United Nations Conference on Trade and Development (UNC-TAD), *The Besieged Palestinian Agricultural Sector*, 2015, 7–8, https://unctad.org/en/PublicationsLibrary/gdsapp2015d1_en.pdf.

3. Ibid., 9.

4. Ibid., 8.

5. Palestinian Central Bureau of Statistics, *Statistical Yearbook 2019* [in Arabic and English], Ramallah, December 2019, 225–27, http://www.pcbs.gov.ps/Downloads/book2495.pdf. Palestinian imports for 2018 totaled USD $6.54 billion; exports totaled $1.15 billion (225–26). Palestinian exports to Israel for 2018 totaled $967.5 million; imports from Israel totaled $3.62 billion (227). Palestinian imports of food and livestock for 2018 totaled $1.45 billion; exports of food and livestock totaled $177.4 million (225–26).

6. In 2019 the Israeli NGO Peace Now estimated the Palestinian population in east Jerusalem at 341,729 and the Jewish population at 215,067; the group also estimated that Israeli settlers constituted 13 percent of the West Bank population, citing a Palestinian population figure of 2.9 million (indicating approximately 430,000 Israeli settlers); see "Israeli Settlements 2019/East Jerusalem 2019," http://peacenow.org.il/wp-content/uploads/2019/08/settlements_map_eng-2019.pdf. The Palestinian population of the West Bank at the end of 2019 was cited as 3,019,948 by the Palestinian Central Bureau of Statistics (*Palestine in Figures 2019*, March 2020, 8, http://pcbs.gov.ps/Downloads/book2513.pdf).

Media reports in late 2019–early 2020 indicated an overall Israeli settler population in the West Bank and east Jerusalem of 700,000. See Heller and Lee, "Trump Peace Plan Delights Israelis"; Lee, "US Angers Palestinians"; DeYoung, Hendrix, and Hudson, "Trump Administration Says Israel's West Bank Settlements Do Not Violate."

7. Jacob Magid, "Settler Growth Rate Declines for Sixth Straight Year," *Times of Israel*, Jan. 21, 2018, https://www.timesofisrael.com/settler-growth-rate-declines-for-sixth-straight-year/. The report cites Israeli Interior Ministry data.

8. While the Israel Central Bureau of Statistics indicated 126 West Bank settlements in December 2017, in September 2018 the Israeli NGO Peace Now reported 130 government-recognized settlements in the West Bank (excluding east Jerusalem) and 101 outposts ("Settlement Watch/Data/Population," http://peacenow.org.il/en/settlements-watch/settlements-data/population).

9. Interview with Reja-e and Musaab Fayyad, Zababdeh, West Bank, May 3, 2016.

10. Some military campaigns by the prestate Jewish forces (Haganah) were designed to expel Palestinian Arabs living in areas designated for Jewish statehood as designated in the November 1947 UN Partition of Palestine (General Assembly Resolution 181) for the express purpose of establishing a Jewish majority. According to Israeli historian Benny Morris, the partition "did not provide for population transfers and, indeed, left in the areas designated for Jewish statehood close to 400,000 Arabs (alongside some 500,000 Jews)"—nearly 45 percent; Benny Morris, *The Birth of the Palestinian Refugee Problem Revisited* (Cambridge: Cambridge University Press, 2004), 60. At the time of the partition, which designated 55 percent of the land in Palestine for the Jewish state, the Arab population numbered approximately 1.3 million and the Jewish population some 600,000. "Plan Dalet" (Plan D) was a major expulsion campaign; carried out by Haganah units in April–May 1948, it led to some 250,000–300,000 largely unarmed Palestinians becoming refugees—nearly 40 percent of the 700,000–725,000 total—before the war between Israel and surrounding Arab states broke out on May 15 (Morris, *Birth of the Palestinian Refugee Problem Revisited*, 262–63).

11. Interview with Nasser Abufarha, Burqin, West Bank, Dec. 28, 2015. Data updates from Canaan Fair Trade in January 2020.

12. Originally established as Canaan Fair Trade, the company is also variously identified as Canaan and/or Canaan Palestine in its marketing and media outreach; see https://canaanpalestine.com/.

13. Robin Emmott, "EU Defends Labeling Goods Made in Israeli Settlements," Reuters, Jan. 18, 2016, https://www.reuters.com/article/us-israel -palestinians-eu/eu-defends-labeling-goods-made-in-israeli-settlements -idUSKCN0UW24P.

14. Human Rights Watch, *Occupation, Inc.: How Settlement Businesses Contribute to Israel's Violations of Human Rights*, 2016, 101–2, https://www .hrw.org/sites/default/files/report_pdf/israel0116_web2.pdf. The report states: "In 2012, Israel told the World Bank that the value of exports from settlements to Europe, Israel's largest trade partner, was $300 million per year, but the World Bank notes that other analyses, which take into account goods partially produced in settlements, estimated the value of European imports of such goods to be significantly higher." The reference to "settlements" presumably means those located in the West Bank, not the Golan Heights or east Jerusalem—territories that Israel has exerted its control over in contravention of international law. The Human Rights Watch report called on Israeli and international companies to stop doing businesses "inside or for the benefit of settlements" but stopped short of advocating a boycott of settlement products.

15. The UN Security Council adopted Resolutions 446 and 452 in 1979 and Resolution 465 in 1980. All three affirmed the applicability of the Fourth Geneva Convention—which prohibits transfer, including settlement, of an occupying power's own civilian population into occupied territory—"to the Arab territories occupied by Israel in 1967, including Jerusalem." The three resolutions further declared that the settlements built by Israel in those territories have "no legal validity."

16. Jewish Telegraphic Agency, "Obama Administration Reissues Labeling Order on West Bank Products," Jan. 28, 2016, https://www.jta.org/2016/01/28/news-opinion/politics/obama-administration-reissues-labeling-order-on-west-bank-products.

17. Jewish Telegraphic Agency, "Airbnb Gets 140,000-Signature Petition Protesting Settler Rentals," March 10, 2016, https://www.jta.org/2016/03/10/news-opinion/israel-middle-east/airbnb-gets-140000-signature-petition-protesting-settler-rentals.

18. Interview with Areen Shaar, Burqin, West Bank, May 13, 2018.

19. Interview with Faris Hussein, Ti'inik, West Bank, Dec. 28, 2015.

20. Interview with Mohammed Al-Ruzzi, Jenin, West Bank, Dec. 28, 2015.

21. Ma'an News Agency (Palestine), "Israeli Authorities Demolish 3 Wells in Northern West Bank," Nov. 11, 2015, https://www.marsad.ps/en/2015/11/11/israeli-authorities-demolish-3-wells-in-northern-west-bank/?doing_wp_cron=1592408665.1621639728546142578125.

22. Interview with Ciro Fiorillo, Jerusalem, May 2, 2016.

23. UNCTAD, *Besieged Palestinian Agricultural Sector*, 29.

24. Ibid., i.

25. Amira Hass, "Exploitation and Profiteering: Palestinians Forced to Pay a Fortune to Work in Israel," *Haaretz*, Oct. 23, 2019, https://www.haaretz.com/israel-news/.premium-every-third-palestinian-worker-in-israel-is-forced-to-buy-a-work-permit-1.8016313. The report stated that according to a Bank of Israel study published in September 2019, around one-third of 81,000 Palestinian workers in Israel "are forced to buy an Israeli work permit. . . . Thus in 2018 more than 20,000 people paid almost half a billion shekels ($140 million) to brokers and Israeli companies and employers. They each pay between 1,500 shekels and 2,500 shekels a month—between one-third and one-half of their potential earning power in Israel. . . . The new study gives a conservative estimate of the profits in the illegal permits business in 2018: 122 million shekels. This money is divided among brokers, Israeli clerks and the employers whose names appear on the permits."

26. Edo Konrad, "Settlers to Palestinian Laborers: 'Work with Human Rights Groups and Lose Your Job,'" *+972 Magazine*, Feb. 4, 2019, https://www.972mag.com/settlers-palestinian-jobs-human-rights/.

27. Human Rights Watch, *Occupation, Inc.*, 110.

28. "The Separation Barrier," B'Tselem, The Israeli Information Center for Human Rights in the Occupied Territories, Nov. 11, 2017, https://www.btselem.org/separation_barrier.

29. Ibid.

30. Judy Maltz, "For West Bank Settlement Marking 40 Years, Donald Trump Is Just Another Reason to Celebrate," *Haaretz*, Aug. 17, 2018, https://www.haaretz.com/israel-news/.premium.MAGAZINE-to-40-year-old-settlement-trump-is-one-more-reason-to-celebrate-1.6387333.

31. Human Rights Watch, *Occupation, Inc.*, 112.

32. Ibid., 115.

33. Data from Canaan Fair Trade.

34. Palestinian Central Bureau of Statistics, "Projected Mid-Year Population for Jenin Governorate by Locality 2017–2021," http://www.pcbs.gov.ps/Portals/_Rainbow/Documents/JeninE.html.

35. Khaled Abu Toameh, "Palestinian Census: 4.7 Million in West Bank and Gaza Strip," *Times of Israel*, March 28, 2018, https://www.timesofisrael.com/palestinian-census-4-7-million-in-west-bank-and-gaza-strip/.

36. World Bank, *West Bank and Gaza: Area C and the Future of the Palestinian Economy*, Middle East and North Africa Region, Report No. AUS2922, Oct. 2, 2013, 4, http://documents.worldbank.org/curated/en/137111468329419171/pdf/AUS29220REPLAC0EVISION0January02014.pdf. The remaining land in Area C is allocated for closed military areas (approx. 21 percent) and nature reserves (approx. 9 percent).

37. Ibid., x, xi, 34.

38. Human Rights Watch, *Occupation, Inc.*, 1. The report references hectares (1 hectare = 10 dunams), stating: "There are approximately 20 Israeli-administered industrial zones in the West Bank, covering about 1,365 hectares, and Israeli settlers oversee the cultivation of 9,300 hectares of agricultural land. In comparison, the built-up area of residential settlements covers 6,000 hectares (although their municipal borders encompass a much larger area)."

39. UNCTAD, *Besieged Palestinian Agricultural Sector*, 9.

40. Ibid., 12.

41. Ibid., 35.

42. State of Palestine Ministry of Agriculture, "National Agriculture Sector Strategy: 'Resilience and Development,' 2014–2016" (Ramallah: State of Palestine Ministry of Agriculture, 2013), 43.

43. UNCTAD, *Besieged Palestinian Agricultural Sector*, 35.

44. Ibid., 24.

45. Palestinian Central Bureau of Statistics, *Statistical Yearbook 2019*, 225–27.

46. World Bank, "West Bank and Gaza," https://data.worldbank.org /country/west-bank-and-gaza (see chart on GDP).

47. Food and Agriculture Organization of the United Nations, "Palestine Humanitarian Response 2019," http://www.fao.org/3/CA3263EN/ca32 63en.pdf.

48. Ibid.

49. Interview with Basma Qablawi, Zababdeh, West Bank, Jan. 5, 2016.

50. UNCTAD, *Besieged Palestinian Agricultural Sector*, 34.

51. Interview with Naoko Inagaki, Zababdeh, West Bank, Jan. 5, 2016.

52. Interview with Majdi Abu Na'eem, Zababdeh, West Bank, Jan. 5, 2016.

53. Interview with Safaa Jarbou, Zababdeh, West Bank, Jan. 5, 2016.

54. Daniel Estrin, "Israel Expropriated West Bank Land during End of Biden Visit," Associated Press, March 16, 2016, http://www.sun-sentinel.com /florida-jewish-journal/jj-israel-expropriated-west-bank-land-during-end -of-biden-visit-20160316-story.html.

55. The sign was photographed by the author on May 2, 2016. Transliterated, the Hebrew text on the sign read: "zeh hazman l'kabel haḥlata tova l'ḥaim / haharḥava shel kibbutz almog / boh-ooh lagur b'bayit prati al ḥaytzi dunam b'tzafon hakasoom shel yam hamelaḥ."

CHAPTER 2. Lessons in Liberation

1. "Global Teacher Prize 2016: Announcement with Pope Francis and Salma Hayek," Global Education and Skills Forum, Dubai, Varkey Foundation, video, 10:56, March 13, 2016, https://www.youtube.com/watch?v=yt PXBoGUceo. See also "About Global Teacher Prize," Varkey Foundation, https://www.globalteacherprize.org/about-the-global-teacher-prize/about -global-teacher-prize/; "2016 Top 10 finalists," https://www.globalteacher prize.org/finalists/2016-finalists/.

2. Hanan Al-Hroub narrative based primarily on interview with the author in Ramallah on June 6, 2018 (other sources cited).

3. Walid Khalidi, ed., *All That Remains: The Palestinian Villages Occupied and Depopulated by Israel in 1948* (Washington, DC: Institute for Palestine Studies, 1992), 307–8. The population of Al-Qabu according to the 1944–45 census was 260, with 1,669 cultivable dunams.

4. Ibid., 308.

5. Morris, *Birth of the Palestinian Refugee Problem Revisited*, xviii, 519–20.

6. Khalidi, *All That Remains*, 308.

7. "Dheisheh Camp," United Nations Relief and Works Agency for Palestine Refugees in the Near East (UNRWA), https://www.unrwa.org /where-we-work/west-bank/dheisheh-camp; see also "Profile: Dheisheh Camp," http://www.unrwa.org/sites/default/files/dheisheh_refugee_camp .pdf. With a current population of approximately 15,000, the population density of Dheisheh is estimated at 45,454 persons per square kilometer (.386 square miles).

Across the region, by October 2020 UNRWA was supporting approximately 5.6 million Palestinian refugees in five fields of operation: the West Bank (including east Jerusalem), the Gaza Strip, Jordan, Lebanon, and Syria (www.unrwa.org). Since it began operations on May 1, 1950, UNRWA has served four generations of Palestinian refugees, defined as "persons whose normal place of residence was Palestine during the period 1 June 1946 to 15 May 1948, and who lost both home and means of livelihood as a result of the 1948 conflict." According to UNRWA, "The descendants of Palestine refugee males, including legally adopted children, are also eligible for registration." As of October 2020, nearly one-third of registered refugees numbering more than 1.5 million persons live in fifty-eight recognized Palestinian refugee camps across the region; the other two-thirds live "in and around the cities and towns of the host countries, and in the West Bank and Gaza Strip, often in the environs of official camps" (https://www.unrwa.org/palestine-refugees).

8. "Teaching for Peace in Palestine: Hanan Al Hroub, Palestine; Global Teacher Prize," video, 7:12, Feb. 16, 2016, https://www.youtube.com /watch?v=02Z1NpMB2r4; see also "Hanan Al Hroub 2016, The 2016 Global Teacher Prize Winner," Varkey Foundation, https://www.globalteacherprize .org/winners/hanan-al-hroub-2016/.

9. "The Only Thing That Can Change the Future Is Education" [Hanan Al-Hroub profile], UNRWA, March 11, 2016, https://www.unrwa .org/newsroom/features/only-thing-can-change-future-education.

10. Ibid.

11. United Nations Office for the Coordination of Humanitarian Affairs, Occupied Palestinian Territory (OCHA), "Right to Education Deeply Impacted by Ongoing Interference in Schools: Joint Statement by the Humanitarian Coordinator, Jamie McGoldrick, UNICEF Special Representative, Genevieve Boutin, and UNESCO," press release, Jan. 30, 2019, https://www

.ochaopt.org/content/right-education-deeply-impacted-ongoing-interference
-schools.

12. Ibid.

13. World Council of Churches, Ecumenical Accompaniment Programme in Palestine and Israel, *Education under Occupation: Access to
Education in the Occupied Palestinian Territory* (Geneva: World Council
of Churches, 2013), 9, https://www.unicef.org/oPt/UNICEF_Under
_Occupation_final-SMALL.pdf. The report was published with support
from UNICEF and with funding from the Japanese government.

14. Ibid.

15. Ibid., 11.

16. Ibid., 10.

17. United Nations General Assembly/Security Council, *Children and
Armed Conflict: Report of the Secretary-General*, A/73/907–S/2019/509, June
20, 2019, 14–16. The report, which Secretary-General Antonio Guterres presented to the UN Security Council on July 26, 2019, also documented that six
Israeli children had been injured in 2018, including two girls "in their home
by a rocket fired indiscriminately by a Palestinian armed group." See also
Michelle Nichols, "Saudi-Led Forces, Israel among States Rapped by U. N. for
Killing Children," Reuters, July 26, 2019, https://www.reuters.com/article
/us-un-rights-children/saudi-led-forces-israel-among-states-rapped-by-un
-for-killing-children-idUSKCN1UL2SH.

18. Al-Hroub demonstrated these techniques in a master class presented to judges and others the day before she was named winner of the
Global Teacher Prize. "Teacher Masterclass: Lessons from a Palestinian Primary School," Global Education and Skills Forum, Dubai, Varkey Foundation, video, 25:59, March 12, 2016, https://www.youtube.com/watch?v=sie
ZmDHt7ic.

19. UN General Assembly, Resolution 217A, Universal Declaration of
Human Rights (Dec. 10, 1948), https://www.un.org/en/universal-declaration
-human-rights/. Article 26 states in part: "(1) Everyone has the right to education. Education shall be free, at least in the elementary and fundamental
stages. Elementary education shall be compulsory. . . . (2) Education shall be
directed to the full development of the human personality and to the strengthening of respect for human rights and fundamental freedoms." See also UN
General Assembly, Resolution 2200A (XXI), International Covenant on Economic, Social and Cultural Rights (Dec. 16, 1966; entered into force on Jan. 3,
1976), https://www.ohchr.org/en/professionalinterest/pages/cescr.aspx. Article 13 states in part: "1. The States Parties to the present Covenant recognize

the right of everyone to education. They agree that education shall be directed to the full development of the human personality and the sense of its dignity, and shall strengthen the respect for human rights and fundamental freedoms. They further agree that education shall enable all persons to participate effectively in a free society, promote understanding, tolerance and friendship among all nations and all racial, ethnic or religious groups, and further the activities of the United Nations for the maintenance of peace."

20. "Global Teacher Prize 2016." The $1 million Global Teacher Prize, disbursed over ten years, comes with the stipulation that recipients continue teaching for five years. Al-Hroub has contributed a portion of her winnings for scholarships for Palestinian students and to support Palestinian schools in remote areas and schools facing threat of demolition.

21. Interview with Sabri Saidam, Ramallah, June 6, 2018.

22. Saidam earned his PhD from Imperial College, London, in 2000 and his bachelor's degree from Royal Holloway College, London.

23. Isabel Kershner, "Academic Study Weakens Israeli Claim That Palestinian School Texts Teach Hate," *New York Times*, Feb. 3, 2013, https://www.nytimes.com/2013/02/04/world/middleeast/study-belies -israeli-claim-of-hate-in-palestinian-texts.html. The *Times* reported that the Israeli Ministry of Education issued a statement dismissing the study as "biased, unprofessional and significantly lacking in objectivity"; however, fourteen of nineteen members of the scientific advisory panel of experts that oversaw the study issued a statement expressing support for its conclusions. The *Times* also reported that the study—which was originated by Dr. Bruce E. Wexler, professor emeritus of psychiatry at the Yale School of Medicine (Yale University), and led by Daniel Bar-Tal, an Israeli professor of research in child development and education at Tel Aviv University, and Sami Adwan, a Palestinian associate professor of education at Bethlehem University—also included textbooks used in independent ultra-Orthodox Jewish schools and a small number used in independent Islamic Trust schools; research data were "entered remotely into a database at Yale, similar to a blind study."

In a subsequent development, the *Times* reported that in 2013 Hamas, the Islamist Palestinian political party in control of the Gaza Strip, added to the Palestinian Authority curriculum in force there new textbooks for use in a "national education course of study" for fifty-five thousand children in grades 8 to 10, texts that "do not recognize modern Israel or even mention the Oslo Peace Accords." The *Times* report characterized the move as "a salvo in the war for influence between the rival Palestinian factions: Gaza-based Hamas and Fatah, which dominates the Palestinian Authority and the

West Bank." Fares Akram and Jodi Rudoren, "To Shape Young Palestinians, Hamas Creates Its Own Textbooks," *New York Times*, Nov. 3, 2013, https://www.nytimes.com/2013/11/04/world/middleeast/to-shape-young -palestinians-hamas-creates-its-own-textbooks.html.

24. Roger Avenstrup, "Palestinian Textbooks: Where Is All That 'Incitement'?," *New York Times*, Dec. 18, 2004, https://www.nytimes.com/2004 /12/18/opinion/palestinian-textbooks-where-is-all-that-incitement.html. Labeled as "Opinion," the piece identifies Avenstrup as "an international education consultant who has worked in various countries in conflict and post-conflict situations." Jordan controlled the West Bank (including its educational system) from 1948 to 1967; Egypt controlled the Gaza Strip (and its schools) during the same time period. Following the Oslo Accords, the Palestinian Authority, established in 1994, replaced textbooks formerly in use in these territories with those of its own issue.

25. Ibid. According to Avenstrup, analyses of Palestinian textbooks were undertaken in Jerusalem by the Israel/Palestine Center for Research and Information (commissioned by the U.S. Consulate General in Jerusalem) and in Germany by the Georg Eckert Institute for International Textbook Research, among others. "Time and again, independently of each other, researchers find no incitement to hatred in the Palestinian textbooks," Avenstrup noted in the *Times* essay. "On the political level, a U.S. Senate subcommittee on Palestinian education and the Political Committee of the European Parliament have both held hearings on the matter."

26. Harriet Sherwood, "Academic Claims Israeli School Textbooks Contain Bias," *Guardian* (UK), Aug. 6, 2011, https://www.theguardian.com /world/2011/aug/07/israeli-school-racism-claim. The report quotes professor Nurit Peled-Elhanan, author of *Palestine in Israeli School Books: Ideology and Propaganda in Education* (London: I. B. Tauris, 2012).

27. Palestinian Central Bureau of Statistics, "Press Release by Palestinian Central Bureau of Statistics (PCBS) on the Occasion of International Literacy Day, 08/09/2019," Sept. 8, 2019, http://pcbs.gov.ps/site/512/default .aspx?lang=en&ItemID=3543. The PCBS further reported that "for males, the rate fell from 7.8 percent in 1997 to 1.3 percent in 2018, while for females it fell from 20.3 to 4.3 percent over the same period," and that for 2018 the percentage distribution of illiterate persons age fifteen years and above by age group was as follows: ages 15–29, 11.9 percent; 30–44, 8.4 percent; 45–64, 22.9 percent; and 65 and above, 56.8 percent.

28. Palestinian Central Bureau of Statistics, "Percentage Distribution of Persons Aged (15 Years and Over) in Palestine by Educational Attainment, 2017–2018" (table), in *Palestine in Figures 2018* (Ramallah: Palestinian Central

Bureau of Statistics, 2019), 35, http://www.pcbs.gov.ps/Downloads/book 2421.pdf. The PCBS reported the full range (100 percent) of educational attainment for 2018 as follows: illiterate, 2.8 percent; can read and write, 5.2 percent; completion of elementary school, 12.8 percent; completion of preparatory (middle) school, 37.3 percent; completion of secondary school, 21.3 percent; intermediate diploma, 5.6 percent; bachelor's degree and above, 15 percent.

29. Palestinian Central Bureau of Statistics, "Higher Education Indicators in Palestine, 2014/2015–2017/2018" (table), in *Palestine in Figures 2018*, 33. The PCBS reported university graduates at 39,672 for 2014–15; 40,734 for 2015–16; and 43,978 for 2016–17; it reported community college graduates at 3,872 for 2014–15; 3,712 for 2015–16; and 3,390 for 2016–17.

30. Khalidi, *All That Remains*, 359–60. According to Khalidi, "'Aqir was the first village to fall to the Giv'ati Brigade when it implemented the part of Plan Dalet for which it was responsible." Plan Dalet, also known as "Plan D," was a military campaign conducted by Jewish Haganah forces designed to clear areas inhabited by Palestinian Arabs from early April through mid-May 1948, prior to the start of the Arab-Israeli war. After some three thousand villagers had fled and an initial withdrawal, Giv'ati units returned to occupy the village and expelled the remaining population. The Israeli Jewish town of Kiryat Eqron (first named Kfar Eqron) was established on village lands later in 1948; the moshav (cooperative agricultural community) Ganei Yohanan was built on village lands in 1950.

31. Palestinian Central Bureau of Statistics, "Basic and Secondary Education Indicators in Palestine, 2014/2015–2018/2019" (table), in *Palestine in Figures 2018*, 32. The PCBS further reported as follows: government schools, 2,203; UNRWA schools, 370; private schools, 425; male students, 620,597; female students, 632,641.

32. Palestinian Central Bureau of Statistics, "Higher Education Indicators in Palestine." The table also indicates that in 2017/2018 there were 82,877 male university students; female university students, 128,417; male community college students, 5,610; female community college students, 5,870.

33. Daoud Kuttab, "The Man behind the Future of Education in Palestine," Al-Monitor, Feb. 2, 2016, https://www.al-monitor.com/pulse/ru /originals/2016/02/palestinian-minister-reform-education-sector.html; Ahmad Melhem, "What's in Palestine's First Ever Education Law?," Al-Monitor, April 21, 2017, https://www.al-monitor.com/pulse/originals/2017 /04/palestine-education-ministry-law-schools.print.html.

34. Palestinian Central Bureau of Statistics, "On the Occasion of the International Youth Day, the Palestinian Central Bureau of Statistics (PCBS)

Issues a Press Release Demonstrating the Situation of the Youth in the Palestinian Society," Aug. 8, 2019, 3, http://www.pcbs.gov.ps/portals/_pcbs/Press Release/Press_En_International-Youth-Day-2019-en.pdf.

35. Ibid., 1.

36. Ibid., 1–2. The PCBS further reported that according to the 2015 Palestinian Youth Survey, 24 percent of youth ages eighteen to twenty-nine tried to establish their own businesses (3).

37. Sue Surkes, "Public Security Minister Nixes PA Education Minister's East Jerusalem Visit," *Times of Israel*, Feb. 26, 2018, https://www.times ofisrael.com/public-security-minister-nixes-pa-education-ministers-east -jerusalem-visit/.

38. Khaled Abu Toameh, "Palestinian Authority Steps Up Activities in East Jerusalem," *Jerusalem Post*, June 29, 2018, https://www.jpost.com/print article.aspx?id=561162. The *Post* reported that the 1994 Agreement on the Gaza Strip and the Jericho Area—Restriction on Activity, article 3(a), states that "the Palestinian Authority 'shall not open or operate a representative mission, and shall not hold a meeting, in the area of the State of Israel unless written permission for this has been given by the State of Israel or by someone authorized by it to do so.'"

39. Abu Toameh, "Palestinian Authority Steps Up"; Surkes, "Public Security Minister Nixes." Abu Toameh reported: "Trump's decision to recognize Jerusalem as Israel's capital and move the US Embassy to the city has prompted the Palestinians to resume their political activities in the city—a move that has forced the Israel Police to toughen its measures against the Palestinian activists." Surkes reported: "Erdan's office said that the planned visit was part of the 'continuing attempts by the PA to strengthen its status in Jerusalem and demonstrate its presence on the ground. These attempts have been made more often recently, and the Israel Police and Minister Erdan act time after time to prevent them.'"

40. Surkes, "Public Security Minister Nixes."

41. Palestinian Academic Society for the Study of International Affairs (PASSIA), *Education in Jerusalem 2016* (Jerusalem: Palestinian Academic Society for the Study of International Affairs, 2016), 3, http://passia.org /media/filer_public/9a/f5/9af5f866-9b3e-4a0d-8e9a-0f1461e40ff3/edu _final_en2019.pdf.

42. Ibid., 3–4.

43. "Joint Financing Arrangement—Phase II/Palestinian Territory Project Summary," Enabel Belgian Development Agency, n.d., https://open .enabel.be/en/PSE/2175/p/joint-financing-arrangement-phase-ii.html.

44. Interview with Reham Khalaf, Jenin, May 29, 2018.

CHAPTER 3. Beautiful Resistance

1. UNRWA, https://www.unrwa.org/.

2. The Bethlehem-based BADIL Resource Center for Palestinian Residency & Refugee Rights estimated the 2014 Aida population at 5,498 (*Survey of Palestinian Refugees and Internally Displaced Persons 2013–2015*, 8:40); in March 2015 UNRWA estimated the population at 5,500 out of a total 222,500 refugees living in nineteen West Bank camps ("Profile: Aida Camp Bethlehem Governorate," https://www.unrwa.org/sites/default/files/aida _refugee_camp.pdf). A 2017 population figure of 6,400 was cited in Rohini Haar and Jess Ghannam, *No Safe Space: Health Consequences of Tear Gas Exposure among Palestine Refugees* (Berkeley: Human Rights Center, University of California Berkeley School of Law, 2018), 2, https://www.law .berkeley.edu/wp-content/uploads/2017/12/NoSafeSpace_exec_summary 22Dec2017.pdf.

3. UN General Assembly, Resolution 194, Palestine—Progress Report of the United Nations Mediator, A/RES/194 (III) (Dec. 11, 1948), https:// www.refworld.org/docid/4fe2e5672.html. The full text of point 11 reads:

> 11. *Resolves* that the refugees wishing to return to their homes and live at peace with their neighbours should be permitted to do so at the earliest practicable date, and that compensation should be paid for the property of those choosing not to return and for loss of or damage to property which, under principles of international law or in equity, should be made good by the Governments or authorities responsible; Instructs the Conciliation Commission to facilitate the repatriation, resettlement and economic and social rehabilitation of the refugees and the payment of compensation, and to maintain close relations with the Director of the United Nations Relief for Palestine Refugees and, through him, with the appropriate organs and agencies of the United Nations.

4. UN General Assembly, Resolution 217A, Universal Declaration of Human Rights (Dec. 10, 1948), https://www.un.org/en/universal-declaration -human-rights/. Article 13 states: "(1) Everyone has the right to freedom of movement and residence within the borders of each State. (2) Everyone has the right to leave any country, including his own, and to return to his country."

5. Abdelfattah Abusrour narrative based on interviews at Alrowwad, Aida refugee camp, on Dec. 10 and 16, 2018.

6. Khalidi, *All That Remains*, 211–12. The population of Bayt Nattif was reported at 2,150 in 1944–45, with 20,149 of 20,837 cultivable dunams allocated to cereals.

7. According to Khalidi, the *History of the Haganah* (the Haganah was the Jewish army in Palestine preceding the establishment of Israel in May 1948) identifies Bayt Nattif as home to Arabs who attacked and killed thirty-five members of the Palmach, an elite Haganah unit, in January 1948; however, the *New York Times* reported that the unit was ambushed at the nearby village of Surif, and then other Haganah forces encircled three nearby villages including Bayt Nattif "in a 'punitive' attack which lasted over twenty-four hours" (212).

8. Morris, *Birth of the Palestinian Refugee Problem Revisited*, 468.

9. Khalidi, *All That Remains*, 211.

10. Morris, *Birth of the Palestinian Refugee Problem Revisited*, 466.

11. According to Khalidi, in 1944–45 Zakariyya had a population of 1,180, with 7,484 cultivable dunams; main crops included grain, beans, fruit, and olives (*All That Remains*, 224–25).

12. Morris, *Birth of the Palestinian Refugee Problem Revisited*, 521.

13. Aron Shai, "The Fate of Abandoned Arab Villages in Israel, 1965–69," *History & Memory* 18, no. 2 (Fall/Winter 2006): 87, 93. According to Shai, "The operation, which was deliberately planned and executed, unlike its predecessor in the aftermath of the 1948 war, lasted until the few weeks of political and military tension before the June 1967 Six-Day War, and was subsequently continued after the war, and even expanded to include the newly occupied territories."

14. Morris, *Birth of the Palestinian Refugee Problem Revisited*, 73.

15. Ibid., 74.

16. Ibid., 354.

17. Khalidi, *All That Remains*, 212.

18. Ibid., 226.

19. UNRWA, "Profile: Aida Camp." According to Abusrour, by 2018 the number of locales of origin of Aida refugees had increased to forty-three, reflecting continuing displacement of Palestinians since 1948.

20. Abusrour's theater credits include cowriting *Salut C'est Nous* and *Nourrir de Faim* in France and writing and directing *Waiting for the Rain*, *Tent*, *The Orphan*, *We Are the Children of the Camp*, *Blame the Wolf*, and *Handala*. His play *Far Away from a Village Close By* won first prize in the Deir Yassin Remembered Festival London in 2006. In 2014 he directed *The Diary of Anne Frank* at the Burning Coal Theatre in Raleigh, North Carolina, and Samah Sabawi's play *Tales of a City by the Sea* for Alrowwad Theatre. He served as president of the Palestinian Theatre League from 2009 to 2013. "Abdelfattah Abusrour" (bio), Broadway Play Publishing Inc., https://www.broadwayplaypub.com/play-authors/abdelfattah-abusrour/.

21. According to Abusrour, the Israeli separation barrier has partitioned off 14 percent of Palestinian land in the Bethlehem area, and 87 percent of the Bethlehem governorate is controlled by Israel to protect dozens of Israeli settlements and access roads for a settler population of one hundred thousand, with the remaining areas inhabited by two hundred thousand Palestinians under the control of the Palestinian Authority.

22. According to UNRWA, Aida camp covers 0.071 square kilometers; its population before 1967 was 1,977, and it has 5,500 registered persons and an estimated density of 77,464 per square kilometer ("Profile: Aida Camp"). Based on a higher population figure of 6,400, Haar and Ghannam (*No Safe Space*, 2) indicate a population density of 90,000 per square kilometer.

23. UNRWA, "Aida Camp," https://www.unrwa.org/where-we-work/west-bank/aida-camp.

24. UNWRA, "Profile: Aida Camp."

25. Haar and Ghannam, *No Safe Space*, 2. Further, the report indicated: "[Aida] respondents report also being exposed in the past several years to stun grenades (87%), skunk water (85%), pepper spray (54%) and report witnessing the use of rubber bullets (52%) and several also report being witness to live ammunition (6%); 55% of respondents describe between three and ten tear gas exposures in the past month (the month before the survey was carried out), both indoors and outdoors. Over the same period, 84.3% were exposed in the home, 9.4% at work, 10.7% in school, and 8.5% elsewhere."

26. Ibid., 24–25.

27. UN General Assembly, Resolution 3246, Importance of the Universal Realization of the Right of Peoples to Self Determination and of the Speedy Granting of Independence to Colonial Countries and Peoples for the Effective Guarantee and Observance of Human Rights, A/RES/3246 (XXIX) (Nov. 29, 1974), https://unispal.un.org/DPA/DPR/unispal.nsf/0/C867EE1DBF29A6E5852568C6006B2F0C. The resolution states (among other things): "3. *Reaffirms* the legitimacy of the peoples' struggle for liberation form [*sic*] colonial and foreign domination and alien subjugation by all available means, including armed struggle;" and "7. *Strongly condemns* all Governments which do not recognize the right to self-determination and independence of peoples under colonial and foreign domination and alien subjugation, notably the peoples of Africa and the Palestinian people."

See also UN General Assembly, Resolution 37/43, Importance of the Universal Realization of the Right of Peoples to Self-Determination and of the Speedy Granting of Independence to Colonial Countries and Peoples for the Effective Guarantee and Observance of Human Rights, A/RES/37/43 (Dec. 3, 1982), https://unispal.un.org/DPA/DPR/unispal.nsf/0/BAC85A78

081380FB852560D90050DC5F. The resolution states (among other things): "2. *Reaffirms* the legitimacy of the struggle of peoples for independence, territorial integrity, national unity and occupation by all available means, including armed struggle; 3. *Reaffirms* the inalienable right of the Namibian people, the Palestinian people and all peoples under foreign and colonial domination to self-determination, national independence, territorial integrity, national unity and sovereignty without outside interference."

28. See https://www.ashoka.org/en-EG/fellow/abdelfattah-abusrour; https://www.synergos.org/our-network/bio/abdelfattah-abusrour.

29. Shyrine Ziadeh, "Empower through Movement," TEDxMines Nancy, video, 16:03, June 13, 2017, https://www.youtube.com/watch?v=Fj rbXKpkz9A.

30. John Lancaster and Lee Hockstader, "Israel Lifts Siege of Arafat's Offices," *Washington Post*, May 2, 2002, https://www.washingtonpost.com /archive/politics/2002/05/02/israel-lifts-siege-of-arafats-offices/e5b13bcf -11e6-41d5-a89d-772f4891459a/.

31. Narrative based on telephone interviews with Shyrine Ziadeh speaking from Paris on April 18, 2019, and Ramallah on June 16, 2019. Details also taken from "Empower through Movement" and "Princess behind the Wall" videos (notes 29 and 33 in this chapter).

32. Agence France-Presse, France (AFP), "Palestinian Dancer Seeks Change through Ballet," *Prothom Alo* (Bangladesh), Nov. 20, 2014, https:/ /en.prothomalo.com/entertainment/news/56411/Palestinian-dancer-seeks -change-through-ballet.

33. "The Princess behind the Wall" (video), Ramallah Ballet Center Facebook page, posted May 13, 2014, https://www.facebook.com/Ramallah BalletCenterDanceSchool/videos/639773129430364/; https://www.facebook .com/RamallahBalletCenterDanceSchool/videos/639787729428904/.

34. See "West Bank Access Restrictions" (map), OCHA, September 2014, https://www.ochaopt.org/sites/default/files/Westbank_2014_Final.pdf; "The West Bank Settlements and Separation Barrier" (map), B'Tselem, The Israeli Information Center for Human Rights in the Occupied Territories, November 2014, https://www.btselem.org/download/201411_btselem_map _of_wb_eng.pdf.

35. The four universities are University of Clermont Auvergne, Clermont-Ferrand, France; Norwegian University of Science and Technology, Trondheim, Norway; University of Szeged, Szeged, Hungary; and University of Roehampton, London, UK. See Norwegian University of Science and Technology, "Choreomundus—International Master in Dance Knowledge, Practice, and Heritage," https://www.ntnu.edu/studies/choreomundus.

36. Stuart Hall, "Notes on Deconstructing 'The Popular,'" in *People's History and Socialist Theory*, ed. Raphael Samuel (London: Routledge & Kegan Paul, 1981), 239.

37. Raymond Williams, *Culture and Society, 1780–1950* (New York: Columbia University Press, 1958), 295.

38. Ibid., 338.

39. John Paul Lederach, *Preparing for Peace: Conflict Transformation across Cultures* (Syracuse, NY: Syracuse University Press, 1995), 9, cited in Christian Fuchs, "The Self-Organization of the Cultural Subsystem of Modern Society," contribution for the 12th Fuschl Conversations: New Agoras for the 21st Century, Austria, April 2004, 6.

40. Fuchs, "Self-Organization of the Cultural Subsystem," 36.

41. "What Is UNESCO?," United Nations Educational, Scientific and Cultural Organization (UNESCO), https://en.unesco.org/about-us /introducing-unesco.

42. Office of the United Nations Special Coordinator for the Middle East Peace Process, *Palestinian State-Building: A Decisive Period*, report on Ad Hoc Liaison Committee meeting, Brussels, April 13, 2011 (n.p.: United Nations, 2011), iii, 29, https://unispal.un.org/pdfs/AHLC-Apr2011_UNSCO rpt.pdf. With regard to Palestinian culture, the report stated "the PA has demonstrated institutional commitment to support the promotion and protection of the richness and diversity of Palestinian culture through effective planning, promotion of standards and legislation and ongoing efforts to manage the cultural resources in the oPt [occupied Palestinian territories]" (11), including strategies for tourism and heritage, updating the cultural heritage law in conformity with international standards, preparing to join UNESCO conventions, and development of best practices to plan and manage heritage sites (22–23).

43. Ethan Bronner, "Bid for State of Palestine Gets Support from I. M. F.," *New York Times*, April 6, 2011, https://www.nytimes.com/2011/04 /07/world/middleeast/07palestinians.html.

44. Ibid.

45. "How Unesco Countries Voted on Palestinian Membership," *Guardian* (UK), Nov. 1, 2011, https://www.theguardian.com/world/2011 /nov/01/unesco-countries-vote-palestinian-membership. The countries voting "no" were Australia, Canada, Czech Republic, Germany, Israel, Lithuania, the Netherlands, Palau, Panama, Samoa, Solomon Islands, Sweden, the United States, and Vanuatu.

46. Steven Erlanger and Scott Sayare, "Unesco Accepts Palestinians as Full Members," *New York Times*, Oct. 31, 2011, https://www.nytimes

.com/2011/11/01/world/middleeast/unesco-approves-full-membership-for -palestinians.html.

47. UN General Assembly, Resolution 67/19, Status of Palestine in the United Nations, A/67/L.28 (Nov. 29, 2012), https://www.securitycouncil report.org/atf/cf/%7B65BFCF9B-6D27-4E9C-8CD3-CF6E4FF96FF9%7D /a_res_67_19.pdf. Vote tally on the Internet Archive at https://web.archive .org/web/20140714201926/https://pbs.twimg.com/media/A851fHTCMAIW 8Xg.jpg:large.

48. Erlanger and Sayare, "Unesco Accepts Palestinians."

49. Ibid.

50. Steven Erlanger, "Cutoff of U.S. Money Leads Unesco to Slash Programs and Seek Emergency Aid," *New York Times*, Oct. 11, 2012, https:// www.nytimes.com/2012/10/12/world/cutoff-of-us-money-leads-unesco-to -slash-programs.html.

51. Erlanger and Sayare, "Unesco Accepts Palestinians."

52. Erlanger, "Cutoff of U.S. Money." Erlanger reported: "When Unesco did not receive the American money late last year, it immediately used its working capital fund of $31 million for the budget, froze all programs, canceled any program in the pipeline, ended some programs, froze hiring, initiated a voluntary retirement plan, changed its travel rules, reduced translations, renegotiated contracts and limited the use of outside consultants."

53. Ruth Eglash, "Israel Suspends Cooperation with U.N. Cultural Agency over Jerusalem Resolution," *Washington Post*, Oct. 14, 2016, https:// www.washingtonpost.com/world/middle_east/israel-suspends-cooperation -with-un-cultural-agency-over-jerusalem-resolution/2016/10/14/5f85cbb4 -922f-11e6-9c85-ac42097b8cc0_story.html.

54. Ibid.

55. Peter Beaumont, "Unesco Adopts Controversial Resolution on Jerusalem Holy Sites," *Guardian* (UK), Oct. 26, 2016, https://www.the guardian.com/world/2016/oct/26/unesco-adopts-controversial-resolution -on-jerusalem-holy-sites-israel.

56. Isabel Kershner, "Unesco Declares Hebron's Core as Palestinian World Heritage Site," *New York Times*, July 7, 2017, https://www.nytimes .com/2017/07/07/world/middleeast/unesco-hebron-world-heritage-site -israel-palestinians.html.

57. Gardiner Harris and Steven Erlanger, "U.S. Will Withdraw from Unesco, Citing Its 'Anti-Israel Bias,'" *New York Times*, Oct. 12, 2017, https://www.nytimes.com/2017/10/12/us/politics/trump-unesco-withdrawal .html.

58. Ibid.

59. Thomas Adamson, "US, Israel Exit UN Cultural Agency, Claiming Bias," Associated Press, Jan. 1, 2019, https://www.apnews.com/abfcb84 a48f14f41ab1ce6b7045e6794. Claiming UNESCO budgetary mismanagement and biases against Israel and in favor of the Soviet Union, the U.S. had withdrawn from the agency in 1984 under the Reagan administration, rejoining in 2002 under the administration of George W. Bush, according to Colum Lynch, "U.S. to Pull Out of UNESCO, Again," *Foreign Policy*, Oct. 11, 2017, https://foreignpolicy.com/2017/10/11/u-s-to-pull-out-of-unesco-again/.

60. Permanent Observer Mission of the State of Palestine to the United Nations New York, "Diplomatic Relations," https://palestineun.org/about -palestine/diplomatic-relations/.

61. Interview with Madees Khoury, Taybeh, West Bank, June 5, 2018.

62. Lizzie Porter, "How a Palestinian Brewery Is Taking on the US," *Al Jazeera*, May 27, 2017, https://www.aljazeera.com/indepth/features/2017 /04/palestinian-brewery-170426081708026.html; Dov Lieber and Luke Tress, "Straight outta Taybeh: Beer, Good Times Flow at Palestinian Oktoberfest," *Times of Israel*, Sept. 27, 2016, https://www.timesofisrael.com/straight-outta -taybeh-beer-good-times-flow-at-palestinian-oktoberfest/. Nadim Khoury told the *Times*: "Making business in Palestine, especially beer business, is not like anywhere in the world. We have no borders, no airport, no ports. Religion, culture, education, advertisement, there are so many obstacles. But we are determined to produce good quality beer and show the whole world Palestinians are normal and love to enjoy life."

63. Fanack, "Water Resources," updated April 13, 2017, https://water .fanack.com/palestine/water-resources/. According to Fanack, a Netherlands-based, independent online media organization that publishes data and analysis on countries of the Middle East and North Africa, Palestinians in the West Bank do not have access to the Jordan River, and so they must rely on the Mountain Aquifer. The aquifer lies under both the West Bank and Israel, is "fed mainly by rainwater falling over the mountains of the West Bank," and is controlled by Israel.

Fanack reports that the aquifer contributes about 25 percent of Israel's total water budget and that "Israel extracts about 80 percent of the Mountain Aquifer's potential yield and restricts Palestinians to only about 20 percent of its estimated potential. Furthermore, Israel reportedly withdraws water from the Mountain Aquifer up to 50 percent beyond its sustainable yield to provide water for its citizens [in Israel proper] and settlers in the West Bank."

64. Based on annual growth rates at the time, the Palestinian population in the West Bank was projected to reach 933,577 by the end of 1990, according to UNCTAD, *Population and Demographic Developments in the West*

Bank and Gaza Strip until 1990, UNCTAD/ECDC/SEU/1, June 28, 1994, 22, paragraph 47, https://unctad.org/en/docs/poecdcseud1.en.pdf. The census taken by the Palestinian Central Bureau of Statistics from 2015 to 2017 indicated that the West Bank Palestinian population had reached 2.88 million by the end of 2017, according to Khaled Abu Toameh, "Palestinian Census: 4.7 Million in West Bank and Gaza Strip," *Times of Israel*, March 28, 2018, https://www.timesofisrael.com/palestinian-census-4-7-million-in-west-bank-and-gaza-strip/.

65. Fanack, "Water Resources": "Palestine's share of the Mountain Aquifer's resources has declined over the last 10 to 15 years because of Israeli over-extraction, reduced natural recharge and restrictions on well drilling. In 1999, for example, overall Palestinian water extraction from the Mountain Aquifer was 138 MCM [million cubic meters], dropping to 113 MCM in 2007 and 87 MCM in 2011, which is less than the 118 MCM/yr that was allocated to Palestinians in the 1996 [*sic*; 1995] Oslo agreement."

66. The 2017 Palestinian census found that 97.9 percent of Palestinians in the West Bank and Gaza Strip were Muslims, with the overall Christian population in both territories estimated at less than 1 percent. A Palestinian Central Bureau of Statistics official indicated that Christians were one-third of the Palestinian population in 1948; emigration has accounted for the decline since, according to Abu Toameh, "Palestinian Census." In 2012 the Institute for Middle East Understanding, citing "a lack of official figures on the number of Palestinian Christians in the occupied territories," estimated that at roughly fifty thousand, Christians accounted for approximately 2 percent of the West Bank population; and at three thousand, less than 1 percent of Gaza's population. "Palestinian Christians in the Holy Land," Dec. 17, 2012, https://imeu.org/article/palestinian-christians-in-the-holy-land.

67. Lieber and Tress, "Straight outta Taybeh." The report identified the source as a "Jewish-American Israeli from Jerusalem, who asked to remain anonymous for work-related reasons."

CHAPTER 4. Day by Day in Jerusalem

1. Also known variously as the Flower or Flowers Gate.

2. Interviews with Imad Khatib, Jerusalem, Dec. 9 and 14, 2018.

3. UNCTAD, *The Palestinian Economy in East Jerusalem: Enduring Annexation, Isolation and Disintegration* (Geneva: UNCTAD, 2013), 5, https://unctad.org/en/PublicationsLibrary/gdsapp2012d1_en.pdf; "East Jerusalem 2018" (map), Peace Now, http://peacenow.org.il/wp-content/uploads/2018/07/Peace-Now-Map-2018-East-Jerusalem-ENG.pdf.

4. "Jerusalem Municipal Data Reveals Stark Israeli-Palestinian Discrepancy in Construction Permits in Jerusalem," Peace Now, Sept. 12, 2019, https://peacenow.org.il/en/jerusalem-municipal-data-reveals-stark-israeli-palestinian-discrepancy-in-construction-permits-in-jerusalem. By the end of 2017, the total Jewish population of Jerusalem was 559,571 (62 percent, including 215,067 living in east Jerusalem and 344,504 living in west Jerusalem), and the Palestinian population (all living in east Jerusalem) was 341,729 (38 percent).

East Jerusalem, which is under Israeli control, constitutes what the Palestinian Authority designates as the "Area J1" subdistrict of the Jerusalem governorate (one of eleven governorates in the West Bank and five governorates in the Gaza Strip under Palestinian control). "Area J2" comprises the rest of the Jerusalem governorate, which is under Palestinian control, including approximately twenty-five villages and neighborhoods, the Qalandia refugee camp, and Bedouin communities. According to the 2017 Palestinian census, the entire Jerusalem governorate (including east Jerusalem) had a population of 435,753, constituting 9.1 percent of the total population of Palestine and 15.1 percent of the Palestinian population in the West Bank. Palestinian Central Bureau of Statistics, "Jerusalem Statistical Yearbook 2018 Summary," *Jerusalem Quarterly* 76 (Winter 2018): 88–89.

5. Ir Amim, *Destructive Unilateral Measures to Redraw the Borders of Jerusalem* (Jerusalem: Ir Amim, 2018), 5, http://www.ir-amim.org.il/sites/default/files/Destructive%20Unilateral%20Measures%20to%20Redraw%20the%20Borders%20of%20Jerusalem.5.7.pdf.msg_.pdf; Jonathan Blake, Elizabeth M. Bartels, Shira Efron, and Yitzhak Reiter, *What Might Happen If Palestinians Start Voting in Jerusalem Municipal Elections?* (Santa Monica, CA: RAND Corporation, 2018), 10, https://www.rand.org/content/dam/rand/pubs/research_reports/RR2700/RR2743/RAND_RR2743.pdf.

6. Michal Korach and Maya Choshen, *Jerusalem Facts and Trends* (Jerusalem: Jerusalem Institute for Policy Research, 2019), 58, https://jerusaleminstitute.org.il/wp-content/uploads/2019/05/PUB_505_facts-and-trends_eng_2019_web.pdf. The 45 percent poverty rate for Jerusalem (25 percent for Jews and 78 percent for Arabs) in 2017 was significantly higher than "the rates in Israel at large and in its other major cities (4 percent–23 percent)."

7. Ir Amim, *Jerusalem Municipality Budget Analysis for 2013: Share of Investment in East Jerusalem* (Jerusalem: Ir Amim, 2014), 2, http://www.ir-amim.org.il/sites/default/files/PL_Investment%20in%20East%20Jerusalem%20December%202014-2%2025%2015%20%281%29.pdf. The 10.1 percent figure includes staffing costs; when these costs were removed, the figure rose to 13.6 percent. The report also noted that the share of funding for east Jeru-

salem was below 5 percent in the following municipal departments: culture, 3.4 percent; sports, 0.6 percent; welfare, 4.2 percent; business promotion, 1.5 percent; and youth promotion, 2.5 percent.

8. Ir Amim, *Fifty Years of Neglect: East Jerusalem Education Report* (Jerusalem: Ir Amim, 2017), 6, http://www.ir-amim.org.il/sites/default/files /Education_Report_2017-Fifty_Years_of_Neglect.pdf.

9. Association for Civil Rights in Israel, *East Jerusalem: Facts and Figures 2017* (Tel Aviv: Association for Civil Rights in Israel, 2017), 2, https:// law.acri.org.il/en/2017/05/24/east-jerusalem-facts-and-figures-2017/.

10. Korach and Choshen, *Jerusalem Facts and Trends*, 15. In 1967 the Arab population of Jerusalem was approximately 69,000, 26 percent of the total 266,300; in 2017 it was approximately 342,500, 38 percent of the 901,300 total—an increase of 396 percent. In 1967 the Jewish population of Jerusalem was approximately 197,000, 74 percent of the total 266,300; in 2017 it was approximately 558,800, 62 percent of the 901,300 total—an increase of 183 percent.

11. "East Jerusalem 2019," Peace Now, http://peacenow.org.il/wp -content/uploads/2019/08/settlements_map_eng-2019.pdf.

12. Nir Hasson, "Panel Rejects Protocol Allowing Palestinian Construction in East Jerusalem," *Haaretz*, March 3, 2019, https://www.haaretz .com/israel-news/.premium-jerusalem-rejects-procedure-allowing-palestinian -construction-in-east-jerusalem-1.6982181.

13. Nir Hasson, "Only 7% of Jerusalem Building Permits go to Palestinian Neighborhoods," *Haaretz*, Dec. 7, 2015, https://www.haaretz.com /israel-news/.premium-only-7-of-jlem-building-permits-go-to-palestinian -neighborhoods-1.5432437.

14. "Jerusalem Municipal Data." The data analysis showed that the Jerusalem municipality approved a total of 57,737 construction permits from 1991 to 2018: 21,834 (37.8 percent) for Israeli (Jewish) neighborhoods in east Jerusalem; 26,367 (45.7 percent) for Israeli neighborhoods in west Jerusalem; and 9,536 (16.5 percent) for Palestinian (Arab) neighborhoods in east Jerusalem.

15. Joseph Krauss and Mohammed Daraghmeh, "New Data Shows Israeli Settlement Surge in East Jerusalem," Associated Press, Sept. 12, 2019, https://apnews.com/98e4ad57e0784e05b9fdde2e0ffd7439.

16. "Jerusalem Municipal Data." The data analysis also showed that in 2017–18 the city issued 1,233 permits for construction in Palestinian neighborhoods in east Jerusalem, up 25.8 percent from the 980 such permits issued in 2015–16.

17. Ibid.

18. Association for Civil Rights in Israel, *East Jerusalem*, 4.

19. "Statistics on Demolition of Houses Built without Permits in East Jerusalem," B'Tselem, The Israeli Information Center for Human Rights in the Occupied Territories, Nov. 14, 2019, https://www.btselem.org/planning _and_building/east_jerusalem_statistics.

20. Lee and Klapper, "Trump Declares Jerusalem Israeli Capital."

21. Reuters, "Trump Cuts $25 Million in Aid for Palestinians."

22. Lee, "U.S. Cuts Aid to Palestinians." The report stated that the aid cut "comes as President Donald Trump and his Middle East pointmen, Jared Kushner and Jason Greenblatt, staff up their office to prepare for the rollout of a much-vaunted but as yet unclear peace plan for Israel and the Palestinians."

23. Sleiman Jad, "In Jerusalem's Cramped Old City, Christians Feel the Squeeze," Reuters, June 21, 2016, https://www.reuters.com/article/us-israel -palestinians-oldcity-idUSKCN0Z71DD. In 2010 the population of the Old City was estimated at 40,607, with 31,182 residents in the Muslim Quarter, 4,707 in the Christian Quarter, 3,105 in the Jewish Quarter, and 1,613 in the Armenian Quarter, according to United Nations Conference on Trade and Development, "Palestinian Economy," 52.

24. Nir Hasson, "All the Ways East Jerusalem Palestinians Get Rejected in Bid to Become Israelis," *Haaretz*, Jan. 15, 2019, https://www.haaretz.com /israel-news/.premium-east-jerusalem-palestinians-face-uphill-battle-in-bid -for-israeli-citizenship-1.6844543.

25. "Statistics on Revocation of Residency in East Jerusalem," B'Tselem, The Israeli Information Center for Human Rights in the Occupied Territories, updated May 23, 2019, https://www.btselem.org/jerusalem/revocation _statistics. Residency permits of 14,481 Palestinian Jerusalemites were revoked from 1967 to 2014, with only four months' data available for 2001 and no data available for 2002. Of 10,973 permits revoked from 1997 to 2011, the Ministry of the Interior indicated 10,376 were for relocation abroad and 597 for relocation to the occupied territories. According to UNCTAD ("Palestinian Economy," 6), from 1967 to 1994, more than 140,000 Palestinians, including approximately 14,000 from east Jerusalem, were estimated to have lost their residency rights due to extended physical absence.

26. Tamara Tawfiq Tamimi, "Revocation of Residency of Palestinians in Jerusalem: Prospects for Accountability," *Jerusalem Quarterly* 72 (Winter 2017): 40–41.

27. Hasson, "All the Ways." The report notes: "Simply getting an appointment to present the necessary documents has taken three years."

28. Imad 'Afif Al-Khatib and Aziz Mahmoud Al-'Assa, *Maqdisiyyūn Sana'ū Tarīkhan* [Jerusalemites making history] (Al-Bireh, Palestine: Palestinian Authority Ministry of Culture, 2018).

29. "Kalimat Literature Festival in Ramallah," video, 47:05–57:18, Nov. 5, 2018, https://www.youtube.com/watch?v=XlnYy8M_8P4.

30. Abulhawa was detained at Ben-Gurion Airport on Nov. 1, 2018, and deported on Nov. 2 for reportedly not having coordinated her arrival in advance, a condition that Israeli authorities imposed on her following an incident in 2015, when she was denied entry to Israel from Jordan at a land border crossing, according to AFP (Agence France-Presse, France), "Palestinian-American Woman Detained at Airport, to Be Deported," *Times of Israel*, Nov. 2, 2018, https://www.timesofisrael.com/palestinian-american-woman -detained-at-airport-to-be-deported/.

31. "Kalimat Literature Festival," 57:42–59:36.

32. Interview with Mahmoud Muna, Jerusalem, Dec. 11, 2018.

33. Mahmoud Muna, "Not for Entertainment: Jerusalem, the Eternal Cultural Capital of the Arab World," *Perspectives: Political Analysis and Commentary* 12 (August 2017): 46 (published by the Heinrich Böll Foundation [Stiftung], Middle East & North Africa).

34. Kalimat: The Palestinian Literature Festival was held Nov. 3–7, 2018. Muna estimates that the public evening events and university workshops drew a total of six hundred to seven hundred attendees. Funded by The British Council/Occupied Palestinian Territories (https://www.british council.ps/en) and Friedrich-Ebert-Stiftung Ost-Jerusalem (https://www.fes -palestine.org/), the festival was organized by the Educational Bookshop (https://www.educationalbookshop.com/) and the Kenyon Institute, Council for British Research in the Levant (http://cbrl.ac.uk/kenyon-institute), with additional support from Institut Français de Jérusalem—Chateaubriand; the Goethe-Institut Ramallah; and Al-Qattan Foundation. Palestinian writers attending were Raja Shehadeh, Suad Amiry, Nur Masalha, Nasab Hussein, Maya Abu Al-Hayat, Salim Tamari, Susan Abulhawa (remote), Ala Hlehel, Fida Jiryis, and Asmaa Azaizeh; international writers attending were Sylwia Chutnik (Poland), Marcello Di Cintio (Canada), Gavin Francis (UK), and Cathy Otten (UK); bios at http://palestine.mei.columbia.edu/news-1/kalimat -the-palestinian-literature-festival.

35. The term "Palestinian territories" was in vogue at that time; in November 2012, the United Nations General Assembly recognized Palestine as a nonmember observer state.

36. Muna, "Not for Entertainment," 48.

37. Ibid.

38. Walid Salem, "The East Jerusalem Municipality: Palestinian Policy Options and Proposed Alternatives," *Jerusalem Quarterly* 74 (Summer 2018): 120.

39. Blake et al., *What Might Happen*, 11–12.

40. Ir Amim, *Jerusalem Municipality Budget Analysis*, 2.

41. Amjad Samhan, "Jerusalem: Arab Cultural Capital of 2009?," *Jerusalem Quarterly* 34 (Spring 2008): 7; Varsen Aghabekian, "Under Occupation: Celebrations and Contradictions of al-Quds Capital of Arab Culture 2009," *Jerusalem Quarterly* 38 (Summer 2009): 81.

42. Muna, "Not for Entertainment," 48–49.

43. Samhan, "Jerusalem: Arab Cultural Capital," 5–6.

44. Ibid., 7–10.

45. Aghabekian, "Under Occupation," 79.

46. Samhan, "Jerusalem: Arab Cultural Capital," 11.

47. Varsen Aghabekian as told to Andrea D'Cruz, "Time for Jerusalem's Arab Culture," *Guardian* (UK), April 10, 2009, https://www.theguardian.com/world/2009/apr/10/israel-palestinian-territories.

48. Etgar Lefkovits, "Police Break Up 8 PA Events in E. J'lem," *Jerusalem Post*, March 21, 2009, https://www.jpost.com/printarticle.aspx?id=136639.

49. Ivan Karakashian, "Israeli Police Shut Jerusalem Book Fest, Again," Reuters, May 28, 2009, https://www.reuters.com/article/us-palestinians-israel-arts-jerusalem-sb/israeli-police-shut-jerusalem-book-fest-again-idUSTRE54R6VN20090528.

50. Aghabekian, "Under Occupation," 81.

51. Edward W. Said, *Culture and Imperialism* (New York: Knopf, 1993), xiii.

52. Nadia Harhash narrative is based on an interview with her in Jerusalem on Dec. 15, 2018, and on her book *In the Shadows of Men*, citations from which appear in italics (original Arabic: *Fi Dhilāl al-Rijāl* [Cairo: Ibn Rushd, 2016]; English translation, Ramallah: Dar al-Ru'at, 2020).

53. Juzoor for Health and Social Development, "Empowering Jerusalem's Most Marginalized Palestinian Women," *Jerusalem Quarterly* 74 (Summer 2018): 137–43. The study reported on 953 women aged eighteen to sixty-eight, half of whom finished high school and a third of whom had married before age eighteen. (See also Juzoor for Health and Social Development, "Women Empowerment [*sic*] in Marginalized East Jerusalem Communities" [graphic], *Jerusalem Quarterly* 73 [Spring 2018]: 143.)

54. Juzoor for Health and Social Development, "Empowering Jerusalem's Most Marginalized," 139. The report characterized "Israeli-sponsored military and settler violence" as significant: "While incidents of women's family members being detained, arrested, and injured by Israeli military were widespread, fully half of women [study] participants also had their homes seized, demolished or under threat of demolition by the Israeli government."

55. Ibid., 138.

56. Ibid., 138–39.

57. Nadia Harhash, "Debating Gender: A Study of Medieval and Contemporary Islam" (master's thesis, Freie Universität Berlin, 2015, English); "The Growth and Development of the Palestinian Women's Movement in Jerusalem during the British Mandate" (master's thesis, Al-Quds University, published in Arabic, Ramallah: Dar al-Ru'at, 2016).

58. Nadia Harhash, "Essere una madre single a Gerusalemme: E preoccuparsi, ogni mattina, per i miei figli," Huffington Post Italian edition, Oct. 22, 2015; English translation: "Being a single mother in Jerusalem. And worry, every morning, for my children," https://translate.google.com/translate?hl=en&sl=it&u=https://www.huffingtonpost.it/nadia-harhash/essere-una-madre-single-a-gerusalemme_b_8357760.html&prev=search.

59. nadiaharhash.com (blog posts in English and Arabic).

60. Nadia Harhash, "سهى جبارة.. الحرية المفقودة والقمع الذكوري في هيئة أجهزة الأمن" (Arabic; approximate translation: "Suha Jbara: The embodiment of lost freedom and patriarchal oppression at the hands of the security apparatuses"), Wattan (Palestine), Dec. 9, 2018, https://www.wattan.net/ar/news/270817.html.

61. Amnesty International, "Palestine: Social Justice Activist Tortured and Punished for Going on Hunger Strike," news release, Dec. 5, 2018, https://www.amnesty.org/en/latest/news/2018/12/palestine-social-justice-activist-tortured-and-punished-for-going-on-hunger-strike; Amnesty International, "Social Justice Activist on Hunger Strike," Urgent Action 203/18, Nov. 29, 2018, https://www.amnesty.org/download/Documents/MDE1594782018ENGLISH.pdf.

62. Nadia Harhash, 'Ala Darb Maryam [On the path of Maryam] (Ramallah: Dar al-Ru'at, 2019).

CHAPTER 5. In Gaza, They Are Not Numbers

1. Areej Al-Madhoun's narrative is based on four extended voice interviews conducted via WhatsApp on April 12, 19, and 26 and May 24, 2019. Details also taken from "IMA International Competition 2012—Highlight Version," Intelligent Mental-Arithmetic Competition, Malaysia, Dec. 16, 2012, video, 5:22, posted Jan. 2, 2013, https://www.youtube.com/watch?v=yH_mvGs7bS4.

2. Hamas (the acronym for Harakat al-Muqāwamah al-'Islāmiyyah, or Islamic Resistance Movement) came to power in the Gaza Strip in 2007. The 2012 Gaza war between Israel and Hamas occurred Nov. 14–21.

3. Rafeef Ziadah, "We Teach Life, Sir." See, among other sources, https://www.tandfonline.com/doi/abs/10.1080/02690055.2012.718879?journal Code=rwas20.

4. Yael Stein, *Human Rights Violations during Operation Pillar of Defense, 14–21 November 2012*, trans. Deb Reich, ed. Shuli Schneiderman (Jerusalem: B'Tselem, The Israeli Information Center for Human Rights in the Occupied Territories, 2013), 9, https://www.btselem.org/download /201305_pillar_of_defense_operation_eng.pdf. The report states: "According to B'Tselem's investigation, 167 Palestinians were killed by the Israeli military during Operation Pillar of Defense, including at least 87 who did not take part in the hostilities, 32 of whom were minors." The report further states that during the war four Israeli civilians were killed by rockets fired into Israel by militants in Gaza, and two Israeli soldiers were killed by mortar shells (28).

5. "Gaza Strip Schools and Universities," OCHA, December 2018, https://www.ochaopt.org/content/gaza-strip-schools-and-universities -december-2018.

6. In interviews for *Stories from Palestine*, Areej Al-Madhoun and her father, Mahmoud Al-Madhoun, refer to the town colloquially as "Asqalan"; historians tend to refer to it as "al-Majdal" or "Majdal."

7. Morris, *Birth of the Palestinian Refugee Problem Revisited*, 528. According to Morris, "The last major problem in the south was the Arab concentration in al-Majdal (Ashkelon), whose pre-war population had been around 10,000. Almost all had fled their homes in October–November 1948."

8. According to Morris, in an operation to dislodge Egyptian forces, the Israeli army overran much of the southern coastal strip, including al-Majdal, in Operation Yoav, Oct. 15–Nov. 9, 1948, breaking the second truce that had been in place between Israel and forces of the surrounding Arab countries since July 19. Palestinian inhabitants of the region, including al-Majdal, "fled or were expelled, mainly to the Gaza Strip" (ibid., 462).

According to Fawaz Gerges, "In mid-October, Israel broke the truce and singled out the Egyptian forces for an all-out offensive in the south. Israeli forces neutralized the small Egyptian air force and encircled land units in several theatres. This round of fighting witnessed an intensification of Israel's air raids on Egyptian positions." Fawaz A. Gerges, "Egypt and the 1948 War: Internal Conflict and Regional Ambition," in *The War for Palestine: Rewriting the History of 1948*, ed. Eugene L. Rogan and Avi Shlaim (Cambridge: Cambridge University Press, 2001), 164–65.

According to Morris, al-Majdal and other southern locales came under Israeli "bombing and strafing attacks" on Oct. 15–16 (*Birth of the Palestinian*

Refugee Problem Revisited, 465). These operations had caused "despair among the local inhabitants"; and "flight from the coastal towns increased following the Israeli navy shelling of Gaza (17 October) and Majdal (21 October). . . . Majdal was bombed twice on the night of 19/20 October" (ibid., 471).

According to Morris, Israeli forces overran al-Majdal, with much of the population having "evacuated after the start of Operation Yoav, under the impact of the aerial and naval bombardment." The Egyptian brigade headquarters had left for Gaza on Oct. 19, part of the town garrison left on Oct. 30, and the last Egyptian troops left on Nov. 4. On Dec. 1 the Israeli Southern Front command expelled five hundred Palestinian refugees (presumably residents from the surrounding area who had sheltered in al-Majdal) from al-Majdal to the Gaza Strip (ibid., 472).

According to Morris, by late 1949, the number of "infiltrating returnees" and other Arab refugees in al-Majdal "had swelled to 2,600. The Arab inhabitants were placed under military government, concentrated and sealed off with barbed wire and IDF [Israel Defense Forces] guards in a small, built-up area commonly known as the 'ghetto.' In December 1948, the authorities approved the settlement in the town of 3,000 Jews; hundreds of families moved in during 1949" (ibid., 528).

According to Morris, by means of "subtle and not-so-subtle pressure" including "oppressive restrictions of movement and employment and a readiness to exchange Israeli pounds for Palestine pounds . . . at favourable rates," Israel succeeded in removing all Arab inhabitants from the town by October 1950. "At last, [head of the Southern Command Maj. Gen. Moshe] Dayan and [al-Majdal military governor Maj. Yehoshu'a] Varbin had achieved an Arab-free Majdal (or Ashkelon, as it was to be renamed). . . . Majdal was the last big post-1948 transfer operation" (ibid., 529).

According to Ilan Pappé, "The two southern coastal towns of Isdud and Majdal were taken [by Israel] in November 1948 and their populations were expelled to the Gaza Strip. Several thousands of people who had remained in Majdal were expelled in December 1949, shocking some left-wing Israelis as this was done during a 'time of peace.'" Ilan Pappé, *The Ethnic Cleansing of Palestine* (Oxford: Oneworld Publications, 2006), 194.

9. Email interview with Areej's father, Mahmoud Al-Madhoun, May 24, 2019.

10. "Jabalia Camp," United Nations Relief and Works Agency for Palestine Refugees in the Near East, https://www.unrwa.org/where-we-work/gaza-strip/jabalia-camp.

11. "Where We Work/Gaza Strip," UNRWA, https://www.unrwa.org/where-we-work/gaza-strip.

12. "Update on UNRWA Operations in Gaza," UNRWA, April 2019, https://www.unrwa.org/sites/default/files/content/resources/update_on _unrwa_operations_in_gaza_-_april_2019_eng.pdf. Refugees receive primary education (grades 1–9) in UNRWA schools and attend government-run high schools. During the 2018–19 academic year, UNRWA operated 274 elementary and preparatory schools in the Gaza Strip, with 84 schools operating on single shifts, 177 on double shifts, and 13 on triple shifts and serving approximately 279,000 pupils, an increase of about 7,000 over the previous school year.

13. "Jabalia Camp." By 2019 Jabalia's 113,990 residents were being supported by UNRWA with one food distribution center, three health clinics, two relief and social services offices, twenty-five schools housed in sixteen school buildings, one public library, seven water wells, and one maintenance and sanitation office.

14. "Where We Work/Gaza Strip," citing unemployment statistics and characterization from the World Bank.

15. In an April 2019 interview, Areej Al-Madhoun stated that the cost of one kilowatt hour of electricity from Gaza's main power grid was 0.5 shekel, or approximately 14.3 cents USD; the cost of one kilowatt hour of electricity powered by generators was 3.5 to 4.5 shekels, or about 97 cents to $1.25 USD.

16. Due to the difficulty of traveling to the Gaza Strip, the author conducted interviews with Areej Al-Madhoun and two other sources in Gaza via WhatsApp.

17. "Gaza Strip/The Humanitarian Impact of Major Escalation of Hostilities," OCHA, Dec. 21, 2017, https://www.ochaopt.org/content/gaza-strip -humanitarian-impact-major-escalation-hostilities.

18. Raphael S. Cohen, David E. Johnson, David E. Thaler, Brenna Allen, Elizabeth M. Bartels, James Cahill, and Shira Efron, *Lessons from Israel's Wars in Gaza* (Santa Monica, CA: RAND Corporation, 2017), 2, https:// www.rand.org/pubs/research_briefs/RB9975.html, based on Cohen et al., *From Cast Lead to Protective Edge: Lessons from Israel's Wars in Gaza* (Santa Monica, CA: RAND Arroyo Center, 2017), https://www.rand.org/pubs /research_reports/RR1888.html.

19. *World Report 2020: Events of 2019* (n.p.: Human Rights Watch, 2020), 302–5, hrw.org/sites/default/files/world_report_download/hrw_world _report_2020_0.pdf. The report stated: "Israeli forces stationed on the Israeli side of fences separating Gaza and Israel continued to fire live ammunition at demonstrators inside Gaza who posed no imminent threat to life, pursuant to open-fire orders from senior officials that contravene international human rights standards." By mid-November 2019, HRW reported (citing OCHA)

that lethal force used by the Israeli military had resulted in the killing of 71 and injuring of 11,453 Palestinians in Gaza and reported (citing the Meir Amit Intelligence and Terrorism Information Center) that Palestinian armed groups in Gaza had fired 1,378 rockets at Israel, killing 4 Israeli civilians and injuring more than 123.

20. "Gaza Strip," OCHA, https://www.ochaopt.org/location/gaza-strip.

21. "Access Restricted Areas (ARA) in the Gaza Strip," OCHA, July 2013, https://reliefweb.int/sites/reliefweb.int/files/resources/ocha_opt_gaza _ara_factsheet_july_2013_english.pdf. According to OCHA, in 2013 the ARA included "up to 35 percent of Gaza's agricultural land and as much as 85 percent of its fishing waters having been affected at various points; access to farming land within 300 meters of the perimeter fence separating Gaza from Israel being largely prohibited, while presence for several hundred meters beyond this distance is risky; and fishermen being allowed to access less than one-third of the fishing areas allocated under the Oslo Accords (6 out of 20 nautical miles from the coast)."

22. United Nations General Assembly Human Rights Council, *Human Rights Situation in the Occupied Palestinian Territory, Including East Jerusalem: Report by the Secretary-General*, A/HRC/24/30 (Aug. 22, 2013), 8, https://unispal.un.org/DPA/DPR/unispal.nsf/5ba47a5c6cef541b802563e000 493b8c/fca448af7fc6c9c085257be10051a1d3?OpenDocument.

23. Ibid.

24. Ibid., 18.

25. "Key Figures on the 2014 Hostilities," OCHA, June 23, 2015, https://www.ochaopt.org/content/key-figures-2014-hostilities (excerpted from United Nations General Assembly Human Rights Council, *Report of Detailed Findings of the Independent Commission of Inquiry Established Pursuant to Human Rights Council Resolution S-21/1*, A/HRC/29/52 (June 24, 2015).

26. Ibid. Compared with the UN's 2,251-Palestinian-death figure including 1,462 (or 65 percent) civilians, in May 2015 the Israeli government asserted that of approximately 2,125 Palestinians killed, at least 936 (44 percent of the total) had been "positively identified" by the Israeli military as having been affiliated with Hamas and other armed organizations, 36 percent identified as civilians, and 20 percent yet to be identified as civilians or combatants. Israel Ministry of Foreign Affairs, *The 2014 Gaza Conflict, 7 July–26 August 2014: Factual and Legal Aspects*, May 2015, 55–56, https://mfa.gov.il /ProtectiveEdge/Documents/2014GazaConflictFullReport.pdf.

27. "Key Figures on the 2014 Hostilities."

28. Ibid.

29. United Nations Human Rights Council, *Report of the Detailed Findings of the Independent Commission of Inquiry Established Pursuant to Human Rights Council Resolution S-21/1*, A/HRC/29/CRP.4 (June 22, 2015), 152, https://reliefweb.int/sites/reliefweb.int/files/resources/A_HRC_CRP_4.pdf.

30. Noah Browning, "Palestinians Put Gaza Reconstruction Cost at $7.8 Billion," Reuters, Sept. 4, 2014, https://www.reuters.com/article/us-mideast-gaza-reconstruction/palestinians-put-gaza-reconstruction-cost-at-7-8-billion-idUSKBN0GZ1N720140904.

31. Sultan Barakat and Firas Masri, *Still in Ruins: Reviving the Stalled Reconstruction of Gaza*, Brookings Doha Center Policy Briefing, (Washington, DC: Brookings Institution, 2017), 3, https://www.brookings.edu/research/reviving-the-stalled-reconstruction-of-gaza/.

32. Interview with Najwa Sheikh-Ahmad, acting public information officer, UNRWA Gaza field office, May 25, 2019, via WhatsApp.

33. UNRWA statistics supplied by Najwa Sheikh-Ahmad.

34. UNRWA, *Occupied Palestinian Territory Emergency Appeal 2019*, Jan. 29, 2019, 8, https://www.unrwa.org/sites/default/files/content/resources/2019_opt_ea_final.pdf.

35. UNRWA, *Occupied Palestinian Territory Emergency Appeal 2019* (updated summary), May 14, 2019, https://www.unrwa.org/resources/emergency-appeals?field_program_target_id=All&field_country__target_id=All&page=3.

36. UNRWA, *Occupied Palestinian Territory Emergency Appeal 2019*, 9–10.

37. Ibid., 8. According to OCHA, the rate of potable piped water in the Gaza Strip is 5 percent. "Refugee Needs in the Gaza Strip" (map), October 2018, https://www.un.org/unispal/document/refugee-needs-in-the-gaza-strip-oct-2018-ocha-map-2/.

38. UNRWA, "UNRWA Launches 2019 Emergency Appeals and Budget Requirement Totaling US$ 1.2 Billion," news release, Jan. 29, 2019, https://www.unrwa.org/newsroom/press-releases/unrwa-launches-2019-emergency-appeals-and-budget-requirement-totaling-us-12. The agency reported that the $1.2 billion total also included $277 million to support the Syria Regional Crisis Emergency Appeal in Syria and for Palestinian refugees from Syria in Lebanon and Jordan.

39. UNRWA, *Occupied Palestinian Territory Emergency Appeal 2019*, 7.

40. UNRWA, *Occupied Palestinian Territory Emergency Appeal 2019* (updated summary). Palestinian refugees in Gaza accounted for 74.5 percent of its total population of 1.9 million, with approximately 1 million in need of emergency food assistance amid a 54.9 percent unemployment rate. Palestinian

refugees in the West Bank (including east Jerusalem) accounted for 29.2 percent of its total population of 2.9 million, with 37,000 "individuals from Bedouin and herder communities" in need of emergency food assistance amid a 19 percent unemployment rate.

41. UNRWA, "Statement by UNRWA Spokesperson Sami Mshasha on Implications of Funding Shortfall on Emergency Services in OPT [Occupied Palestinian Territory]," news release, July 26, 2018, https://www.unrwa.org /newsroom/official-statements/statement-unrwa-spokesperson-sami-mshasha -implications-funding. The agency reported that it had raised $238 million in new funding for Palestinian refugees and that, following a pledging conference held in June 2018 at the UN in New York, it had reduced its $446 million deficit to $217 million, necessitating elimination of employment and mental health programs and mobile health clinics and the nonrenewal of 154 staff contracts attached to emergency programs.

42. [Author's name redacted], "U.S. Foreign Aid to the Palestinians," RS 22967 (Washington, DC: Congressional Research Service, updated December 12, 2018), 4–5. The report further states that "since UNRWA's inception in 1949, the United States has been the agency's largest donor" (21) and that since the agency began operations in 1950, U.S. contributions to UNRWA have totaled approximately $6.248 billion, dropping to $65 million in fiscal year 2018 (before being eliminated by the Trump administration) from $359.3 million in fiscal year 2017 (6).

43. OCHA, "Refugee Needs in the Gaza Strip," October 2018, https:// www.un.org/unispal/document/refugee-needs-in-the-gaza-strip-oct-2018 -ocha-map-2/. The agency reported:

> The restrictions on the movement of people and goods, and the dire socio-economic situation, have had serious repercussions on the psychosocial well-being of Palestine refugees in Gaza. UNRWA's Community Mental Health Programme conducted a study in May 2017 assessing the psychosocial well-being of 2,262 adult refugees and 3,142 refugee students. The study found a high level of psychosocial stress among both refugee students and adults, with almost one half of adults (48.9 percent) experiencing poor well-being, with 63 percent of these warranting further screening for depression, and almost 30 percent of children experiencing serious difficulties,

with some 290,000 children in need of psychosocial support.

44. Ahmed Alnaouq, "One Year Later: Ayman Is Not a Number," We Are Not Numbers, July 18, 2015, https://wearenotnumbers.org/home/Story /One_year_later:_Ayman_is_not_a_number_.

45. Ibid.

46. Ibid.

47. Ibid.

48. Ibid.

49. Ibid.

50. Ahmed Alnaouq's narrative is based on three extended voice interviews conducted via WhatsApp on June 29, July 8, and July 13, 2019, with updates in November 2019 and October 2020.

51. Ahmed Alnaouq, "The Return of the Apache," We Are Not Numbers, Dec. 14, 2017, https://wearenotnumbers.org/home/Story/The_return _of_the_Apache.

52. Ahmed Alnaouq, "Letter to a Drone," We Are Not Numbers, Nov. 2, 2017, https://wearenotnumbers.org/home/Story/Letter_to_a_drone.

53. Ahmed Alnaouq, "Ayman: To Israel a Target, to Me My Best Friend and Brother," We Are Not Numbers, Dec. 29, 2014, https://wearenot numbers.org/home/Story/Ayman_to_Israel_a_target_to_me_my_best_friend _and_brother.

54. Email interview with Pam Bailey, July 21, 2019, with update in October 2020. See also https://wearenotnumbers.org/home/Contributor/Pam _Bailey.

55. According to Bailey, these have included The New Arab, *Mondoweiss*, Middle East Eye, the *Electronic Intifada*, *Gulf News*, and *+972 Magazine*.

56. Euro-Mediterranean Human Rights Monitor, https://euromed monitor.org/. Established in 2011 and based in Switzerland, Euro-Med defines itself as "a youth-led independent, nonprofit organization that advocates for the human rights of all persons across Europe and the MENA [Middle East and North Africa] region, particularly those who live under occupation, in the throes of war or political unrest and/or have been displaced due to persecution or armed conflict."

57. According to Bailey, WANN's $30,000 annual budget covers three full-time and three part-time staffers in Gaza City as well as office space and furnishings, Wi-Fi, and equipment rental. We Are Not Numbers's crowdfunding source is LaunchGood (https://www.launchgood.com/#!/). CODEPINK (https://www.codepink.org/) has been its single largest consistent donor.

58. Rebuilding Alliance (RA), http://www.rebuildingalliance.org. Established in 2003 and based in Burlingame, California, the organization states that it is "dedicated to advancing equal rights for the Palestinian people through education, advocacy, and support that assures Palestinian families the right to a home, schooling, economic security, safety, and a promising future" and that it works to "amplif[y] the voices of Palestinian and Israeli peacemakers and their

communities." We Are Not Numbers has provided story content—for which its writers have been paid—and social media support for RA.

59. Nonviolence International, nonviolenceinternational.net. Established in 1989 and based in Washington, DC, the organization "researches and promotes nonviolent action, a culture of peace, and seeks to reduce violence and passivity worldwide." According to Bailey, NI has channeled tax-deductible contributions to We Are Not Numbers for a 7 percent fee.

60. "First 'Class' Graduates from Journalism Training," We Are Not Numbers, https://wearenotnumbers.org/home/News/First_class_graduates_from_journalism_training.

61. Ali Abusheikh, "Bridge-Building: An Unexpected Benefit of 'WANN,'" We Are Not Numbers, June 2, 2019, https://wearenotnumbers.org/home/Story/Bridge-building_an_unexpected_benefit_of_We_Are_Not_Numbers. See also "Ali Abusheikh" (bio), https://wearenotnumbers.org/home/Contributor/Ali_Abusheikh.

62. Ahmed Alnaouq, "Gazans Send Kites over the Border to Freedom during Great Return March," We Are Not Numbers, May 7, 2018, https://wearenotnumbers.org/home/Story/Gazans_send_kites_over_the_border_to_freedom_during_Great_Return_March; "Gaza NGOs in 'Catastrophic Crisis,'" April 9, 2018; also published in *The New Arab*, https://wearenotnumbers.org/home/Story/Gaza_NGOs_in_catastrophic_crisis_in_face_of_aid_cuts_Israeli_restrictions_and_PA_pressure; "Syrians make new home in Gaza," Aug. 10, 2017, https://wearenotnumbers.org/home/Story/Syrians_make_new_home_in_Gaza_.

63. Ahmed Alnaouq, "Tribute to Jamal Khashoggi: When Death Is an Inspiration," We Are Not Numbers, Oct. 31, 2018, https://wearenotnumbers.org/home/Story/Tribute_to_Jamal_Khashoggi_when_death_is_an_inspiration_.

64. Alnaouq, "Ayman: To Israel a Target."

CHAPTER 6. Imperatives of Narrative

1. bell hooks, "marginality as site of resistance," in *Out There: Marginalization and Contemporary Culture*, ed. Russell Ferguson, Martha Gever, Trinh T. Minh-ha, and Cornel West (Cambridge, MA: MIT Press, 1990), 343.

2. Ibid.

3. Teju Cole, "The White-Savior Industrial Complex," *Atlantic*, March 21, 2012, https://www.theatlantic.com/international/archive/2012/03/the-white-savior-industrial-complex/254843/.

4. John Berger, *Ways of Seeing* (London: British Broadcasting Corporation and Penguin Books, 1972), 1–2.

5. A prime example of such work is carried out by OCHA, United Nations Office for the Coordination of Humanitarian Affairs, Occupied Palestinian Territory, data from which is cited extensively in *Stories from Palestine*.

6. Richard Falk, *Report of the Special Rapporteur on the Situation of Human Rights in the Palestinian Territories Occupied since 1967*, UN General Assembly, Human Rights Council, A/HRC/25/67, Jan. 13, 2014, 3.

7. Michael Lynk, *Report of the Special Rapporteur on the Situation of Human Rights in the Palestinian Territories Occupied since 1967*, UN General Assembly, Human Rights Council, A/HRC/34/70, March 16, 2017, 2.

8. Unnamed author, *Report of the Special Rapporteur on the Situation of Human Rights in the Palestinian Territories Occupied since 1967*, UN General Assembly, Human Rights Council, A/HRC/37/75, March 15, 2018, 2; unnamed author, *Report of the Special Rapporteur on the Situation of Human Rights in the Palestinian Territories Occupied since 1967*, UN General Assembly, Human Rights Council, A/HRC/40/73, March 15, 2019, 2.

9. Interview with Atef Qasrawi at the Arab American University, Jenin, West Bank, May 12, 2018.

10. Interview with Mohammad Abu Taleb, Jenin, West Bank, June 1, 2019.

11. *Annual Report 2018*, Palestine Institute for Biodiversity and Sustainability, https://www.palestinenature.org/about-us/Annual-Report-2018.pdf. See also "PMNH: Nature and People Prosper," video, 9:21, May 4, 2016, https://www.youtube.com/watch?v=BPhFLOsEIM0&t=44s.

12. *Annual Report 2019*, Palestine Institute for Biodiversity and Sustainability, https://www.palestinenature.org/about-us/final-annual-report.pdf.

13. Interview with Mazin Qumsiyeh at the Palestine Institute for Biodiversity and Museum of Natural History, Bethlehem, June 7, 2018.

14. As in the introductory chapter, note 4, the source of this quotation is the same peer reviewer of the *Stories from Palestine* manuscript, whose identity is not known to the author.

15. Said, *Orientalism*, 12.

16. Cole, "White-Savior Industrial Complex."

17. "U.S. Public Has Favorable View of Israel's People but Is Less Positive toward Its Government," Pew Research Center, April 24, 2019, https://www.people-press.org/2019/04/24/u-s-public-has-favorable-view-of-israels-people-but-is-less-positive-toward-its-government/. The survey, conducted April 1–15, 2019, among 10,523 U.S. adults, also reflected differences toward

Israelis, Palestinians, and their governments along Democratic and Republican party lines.

18. "Republicans and Democrats Grow Even Further Apart in Views of Israel, Palestinians," Pew Research Center, Jan. 23, 2018, https://www.people-press.org/2018/01/23/republicans-and-democrats-grow-even-further-apart-in-views-of-israel-palestinians/. The survey, conducted Jan. 10–15, 2018, among 1,503 adults, indicated that 5 percent of respondents said their sympathies are with both Israelis and Palestinians; 14 percent said with neither; and 19 percent said they did not know. Pew further reported that "the overall balance of opinion has fluctuated only modestly since 1978, when 45 percent said they sympathized more with Israel, 14 percent with the Palestinians, and 42 percent could not decide."

19. The Arabic reads: نموت واقفين كأشجار فلسطين —*namūt waqifīn ka'ashjār Falastīn.*

20. Interview via WhatsApp with Nazmi Jubeh speaking from Jerusalem, March 17, 2019.

INDEX

MARDA DUNSKY,

assistant professor in residence at Northwestern University in Qatar, is a print journalist and journalism scholar. Her research focuses on underreported aspects of the Israel-Palestine conflict. Her teaching focuses on best practices of reporting and writing. She has taught global journalism on the faculty of the Medill School of Journalism at Northwestern University and has held editing and reporting positions at the *Chicago Tribune* and *Jerusalem Post*. She is the author of *Pens and Swords: How the American Mainstream Media Report the Israeli-Palestinian Conflict*, among other works.